Sartre's Second Critique

Sartre's Second Critique

Ronald Aronson

The University of Chicago Press   *Chicago and London*

Ronald Aronson is professor of humanities at Wayne State University. He is the author of *Jean-Paul Sartre—Philosophy in the World*, and *The Dialectics of Disaster: A Preface to Hope*.

The University of Chicago Press, Chicago 60637
The University of Chicago Press, Ltd., London

Library of Congress Cataloging-in-Publication Data

Aronson, Ronald, 1938–
  Sartre's second Critique.

  Includes index.
  1. Sartre, Jean Paul, 1905–80. Critique de
la raison dialectique.   2. Dialectical materialism.
3. Existentialism.   I. Title.
B2430.S33C723   1987   142'.78   86-30707
ISBN 0-226-02804-6
ISBN 0-226-02805-4 (pbk.)

Contents

Acknowledgments

I would like to acknowledge assistance from the American Council of Learned Societies and the National Endowment for the Humanities, as well as from Wayne State University. I spent 1983–84 as Honorary Research Fellow at University College London, where most of this study was written. Neil Belton of Verso Editions generously made available to me that publisher's copy of Sartre's handwritten manuscript. I would also like to thank the following people for their encouragement, support, discussion, critical reading, and various other forms of assistance: Fredric Jameson, Christopher Johnson, Mark Poster, Paul Arthur Schilpp, Michel Contat, Robert Stone, Geneviève Idt, Howard Davies, Adrien van den Hoven, Richard Schmitt, André Gorz, Patrick Camiller, Perry Anderson, Michael Sprinker, Moshe Lewin, Eugene Genovese, William McBride, and Douglas Kellner.

Introduction:

Life after Death

Less than a decade after his death, the Sartre revival is upon us already. Like everything else about Sartre, he has been unpredictable in death. The scandalous side of it is predictable, of course: were the two volumes of Sartre's letters, published by Simone de Beauvoir in 1983, best-sellers in France and widely reviewed in England because of their inherent charm or genuine literary interest, or rather because they permitted an insider's look at Sartre's complicated amorous life? The signs of scholarly interest by the wider world have remained modest enough. The mainstreams in the United States, Britain, and France are increasingly uncomprehending, as evidenced by the moment of play Vladimir Jankélévitch's attack on Sartre's Resistance years received in *Le Monde* and *Libération* in June 1985, which echoed as far west as the *Village Voice* that December. More to the point, there is not yet, for example, a chair of Sartre studies at an American or British university.

But if the revival does not come from the academic or intellectual mainstream, neither does it come, in the words of de Beauvoir's dedication of *Adieux*, from the devoted labors of "those who loved Sartre, do love him, who will love him."[1] To be sure, there has been a small, steady stream of books by Sartre scholars, including two biographies, retrospective issues of journals such as *Yale French Studies* and *Revue Internationale de Philosophie*. But the handful of Sartre conferences is attended by a distressingly tiny band of scholars who are far from being counted in the thousands or even hundreds. Remarkably, then, the Sartre revival is the work of Sartre himself, directly communicating with his readers. It is measured in the presence and relevance of *his own* books, measured indeed in announcements, reviews, and sales figures of books never before published.

In his last years, a posthumous air increasingly came to surround Jean-

---

1. *Adieux: A Farewell to Sartre,* trans. Patrick O'Brian (New York, 1984), v.

Paul Sartre. Nearly blind, recurrently ill, his intellectual powers deteriorating, unable to write, used for his reputation by his young *gauchiste* friends, he seemed to have outlived his great work and life itself. Accordingly, even if tens of thousands turned out for his funeral, the literary, philosophical, and political/intellectual worlds mourned his passing in 1979 with sad retrospection rather than grief—confirming the thought to be found in what follows, that we die too early or too late. In Sartre's case it was too late; his life's work was over, or because of failing sight and health could not and would not be completed. Sartre himself fueled this perception by sometimes regarding his monumental biography of Gustave Flaubert, published in 1971 and 1972, half-apologetically: the remnant of a bourgeois self-indulgence the sexagenarian was too old to suppress completely. In any case, *The Family Idiot* would remain forever suspended, bereft of the never-to-be-achieved study of *Madame Bovary* needed to make the sections on Gustave into more than an endless tale, however ground-breaking, of personal defeat.

In one way or another, then, we have been mourning Sartre for well over a dozen years. Knowing that no great book was interrupted by death, we have been unable to wait upon any decisive but half-finished work. Yes, we knew that his abandoned projects would be faithfully published by Gallimard, and that they would fill in various blank spots about the man, his thought, and his time. But we thought they were destined to remain in the past: dutifully reviewed, they would then find their way into the fifty volumes of collected works, eventually to be taken up by scholars pursuing articles and dissertations.

Since the appearance of *War Diaries* (the first of the posthumous works to be translated), it has been clear that something rather unusual is taking place. The writings Sartre withheld until after his death are too rich, too *present*—even when they deal with the Phony War of 1939–40—to be immediately relegated to the past or easily absorbed into a Sartre industry. Freed by death from reticence about his unfinished and personal writings, Sartre, safely past, seems to be projecting himself beyond the simple grave in the Montparnasse Cemetery and into our midst once again.

It was hardly surprising that Sartre's letters should become read so widely, considering their easy accessibility and the light they throw on Sartre's often-tumultuous personal life. And, of course, *Adieux,* de Beauvoir's account of his last years is attractive as a clear, restrained conclusion of her memoirs of their shared life, telling her intimate story of how the great man lived his declining years. Yet scarcely anyone anticipated the richness, brilliance, and beauty of the treasure trove of other works.

Sartre's 1947–48 ethics, *Cahiers pour une morale* (the sequel to *Being and Nothingness*) is the work for which Sartre students have been waiting the longest. Because it attempts to answer the famous concluding questions of *Being and Nothingness* at the very moment Sartre was discovering society and history, the *Cahiers* is a major philosophical contribution in its own right, even if presented abominably, as one endless sea of words. The *War Diaries* are an altogether disarming masterpiece. These five surviving notebooks of the fourteen Sartre kept during the war are cheerful and kaleidoscopic journals of self-analysis, descriptions of Sartre's experiences as a soldier, and drafts of the ideas of *Being and Nothingness*.

Sartre's *Freud Scenario* is a riveting masterpiece, one of the rare interpretations of one genius by another. At its end, Freud, standing by his father's grave, reconciles with Joseph Breuer while acknowledging that he, Freud, must continue his monumental labors alone. He has overcome the need for a substitute father that has been so important during these years of discovery, and so can now say farewell to Jacob Freud. The old man died earlier, broken by antisemitism (see below, chapter six, note 10) and business failure, shunned by the son who has only just now become conscious of his Oedipal hatred. Freud cries, and then he walks off alone, cured of his rivalry, finally fully mature, having dared to pursue his discoveries to their conclusion and now prepared to continue on his fateful course.

II

Of all the published posthumous works, volume two of the *Critique of Dialectical Reason* most strongly shows why Sartre is alive to us today— we who live at a time when the future itself is in question, when the human world has never seemed more out of human control. Unique among this century's great writers, Sartre—especially in his *Critique II*—points toward understandings and actions which may possibly return the world to its creators and so let there be a future.

Mainstream incomprehension of Sartre might be appropriate had the world resolved the political problems which preoccupied him. But, alas, we have not yet become free of colonialism and its heritage, or the capitalist-Communist confrontation, or the blockage of hope represented by the Communist states. For half his life Sartre searched, and struggled for, a meaningful politics of liberation: for those who still care, the search and struggle continue today. Along his way Sartre sought to reflect on, and develop, appropriate forms of intellectual involvement. He also sought to recover theoretical Marxism's revolutionary force by a grounding and reshaping that would found it as *the* human science. Certainly no better answers to these political-intellectual problems lie ready to hand today, and the problems themselves have hardly lost their urgency.

On a more purely theoretical level, Sartre's abiding concern with freedom and praxis, which yielded a lifetime of exploration of the ways in which the individual is shaped, shapes him- or herself, and takes shape, has not been rendered obsolete by recent wisdom on the subject, any more than his studies of the individual's relationship with society and of the dynamics of social formation have been dated by subsequent research. Sartre's questions have not been better answered elsewhere: they are not being asked. This says less about their intrinsic importance or the merits of his answers than about today's fashions. Behind such stylish watchwords as "poststructuralism," "new philosophy," and "postmodernism," current intellectual-political postures, especially in France, pronounce all these concerns obsolete. When interest reawakens in such questions, there is no doubt that the paths to be taken by those who ask them will lead in each case through Sartre's works. His insights, his concerns, his answers are in no case definitive; but politically and theoretically he commands attention for having lived and thought them so fully, so courageously, so deeply.

Yet even since Sartre's death times have worsened. The development of the atomic bomb, which Sartre indicated in the late 1940s as having transformed our world, has indeed changed everything. The threat has broadened, deepened, become part of our daily lives. The kind of terror mentioned only briefly by Sartre at the darkest days of the Cold War is imposed on us at every moment of every day by strategic policies making us all hostages during "peacetime." Similarly, Sartre's pitched struggle for political hope chronicled in his changing attitudes toward Communism and his efforts to create a new Left, can be seen as remarkably optimistic in the face of that new Left's subsequent collapse everywhere, of martial law in Poland, of the (momentary) exhaustion of the forces for progressive social change in the West, their (equally temporary) containment in the East, and the general absence of any hopeful alternative in the Third World. The zones of hope for which Sartre searched and to which he attached his support and analysis have become, one by one, frozen by events, leaving us today facing the greatest danger in memory with the greatest sense of disarray. As a consequence, hope itself has not been more in jeopardy since the beginning of the modern world.

If times have indeed darkened since the optimistic postwar decade and a half of Sartre's richest productivity, a way out will not be found by abandoning his chosen terrain for various modes of sophisticated evasion, clothed in fashionable "post-" prefixes. Comparing them with the ambitions of thinkers much in vogue today we can only be struck by Sartre's courage, his conviction that anything human can be understood, his indefatigable insistence on seeing human action and intention, however deviated, as the world's source. If we are indeed to survive and flourish, it will probably only be by a concerted intellectual-political practice paralleling his own: of deconstructing the fixed, frozen, menacing entities—above all, the Bomb—created by us but placed beyond our control by determinate and *comprehensible* human intentions and institutions, and of reconstructing the world so that the human intentionality insisted on at the end of *Critique II* prevails with as few deformations as possible. The only hopeful politics for today and the future will seek to return this world gone mad to its human source.

III

I have, of course, been speaking of what Sartre has to tell us today, especially in volume two of *Critique of Dialectical Reason*. I first examined the massive typescript of this volume in December 1977, at the behest of Perry Anderson. In his capacity as my editor, he thought it would be important to include a brief discussion of it in my study of Sartre's career. Sartre had given a copy of the handwritten 781-page manuscript to the editors of *New Left Review*, from which they extracted and translated a section for inclusion in the review's special hundredth issue. I spent a month studying it, and wrote a fifteen-page summary and commentary published as part of my book.

I returned to the manuscript in the summer of 1980 for another period of study, focusing on Sartre's discussion of the Soviet Union. My mind then was not on Sartre but was rather preoccupied with the Holocaust and Stalinism in my analysis of the contemporary barriers to hope. Absorbed in asking and answering the question, Is there reason to hope today? I was beginning what I now project as a three-volume study—encompassing the catastrophes of the twentieth century, the idea and reality of human progress, and the idea and reality of socialism.

As I was finishing *The Dialectics of Disaster: A Preface to Hope*, my mind could not have been further from Sartre's second *Critique*—until it came time to acknowledge the sources of my thinking. Herbert Marcuse, who had been my teacher, was an obvious wellspring, to whom I referred in no less than eight places. But, I discovered, I referred to Sartre twice as often. Sartre was, obviously, a decisive source. In repeatedly trying to understand the worst, and indeed to make way for change within it, he provides major keys and encouragement. As he acted, so did he write: moving toward the most intractable and painful problems of his lifetime, locating the point of most extreme tension between threatened hope and crushing reality, working within the tension, and from there insisting on finding a way forward.[2]

The theory of this practice of radical hope in extreme situations is perhaps the most important of all of Sartre's ideas: that human beings are the source of the human world. If we live entranced by a network of material and ideological mystification that raises our creations beyond our control, Sartre insists on revealing the praxis at their origin. Both those who would demonize the human world on the one hand and those who would remove its human, *moral* dimension on the other can be educated by Sartre's emphasis on human responsibility and intentionality, on choice and action even in the most difficult situations. Neurosis, for example, is the path chosen by the organism "in order to be able to live an unlivable situation."[3] With such concepts Sartre can help us to grasp the logic of evil and defeat: nuclear madness, the destructiveness that has so marked our century, the partially realized but repeatedly betrayed hopes of socialism, the dispiriting course taken by Third World revolutions.

Nowhere is this presented more clearly and strongly than *Critique II*. And so, before continuing with my "Dialectics of Hope Today," I decided to return to volume two for another period of close examination. It seemed clear that the path to my next questions, about the meaning and direction of history, wound through Sartre's reflections on the dialectic. I concluded that, whatever their limitations, they are so rich and important as to demand a study devoted to them.

Accordingly, my first purpose in this book is simply to present Sartre's argument as faithfully as possible. The reader who has not yet studied *Critique II* will find its main lines distilled below, in a discussion that follows Sartre closely until the last quarter of his manuscript. There, the sheer difficulty and repetitiveness forces me to abridge and summarize more actively. On the whole, however, the reader can expect this study to present the essence of Sartre's second *Critique*.

Yet even a reader who has worked with, or is presently studying, *Cri-*

2. Sartre was self-conscious about this approach. See Simone de Beauvoir, *The Force of Circumstance*, trans. Richard Howard (New York, 1965), 261–2.

3. Sartre's foreword to R. D. Laing and D. G. Cooper, *Reason and Violence* (London, 1964), 7.

tique II, is likely to lose his or her way often. Sartre never prepared the manuscript for publication, and thus left undeveloped many key themes, left unresolved many problems of conception, and left intact many blind allies. Accordingly, reading *Critique II* requires interpreting it: taking a position on what Sartre is saying and where he is going, deciding which are Sartre's main paths and which are brief diversions, constantly interrogating what he means. Because the direction is not always clear or self-evident, it is necessary to take bearings frequently, setting a given passage in the light of the logic of volume two as well as in relation to the *Critique* project as enunciated by volume one. And so the reader who opens Sartre's text alongside of mine will be able to use this book as a step-by-step guide through its dense terrain.

If it is a guide, this book is also a commentary. In addition to frequently discussing the flow of Sartre's argument, I have gone beyond the task of closely explicating the text in two respects. First, where necessary I situate Sartre's analyses within his philosophical and political development and in relation to the larger historical and intellectual context. The reader will find frequent references not only to *Being and Nothingness* but also to Maurice Merleau-Ponty's renunciation of Marxism and indeed to the "crisis of Marxism" at the time Sartre was absorbing historical materialism. Furthermore, as will come as no surprise to readers of my *Jean-Paul Sartre—Philosophy in the World*, I evaluate *Critique II* critically, discussing its achievements and its weaknesses. I explain why it is a tremendously important work, even if undermined not only by its unfinished state, but by certain conceptual flaws.

This study, however, is not primarily a critique of Sartre: I am less concerned to demonstrate that the *Critique* "had to" fail because of Sartre's unresolved conceptual weaknesses than to *present* Sartre. Over the years my appreciation for Sartre's genius has only grown, even if my argument with him has not changed, and I think it vitally important that the Sartre revival put at its center his most advanced thought. Accordingly, I have wanted the powerful main currents of *Critique II*, and not my criticism of Sartre, to set the course of this book. As a result, for most of this study my evaluative comments follow directly on his specific analyses, as brief commentaries, rather than structuring my presentation of Sartre. The reader should be able to distinguish Sartre's voice from my own—even where I am trying to explain what I think he is saying. In a concluding chapter, I sketch more fully than elsewhere what I believe to be the *Critique*'s conceptual weaknesses and show how, corrected, the Sartrean dialectic makes a formidable analytical tool. With the benefit of hindsight, I return at the end to develop my own comments on the situation

Sartre reflected on in volume two, the possible evolution of the Soviet Union.

IV

In November 1985, as I was finishing this book, Gallimard at long last published volume two, in a splendid edition prepared by Arlette Elkaïm-Sartre. Unlike the *Cahiers pour une morale*, *Critique II* has been divided into parts, chapters and sections and is accompanied by extremely helpful editor's footnotes. Even if some of her divisions might be quarrelled with, Elkaïm-Sartre has succeeded in making the manuscript accessible.[4] Her work provided numerous corrections of my own. In addition, she organized and presented the fifty pages of notes Sartre made when he briefly returned to the *Critique* in 1961–62.

Elkaïm-Sartre's careful scholarship helps to remind us of something easy to forget when reading and discussing a manuscript such as this which has found its way into book form: *Critique II* never achieved whatever finished form Sartre may have given it. For example, Sartre himself presents its planned organization on pages 451–52, but the manuscript does not follow his plan. The editor notes, as I have, decisive places where Sartre diverges from his plan. And so we must insist, from the beginning of this study to its end: Sartre did not complete the manuscript, he did not correct himself.

And yet, it is also important to note from the outset that, with all its flaws, the manuscript is largely well written and coherent. It clearly sets out in pursuit of its goal in its first quarter, carefully framing what the meaning of studying history as a "totalization without a totalizer" is; Sartre then contributes one of the great discussions of the fate of the Bolshevik Revolution; he goes on to rethink the key terms of *Being and Nothingness* according to the Marxist outlook of the *Critique*; and finally Sartre concludes with a forceful tribute to dialectical reason.

It may well be true that Sartre would have corrected himself if he had had the opportunity, or that he would have completed his task. The explicit goal of volume two was to explain history as a "totalization without a totalizer." One of the great puzzles of twentieth-century thought has been that Sartre abandoned this project, unfinished. Yet even if it does not fulfill its promise, volume two will eventually find its place as one of

4. My comments on the edition are contained in "Sartre's Return to Ontology: *Critique II* rethinks the basis for *Being and Nothingness*," *Journal of the History of Ideas*, Winter, 1986–87.

Sartre's major philosophical manuscripts. After all, he did say what was on his mind about dialectical reason in it, and never returned to the subject. We shall see that the manuscript does end with a ringing return to Sartre's starting point, and does convey a sense of completion. Whatever he "might have" written, then, this is all he has given us of *Critique II*. And it is a great deal.

1 Vicissitudes of the Dialectic

Those who have studied volume one of *Critique of Dialectical Reason* will immediately feel at home within the tone, register, and conceptual universe of volume two. In fact, its very first words begin precisely where volume one leaves off. How, Sartre asks at the outset, can we "conceive that a struggle between individuals or between groups is dialectically intelligible?"[1] What enables us to view each side's action according to the terms of dialectical thought—as participating in the creation of history, as leading to progress and development, as proceeding by contradiction and transcendence? This issue is a simple yet absolutely basic one: How can a meaningful larger whole emerge "when we are in the presence of *two* actions, that is of two autonomous and contradictory totalizations?" (II, 13).

Unlike volume one's first words these reveal no sense of starting out afresh, no need to create a place for the entire undertaking in the world of human praxis and discourse—or indeed in the history of thought. Rather they seem merely to pose, after a pause, the next question of a sustained line of thought whose basic concepts and frames of reference have already been carefully established. To be sure, we shall soon see that Sartre devoted considerable energy in volume two's opening dozen pages to specifying, focusing, and circumscribing this line of thought, and we shall travel this path with him to understand better the work and its significance. But it is also clearly indicated as being no more than the continuation and completion of volume one.

---

1. *Critique de la raison dialectique*, Tome II (inachevé): *L'intelligibilité de l'Histoire*, établissement du texte, notes et glossaire par Arlette Elkaïm-Sartre (Paris, 1985), 13. Future references to this volume will be denoted by "II," followed by a page number.

A Glimpse of Volume Two

Nonetheless, for much of the way a single, coherent, and well-developed manuscript, volume two allows us our first clear sense of the *Critique*'s goals. Until now, readings of the first volume have had to assume a self-sufficiency and completeness not inherent in its pages but imposed by Sartre's subsequent decision to break off the project before its completion. As a result, scholars of "the *Critique*" have emphasized specific structures rather than the larger historical process into which they are to be inserted;[2] or they have mistaken the (reversible) passage from one structure to another as a kind of totalizing study of History itself rather than a highly abstract and prefatory sketch of its elements and their modes of combination and transformation.[3] The presence of the second volume imposes new lenses through which to view the purposes and analyses of the first, as well as Sartre's entire career.[4]

In taking up "the same structures as those brought to light by [volume one's] regressive investigation," he now seeks "to rediscover the moments of their interrelations, the ever vaster and more complex movement which totalizes them and, finally, the very direction of the totalization, that is to say, the 'meaning of History' and its Truth."[5] The structures laid out in the first volume—individual praxis, the practico-inert, the series, the group-in-fusion, the sworn group, the institution, social classes—are intended in the second as "the condition of a directed, developing totalization" (I, 184; 156; 69).

Sartre will pursue this in a specific way in the first quarter of volume two, exploring how separate and contending actions conspire to create totalizations. To totalize, we know from volume one, is to draw together into "the developmental unity of a single process" what appear to be

2. See for example Pietro Chiodi, *Sartre and Marxism* (London, 1976).
3. See for example Mark Poster, *Sartre's Marxism* (London, 1980).
4. My own study of Sartre's career benefited from access to volume two. See my *Jean-Paul Sartre—Philosophy in the World* (London, 1981; hereafter cited as *Jean-Paul Sartre*), and also "Sartre's Turning Point: *Critique de la raison dialectique, II*," in Paul Arthur Schilpp, ed., *The Philosophy of Jean-Paul Sartre*, The Library of Living Philosophers (La Salle, Ill., 1981).
5. *Critique de la raison dialectique*, Tome I: *Théorie des ensembles pratiques* (Paris, 1985), 183; this is a newly established and annotated text edited by Arlette Elkaïm-Sartre with an annotated table of contents by Juliette Simont and Pierre Verstraeten. The original edition, still widely used, was published in 1960. The English translation, made from the original edition, is by Alan Sheridan-Smith, *Critique of Dialectical Reason*, I: *Theory of Practical Ensembles*, edited by Jonathan Rée (London, 1976). The statement quoted appears in the 1960 edition on 156, in the English translation on 69. Future references to volume one will be denoted by "I," followed by the page numbers, respectively, of the 1985 edition, the 1960 edition, and the English translation. Spelling has been Americanized throughout.

separate actions and entities—"the reinteriorization of the different moments in a synthetic progression" (I, 135; 115; 15). In volume one we have repeatedly seen individual or group praxis totalize, but volume two turns to the real historical world of fragmented, contending, and conflicting praxes. Can there be a "totalization without a totalizer," one not produced by a single individual or group praxis but which emerges against or in spite of anyone's intentionality yet moves forward some process of historical development? Hegel had spoken of the "cunning of Reason" when lodging the dialectic in a process operating behind the back of individuals. As we shall see, for Sartre any such totalization can only occur through the praxis of individuals.

Thus he will study two boxers, each trying to defeat the other, and will explore the larger totalities they create and which create them. He will then explore the dialectical theme of contradiction, asking how two subgroups in conflict can be said to further the larger group's purposes in their struggle. And then he will describe, in close detail, the deformed yet still significant product of individuals, subgroups, groups, or classes in conflict. Under the concept of antilabor, he will examine entities produced in and by the conflict yet intended by neither participant.

Sartre's example of antilabor, the slogan "socialism in a single country," will be explained as resulting from the conflict between Stalin and Trotsky for Soviet leadership in the 1920s. With this example Sartre will initiate a new direction of volume two, a major interpretation of Stalinism occupying nearly half of its pages. Framed by a variety of formal goals which diverge from Sartre's search for the totalization without a totalizer—to study the action of groups on series, to observe the "totalization of envelopment" under the conditions of individual sovereignty, and to trace the sovereign individual enveloped by his own praxis—these interconnected analyses will show the Revolution deviating far from its original goals *in order to survive.*

The final quarter of volume two will then wander strikingly from this line of thought. It will shift rather abruptly to explore the ontological status of the particular totalization Sartre has been describing, the totalization of envelopment dominated by Stalin. In a change from dialectical reason to ontology Sartre will ask about its "real-being." He will justify this as avoiding the idealism implied by saying that *everything* takes place within the praxis-process of history. This discussion will return to the root terms of *Being and Nothingness*—being-in-itself and being-for itself—but will struggle to connect them with *need* and *praxis,* root terms of the *Critique.* In its last pages, volume two will stress the difference between analytical and dialectical reason. Then, before the manuscript breaks off, its original goals unmet, Sartre will conclude by reaffirming the dialectic as the master logic of the human world.

Sartre and the Dialectic

Aligning himself with some of the most orthodox currents of Marxism—and contradicting the thrust of both Maurice Merleau-Ponty's "post-Marxism" and more skeptical Marxist trends such as those of "Western Marxism" or the Frankfurt School—Sartre starts out by assuming that there is a single, comprehensible meaning and direction of history.[6] He begins volume one by seeing the dialectic as a tool of analysis *and* as a coherent and meaningful sociohistorical process. Indeed, he regards both Stalinism and his own effort to free the dialectic from it as "moment[s] of the totalizing activity of the world" (I, 166; 141; 50). Every individual life "is the direct and indirect expression of the whole" and of every other life. At the same time, Sartre breaks with orthodoxy and aligns himself with Western Marxism by his emphasis on human subjectivity as the source of the dialectic. He seeks to ground the totalizing movement of the whole not in more general currents and structures but in the (conflictual) activities of individuals. Thus he intends to show that human subjects create *and* are controlled by the dialectic.

But what is it that brings Sartre to the dialectic in the first place? And why is it that he comes to it in the particular way he does, simultaneously affirming Communist Party and Soviet orthodoxy and challenging it? More basically, why did Sartre undertake this a priori study of the nature and meaning of dialectical reason, leading to, but never explaining, the totalization without a totalizer? We shall see the answers evolve slowly, internally, in the body of volume two. Before we approach the text, however, the *Critique* demands to be situated beyond itself, in the personal, intellectual, and political history of which it is such an important moment.

Moving toward Marxism

As the culmination of Sartre's complex movement toward Marxism, the *Critique* crowns a period that began twenty years earlier in a prisoner-of-war camp after the fall of France. In slow, definite stages between 1940 and 1957,[7] Sartre first became committed to political activism;[8] to social-

---

6. "We will attempt to establish that there is *one* human history, with *one* truth and *one* intelligibility" (I, 184; 156; 69).

7. The following story is presented in detail in my *Jean-Paul Sartre*, especially 107–242.

8. "But it was above all a moral position, and my ideas were naïve in the extreme"

ism;[9] to developing an integration of thought, writing, and political activity;[10] to building a non-Communist democratic socialist movement;[11] to close relations with the Communist Party and the Soviet Union; to using Marxism as a tool of analysis; and then, in *Search for a Method* and the *Critique*, to Marxism as a philosophy.

Although (as we know from *Nausea*) Sartre was thoroughly alienated from bourgeois France in the 1930s, he enthuasiastically embraced phenomenology but remained largely indifferent to Marxism as providing an alternative orientation. Still, something about Marxism drew and fascinated him, as he later noted in *Search for a Method*: "It was not the idea which unsettled us; nor was it the condition of the worker, which we knew abstractly but which we had not experienced. No, it was the two joined together. It was—as we would have said then in our idealist jargon even as we were breaking with idealism—the proletariat as the incarnation and vehicle of an idea."[12]

In his apolitical days, the appeal of Marxism lay neither in the philosophy nor in the movement but in the *connection* between the two. In this way, historical materialism, criticized by Sartre in his very first published essay, offered something no other philosophy could aspire to and challenged this philosopher to his roots.[13] At the same time it repelled him by its emphasis on dominant structures and forces which are not immediately accessible to translucent and spontaneous consciousness. Man is not free, Marxism was saying to the Sartre bent on demonstrating freedom.

Before the war, Sartre had been yearning to encounter the real world. During the Occupation and after the war the sheer organized power of the Marxist movement of the working class—the French Communist Party (PCF)—continued to draw him toward it and define his capacity to act. In 1945 Sartre, along with Simone de Beauvoir, Maurice Merleau-Ponty, Raymond Aron, and others, launched *Les Temps Modernes*, which soon became a major force as a political and cultural journal of the non-

---

(*Sartre by Himself*, a film directed by Alexandre Astruc and Michel Contat [1977]; screenplay trans. Richard Seaver [New York, 1978], 50).

9. The first political group he formed included Simone de Beauvoir and Maurice Merleau-Ponty. It was a short-lived Resistance organization called Socialisme et Liberté.

10. In *Les Temps Modernes*, which first appeared in October, 1945. See Sartre's editor's introduction to the first issue, in *Situations* II (Paris, 1948), 9–30.

11. The short-lived organization was named the Rassemblement Démocratique et Révolutionnaire. See Sartre, David Rousset, Gérard Rosenthal, *Entretiens sur la Politique* (Paris, 1949).

12. *Questions de méthode*, *Critique*, I, 29 (1960, 23); trans. Hazel Barnes, *Search for a Method* (New York, 1963), 20.

13. *La transcendance de l'ego* (Paris, 1965); trans. Forrest Williams and Robert Kirkpatrick, *The Transcendence of the Ego* (New York, 1957), 105.

PCF Left.[14] Functionally, Sartre and Merleau-Ponty were its coeditors, although the latter, whom Sartre regarded as his political mentor, was the journal's political editor.

By the postwar period Sartre had accepted certain Marxist themes: the class struggle, the goal of a classless society, the leading role of the proletariat in attaining it, and the emphasis on action as central. But his own action, the *engagement* of a writer, still put little weight on the social and economic forces emphasized by Marxism. Again and again he found himself appealing to the spontaneity of consciousness and the power of words to influence it, as in *What Is Literature?*, first published in *Les Temps Modernes* in 1947. And so this socialist activist still kept his distance from Marxism. During this period Sartre saw himself as being to the right of Merleau-Ponty, whose "hard-hitting, severe and disillusioned Marxism"[15] wanted a greater recognition of historical contingency than Marxism had allowed, but who still called for close adherence to "the effective policy of the Communist Party."[16]

With characteristic self-confidence, in 1946 Sartre wrote *Materialism and Revolution* as an *alternative* to Marxism: it offered existentialism to the Left, including the Communists, as a philosophy of freedom befitting a movement of liberation. Sartre attempted to show how human freedom became alienated under capitalism, and could be fully realized under socialism. The original version of this abstract philosophical essay quarrels with Stalin's *Dialectical and Historical Materialism*, but shows neither a direct reading of Marx nor an appreciation of history, economy, and society as central themes underlying political analysis.

It is interesting to note that Merleau-Ponty was presenting his own sophisticated reflections on Communism and history in the journal during this very period. Merleau-Ponty brilliantly laid out the dilemma of the non-Communist sympathetic to proletarian revolution but troubled by its bloody and dictatorial outcome in the Soviet Union as well as by the passivity of the French working class: "It is impossible to be an anti-Communist and it is not possible to be a Communist."[17] Through essays on the writings of Arthur Koestler, the trial of Bukharin and Trotsky's mode of thought, Merleau-Ponty considered the decisive issues of revo-

14. The story of *TM*'s politics is best told by Michel-Antoine Burnier's excellent *Choice of Action* (New York, 1969). See also Anna Boschetti, *Sartre et "les Temps Modernes"* (Paris, 1985). Sartre describes his relationship on the journal with Merleau-Ponty in his eulogy, "Merleau-Ponty vivant," in *Situations* IV (Paris, 1964); trans. Benita Eisler, "Merleau-Ponty," *Situations* (Greenwich, Conn., 1966).

15. "Merleau-Ponty," 168.

16. Quoted in Burnier, 36.

17. *Humanism and Terror,* trans. John O'Neill (Boston, 1969), xxi.

lutionary violence and the deviation of the Soviet Union from original Bolshevik goals. Because history is human contingency and not an inevitable process working itself out, he argued that we must still wait on events before deciding how Communism has turned out. In the meantime, whatever its imperfections in the world before us, Marxism is the only humanistic philosophy committed to realizing itself in the world. Its agent, the proletariat, "has not achieved power anywhere in the world," but still "threatens to make its voice heard again . . . This is enough for us to regard the Marxist attitude as still attractive, not only as moral criticism but also as an historical hypothesis." [18] Merleau-Ponty thus proclaimed a widely influential "Marxist wait-and-see attitude." [19]

Sartre claimed that these essays, published in book form in 1947 as *Humanism and Terror*, caused him to be "converted" from his old individualism to politics. "This small dense book revealed to me the method and object. It gave me the push I had needed to release me from my immobility." [20] Method and object: Merleau-Ponty takes Marxism in its *historical* reality, seeking to deny none of the negative features of Soviet history or daily life, but refusing to divorce Marxism from its embodiment in that society. His realism insists that even if proletarian rule has not yet been realized by Soviet socialism, that society and the Communist movement still deserve sympathy and patient waiting.

Three years later, in notes added for the republication of *Materialism and Revolution*, Sartre foreshadows what will develop into a rather different direction. He distinguishes "the Marxist scholasticism of 1949," which he still criticizes, from Marx's "much deeper and richer conception" [21] and indicates his intention to explore this later. Sartre, unlike Merleau-Ponty, was in the process of discovering a politically relevant *non-Communist* Marxism, one which was in closer sympathy to his own existentialism than Communist orthodoxy had been.

This was to be followed by other decisive steps in Sartre's development which were, at the same time, steps away from Merleau-Ponty. In the intensifying Cold War Sartre chose to side with the PCF and the Soviet Union against the West, citing the government's apparent attempt to suppress the Communist Party in the wake of the anti-NATO riots against

18. *Ibid.*, 156–57.
19. This is Merleau-Ponty's description from *Adventures*, 228. In *Humanism and Terror* he speaks of a "comprehension without adherence" which acknowledges both the negative features of Communism and the fact that Marxism offers the only adequate moral critique of capitalism and the only meaningful philosophy of history (148–57).
20. "Merleau-Ponty," 174.
21. "Matérialisme et révolution," *Situations* III (Paris, 1949); trans. Annette Michelson, "Materialism and Revolution," *Literary and Philosophical Essays* (New York, 1955), 198.

the American general Matthew Ridgeway in May 1952. "In the name of those principles which it had inculcated into me, in the name of its humanism and of its humanities, in the name of liberty, equality, fraternity, I swore to the bourgeoisie a hatred which would only die with me. When I returned precipitately to Paris [from Rome, where he heard about the events], I had to write or suffocate. Day and night, I wrote the first part of *The Communists and Peace*."[22]

This essay set a new pro-Communist direction for *Les Temps Modernes*, which had been drifting since the beginning of the Korean War due to Merleau-Ponty's self-imposed silence. We shall see that Merleau-Ponty in turn attacked this essay for its lack of historical or social grounding. Influenced by the Cold War and discouraged about the Soviet Union, he was then moving in the opposite political direction, away from Marxism. Sartre, however, was simultaneously pursuing this grounding by self-consciously absorbing his own version of realism into his thought and action. Obviously influenced by Marxism and by his own failure to create a non-Communist Left, as well as by Merleau-Ponty's original analyses, Sartre ruminated on what he increasingly came to call his "idealism." He first sought a way of making his ideas effective in the real world, and then sought a basis for action which was committed to liberation *and* grounded in reality. He had already pondered the problem in 1948 in *Dirty Hands*, producing the impressive character of Hoederer but killing him off and generating no resolution. The most successful intellectual and creative fruit of this process, appearing in 1951, was the brilliant dramatic search for a principle of realistic yet humane action, *The Devil and the Good Lord*.

Politically this began the period of Sartre's fellow traveling. However he might disagree with the PCF and the Soviet Union, he now appropriated Merleau-Ponty's earlier argument, in the process of being renounced by its author, that Communism represented the only positive future of the great mass of humankind.[23] Accepting this thesis did not stifle his sharp intellect: these half-dozen years of his closest ties with the Soviet Union and PCF were characterized by Sartre's critical-minded and original absorption of Marxism. By early 1956 he called it "the truth in motion and the royal road of knowledge." He cited Marxism *against* Party versions of it, agreeing that the PCF's positions were usually correct, but declaring that intellectually "Marxism in France has come to a halt."[24] Sartre had begun to see himself as one of the thinkers who would get it

22. "Merleau-Ponty," 198.
23. It is especially striking to see Sartre citing Merleau-Ponty's original words in his 1961 eulogy. See ibid., 183–84.
24. "Le Reformisme et les fétiches," *Situations* VII (Paris, 1965), 117–18. For Sartre's fas-

moving again. By the Hungarian invasion this independent Marxist was ready to break with the Soviet Union (and the PCF for not condemning it) precisely *in the name of socialism and Marxism.*

The Specific Circumstance

Obviously Sartre would sooner or later need to reflect on the relationship of his original philosophical terms—most notably his Cartesian starting point in *Being and Nothingness* and his famous emphasis on individual freedom—to his growing Marxist intellectual and political orientation. Indeed, his abortive first ethics, *Cahiers pour une morale,* began this task in the late 1940s, but at that time he talked of the class struggle "on the level of a concept; so long as it was not felt as a concrete reality, there could be no morality in it." [25] This leads us to one way of framing the *Critique:* Sartre's slow appropriation of Marxism in experience as well as theory, to the point of seeking to examine it—and establish it—philosophically. The general lines of Sartre's itinerary led quite naturally to a full-scale theoretical encounter with the basic principles of historical materialism.

But what provoked Sartre to write the *Critique?* To answer this we must continue looking beyond its texts themselves, even if only to set it alongside another text, by Merleau-Ponty—close friend and collaborator-become-critic of Marxism and Sartre by 1955. The *Critique* project was developed in the context of a specific circumstance: the ending of the personal, intellectual, and political relationship between Sartre and Merleau-Ponty. Its 90,000-word epitaph, *Adventures of the Dialectic,* asserted the obsolescence of Communism and Marxism as well as the philosophical inadequacy of Sartre's alignment with them.

As we shall see, this quarrel focused the political and intellectual tensions of an entire generation. But to inquire about it is to immediately encounter a major problem: the intellectual histories of the postwar non-Communist French Left ignore its decisive links. [26] Indeed, there has

---

cinating rejoinder to a PCF intellectual's reply (in which he emphasizes that the halt is *temporary*), see "Réponse à Pierre Naville," ibid., 119–43.

25. *Sartre by Himself,* 78.

26. George Lichtheim, in *Marxism in Modern France* (New York, 1966), 89–102, develops Merleau Ponty's argument and then notes Sartre's attitude toward Marxism without showing either Sartre's own development or the relationship between the two. Arthur Hirsch, in *The French New Left: An Intellectual History from Sartre to Gorz* (Boston, 1981), indicates that there is a relationship between Merleau-Ponty's *Adventures of the Dialectic* and Sartre's *Critique* in which "Sartre took the criticism seriously and incorporated much of it into his later *Critique* (Hirsch, 49). But after this promising beginning, Hirsch adds not a word to show how Sartre did so. In *Existential Marxism in Postwar France* (Princeton, 1975) Mark Poster

been virtual silence by commentators on the remarkable juxtaposition of two facts—Sartre's political mentor proclaimed his abandonment of the Marxist dialectic in 1955, and his formerly junior collaborator began a major project of affirming it a few months later.[27] Or, yet more remarkably, as we shall see, the one abandons the Marxian dialectic for the same reason that the other attempts to ground it: "it is at the very moment when the machine seems jammed [*semble coincée*] that it is appropriate to disentangle the formal difficulties that have been neglected until now" (II, 25).[28]

Does the incomprehension stem from the inherent difficulty of the two texts? As Raymond Aron wrote of *Adventures of the Dialectic*, "Out of 330 pages I do not think that there are more than half a dozen that would allow a reader who was not a professional philosopher to clearly grasp the point of these subtle analyses or the purpose of this long discussion."[29] Yet Aron, having seemingly grasped their point, made no reference to it when commenting at even greater length on Sartre's *Critique*. I would suggest, rather, that the two texts have simply not been studied side by side. When they are, it becomes evident, as Perry Anderson notes, that the *Critique* "was initially conceived as a direct response to

---

seems totally unaware of any connection between the two works, or that their personal/ political collaboration *should* lead Sartre to take the criticism seriously. In *Choice of Action*, Burnier mentions each work but without suggesting any connection betwen them. Pursuing the development of dialectical Marxism, Scott Warren, in *The Emergence of Dialectical Theory*, (Chicago, 1984), explores Merleau-Ponty's attack but unaccountably ignores Sartre's *Critique* altogether.

27. Thomas R. Flynn, almost alone among students of Sartre, notes that Merleau-Ponty virtually "invite[s] the writings of the *Critique* [by arguing] that Sartre lacks a social philosophy of mediations" (*Sartre and Marxist Existentialism* [Chicago, 1984]). Pietro Chiodi, in *Sartre and Marxism*, spends a good deal of time discussing *Adventures of the Dialectic* but none showing its internal role in the *Critique*. It is surprising that Monika Langer's study of the relationship between *The Communists and Peace* and *Adventures* does not look beyond 1955 to explore Sartre's reflection on the issues raised by his former friend and colleague. Langer rather unhistorically chooses to assert the *correctness* of the Sartre of 1952–54 against the Merleau-Ponty of *Adventures*, instead of following Sartre's own response ("Sartre and Merleau-Ponty: A Reappraisal," in Schilpp, *The Philosophy of Jean-Paul Sartre*). And, most surprisingly, in two separate books Raymond Aron ignores Merleau-Ponty's role in provoking the *Critique* even after contributing a trenchant analysis of *Adventures* which includes reference to de Beauvoir's reply; see *History and the Dialectic of Violence* (New York, 1975).

28. Merleau-Ponty, summarizing his 1946 position before renouncing it in 1955: "But the marxist dialectic continues to play across the world. It jammed [*s'est enrayée*] when the revolution was limited to an undeveloped country, but one feels its presence in the French and Italian labor movements" (*Adventures of the Dialectic*, trans. Joseph Bien [Evanston, Ill., 1973], 288).

29. Raymond Aron, *Marxism and the Existentialists* (New York, 1969), 46.

the criticisms and objections put to [Sartre] by Merleau-Ponty"[30] in *Adventures of the Dialectic.*

Merleau-Ponty's Break with Marxism

Indeed, having moved into Sartre's and Merleau-Ponty's intellectual-political universe of the 1950s, it is impossible *not* to read the *Critique* as a reply to the challenge of Merleau-Ponty. The publication of Merleau-Ponty's self-consciously "post-Marxist" attack on Marxism, Communism, and Sartre immediately caused a great stir. In a major moment in post-war intellectual history, it presented the rationale for Merleau-Ponty's departure from his common project with Sartre. *Adventures of the Dialectic* not only rejected Marxism as having been wrong *all along,* and thoroughly excoriated Sartre for his growing sympathy to Communism, but proposed a "new liberalism" in its place.

In spite of its obtuseness *Adventures* was sufficiently important to draw a response from Aron[31] as well as Roger Garaudy and other Communist intellectuals.[32] And it provoked Simone de Beauvoir herself to write a reply attacking Merleau-Ponty's distortion of Sartre's thought into a "pseudo-Sartrisme" which ignored key conceptions of his ontology as well as his political and philosophical evolution.[33] In his eulogy of Merleau-Ponty, written in 1961, Sartre tersely suggests that he himself identified with her reply. "He wrote a book on dialectic, where he strongly took me to task. Simone de Beauvoir replied to him in *Les Temps Modernes* in terms no less strong. This was the first and last time that we fought in writing. By publishing our dissensions, we almost made them irremediable."[34]

"We fought," but why did he not reply directly? The question is a personal and not a philosophical or political one, and its answer is to be found in Sartre's moving account of a broken comradeship. In his eulogy we can see Sartre treating Merleau-Ponty as an intellectual giant, the "throwback to anarchy" still learning from the man who "converted" him to a genuinely historical and social perspective (ibid., 176). And we see him still disagreeing, over the nature of the dialectic. Yet moving as it

30. Perry Anderson, *In the Tracks of Historical Materialism* (Chicago, 1984), 36.

31. Aron contributed two articles, published in the review *Preuves* in 1956 and translated and republished in *Marxism and the Existentialists.*

32. Roger Garaudy et al., *Mésaventures de l'anti-marxisme* (Paris, 1956).

33. Simone de Beauvoir, "Merleau-Ponty et le pseudo-Sartrisme," *Les Temps Modernes,* June-July 1955, 114–15; her reaction is described in *The Force of Circumstances,* trans. Richard Howard (Harmondsworth, 1968), 331–32.

34. "Merleau-Ponty," 220.

may be, the personal tone of "Merleau-Ponty" tends to downplay the political charge of this historic split.

Sartre first describes the growing closeness of this deep personal-intel-
lectual relationship and indicates his own profound debt to Merleau-
Ponty as his political mentor. The two had shared many of the same
tasks, the same attitudes, the same lines of analyses, a common language. By aligning himself with Communist politics and Marxist realism while Sartre was still seeking a "third way," Merleau-Ponty in fact
drew Sartre along with him.[35] After 1949 Merleau-Ponty inched away
from Communism, and then departed as the Cold War intensified. The
Korean War, at first widely perceived in France as the beginning of
World War III (189–92, 197), was his personal turning point. It told
Merleau-Ponty that the Soviet Union was morally and politically no
better than the great powers of the capitalist West. At *Les Temps Modernes*
he counseled silence—"because brute force will decide the outcome.
Why speak to what has no ears?" (189)—and had less and less to do with
politics (188–97).

Painfully, in great detail, Sartre describes their mounting political-
personal estrangement. During this period of his own rapprochement
with Communism and Marxism, Sartre behaved intemperately toward
his collaborators on *Les Temps Modernes*, especially toward Merleau-
Ponty (see 198–206). The storm began with *The Communists and Peace*. Its
first part, published in July 1952, "seemed as though I had planned a
systematic refutation of our political editor, opposing, point by point,
my views to his" (199). This was followed by Sartre's nasty reply to *Les
Temps Modernes* associate Claude Lefort's[36] harsh criticism, and by his
high-handed excising of Merleau-Ponty's disavowing editor's preface
from the proof of a Marxist essay on "the contradictions of capitalism."
Merleau-Ponty resigned. Then, when *Adventures of the Dialectic* appeared
in early 1955, Sartre demurred. Obviously shaken by the irreversible
rupture with Merleau-Ponty, Sartre would soon make restraint in the
face of attack his customary response.

Western Marxism

Adventures has puzzled analysts in part because of its apparent con-
tradictoriness. After an introduction in which he announces his goal,

35. Sartre suggests that Merleau-Ponty, much closer to the PCF during this period,
accompanied him in his involvement with the RDR only "in order not to disavow me"
(ibid., 180).
36. Lefort had been close to Merleau-Ponty.

the "liquidation of the revolutionary dialectic,"[37] Merleau-Ponty briefly seems to champion the critical, nondogmatic "Western Marxism" developed by Georg Lukács. Lukács's *History and Class Consciousness*[38] had emphasized the subjective revolutionary capacity of the proletariat as Marxism's theoretical and political core. Yet Merleau-Ponty rejects this open-ended Marxism as incapable of capturing the dense social and economic structures that eventually came to dominate Bolshevik action. On the other hand, the variants of Marxism that paid heed to this plane of reality led to theoretical dogmatism and, ultimately but inevitably, political oppression. The problem, he argues, lies with the very notion of a revolutionary dialectic: after devoting nearly one-third of the book to criticizing Sartre's independent effort to justify Communism, Merleau-Ponty renounces both Marxist philosophy and politics.

Merleau-Ponty is first attracted to Lukács because his kind of rigorous Marxism does not study events in order to "justify a preestablished schema. Rather it questions events, truly deciphers them, and gives them only as much meaning as they demand".[39] And yet it remains Marxism, pointing to the proletariat, and its consciousness, as the truth of history.

Merleau-Ponty praises Lukács for being committed to the proletariat as a force for "universal criticism" rather than as a "carrier of myths." Marxism is thus not a positivism which would present the answer to human history. "This 'philosophy of history' does not so much give us the keys of history as it restores history to us as permanent interrogation" (57). Merleau-Ponty values Marxism, then, as a critical coming-to-consciousness. When it "focuses everything through the perspective of the proletariat, it focuses on a principle of universal strife and intensifies human questioning instead of ending it."[40]

Orthodox Marxism versus Western Marxism

If this dialectical Marxism seems to meet Merleau-Ponty's demands, it was suppressed by Leninist orthodoxy, with all its crude naturalism—its emphasis on the weight of the real world, moving on its own, at the ex-

---

37. *Adventures*, 7.
38. Trans. Rodney Livingstone (Cambridge, Mass., 1971).
39. *Adventures*, 44.
40. Ibid., 57. Merleau-Ponty is already being more stringent here than in *Humanism and Terror*, where he argued that "Marxism is not a philosophy of history; it is *the* philosophy of history and to renounce it is to dig the grave of Reason in history. After that there can be no more dreams or adventures" (153). By 1955 he had clearly renounced the possibility of "dreams or adventures."

pense of the subjectivity so central to Lukács. Both poles are present in
Marx himself, but, Merleau-Ponty argues, Marx rejects the first as "pre-
Marxist." What is the reason, within Marxism itself, that the dialectic re-
verts to naturalism?

Dialectical Marxism fits revolutionary moments—"soaring periods,"
according to Marxist philosopher and proponent of Western Marxism
Karl Korsch[41]—when the world seems capable of radical change, when
human relationships appear transparently in social reality, when theory
and practice are united. In other words, it expresses those malleable historical periods when the human subject seems fully able to shape human history. Yet although it achieved power, Marxism "could not maintain itself at that *sublime point*" (*Adventures*, 73) as the weight of economic
reality imposed itself. The sense of human possibility began to recede
before the urgency of material conditions. "The Marxism of the young
Marx as well as the 'Western' Marxism of 1923 lacked a means of expressing the inertia of the infrastructures, the resistance of economic and
even natural conditions, and the swallowing-up of 'personal relationships' in 'things'" (64). Lukács accepted the criticism of his book by the
Comintern "because his too supple and too notional dialectic did not
translate the opacity, or at least the density, of real history" (66).[42]

Having seemed to approve Western Marxism, then, Merleau-Ponty
quickly concedes its limits. Yet Leninist naturalism restored the weight of
the objective world to Marxism by rooting the dialectic in *being* rather
than in human subjectivity. Thus the dialectic is also placed beyond practice. Merleau-Ponty refuses to specifically blame Leninism for the break-
down of the various unifications envisioned by Lukács: it may well be
that no revolution remains critical of itself, but this suggests that the
Lukácsian vision is inherently unstable. Illusions aside of "a historical
time which would be constantly agitated by this critical ferment" (90), the
real revolutionary negativity comes to "be represented by bureaucrats."

The Central Issue

So far, Merleau-Ponty sees himself as having shown that the split between Lukács's dialectic and Lenin's realism betrays an "equivocalness"
in the Marxian dialectic *on the theoretical level*—presumably meaning that
neither side could conceivably sight *both* the power of human subjec-

---

41. For a discussion of and selection from Korsch, see Douglas Kellner, *Karl Korsch:
Revolutionary Theory* (Austin, Tex., 1977).
42. For a discussion of the orthodox criticism of Lukács, see Russell Jacoby, *Dialectic of
Defeat* (Cambridge, 1981), 83–103.

tivity *and* the objective weight of material reality, and that *each* proffered a Marxism of the moment as the whole of Marxism. A single fatal action of Trotsky offers practical confirmation of this inherent theoretical weakness—Trotsky's remarkable passivity in the face of the Party's degeneration and Stalin's rise to power. He seemed unaccountably blind to the fact that the Party of the mid-1920s had ceased being revolutionary and democratic. "The dialectic was put to the test"—and failed—when Trotsky was unwilling and unable to split the Party in order to save it.

He could not conceive of the Party's betraying the Revolution, and this faith paralyzed him, making impossible the call to arms which alone might have saved the Revolution. Merleau-Ponty blames the materialist dialectic, because it "postulates that if truth is anywhere, it resides in the inner life of the Party, which the proletariat has created" (82). The ascription of truth to the Party is based on the belief in an objective historical process operating through, but independently of, human beings. Trotsky's inability to act reveals a "contradiction and ambiguity" in Bolshevism. Yet "it is Marxism, not Bolshevism," which "bases the Party's interventions on forces which are already there and bases praxis on a historical truth" (85).

This last point leads us to the philosophical heart of the book. In *Humanism and Terror* Merleau-Ponty had warned that "there comes a time when a detour ceases to be a detour, when the dialectic is no longer a dialectic and we enter a new order of history which has nothing in common with Marx's philosophy of the proletariat."[43] In 1946 he was not yet ready to say that this time had come, perhaps because he still retained residual hope that the philosophy might be fulfilled. By 1955 he conceded that a new order had been reached. He concluded that this was due to a philosophy which itself had been faulty from the outset. In *Critique II* we shall see Sartre respond by taking up this challenge directly, using the Marxian dialectic itself to explain the deviation of the Marxian dialectic. Indeed, Sartre will develop Merleau-Ponty's very theme of deviation into one of the *Critique*'s most powerful tools, everywhere insisting on laying bare its underlying dialectical logic.

From Philosophy to History: The Obsolescence of Marxism

So far, Merleau-Ponty's discussion may seem a bit puzzling. Any confusion thus far stems from the fact that his argument moves along *two* intersecting axes *and* shifts as it develops. Along one axis he shifts from seeking an authentic Marxism and appearing to find it, to discovering

43. *Humanism and Terror*, 150.

that Western Marxism is unable to express history's density, to concluding that Marxism's natural terminus lies rather in an objectivist dialectic
which exalts the Party as its keeper.[44] After locating what seems to be a
philosophically adequate Marxism, he turns away from it, insisting that
history itself effectively reduces *all* varieties of Marxism to a single one.

But is there no middle ground which stresses subject *and* structure,
activity *and* history, chance *and* objective tendency?[45] Merleau-Ponty's
"post-Marxism" seems to be crying out for precisely the great creative
reconsideration carried out in an Italian prison by Antonio Gramsci, or
in American exile by the members of the Frankfurt School.[46] Indeed,
such a "living Marxism" will become the Sartrean hope, to be voiced immediately after *Adventures* appeared, in essays in *Les Temps Modernes*
(one of which mentions Merleau-Ponty's criticism of Sartre).[47] Sartre
then began to *fullfill the hope* in *Search for a Method* and the *Critique*.

Merleau-Ponty's critique foredooms *all* such efforts to separate a more
authentic Marxism from the official Marxisms, and to find there the possibility of a new political reorientation. His renunciation barred him
from joining with that Marxism which, incubated in defeat, prison, and
exile, as well as in response to his own challenge, would itself become a
political force—in the Italian Communist Party, in the student movements of the 1960s, and in the explosion of the French Left in 1968. Why
did not his formidable intellect seek to *develop* this Marxism?

He takes Marxism *as it is*, rather than seeking to fashion a more adequate one. Philosophically he argues that the entire enterprise is obsolete, and this because wrong in the first place: "There is not much
sense in trying Bolshevism all over again at the moment when its revolutionary failure becomes apparent. But neither is there much sense in trying Marx all over again if his philosophy is involved in this failure, or in
acting as if this philosophy came out of this affair intact and rightfully
ended humanity's questioning and self-criticism" (91).

A second answer, a historical one, lies along the other axis of Merleau-

44. Commentators have remarked on the political ambivalence of *Adventures*. According
to Aron, for example, "Merleau-Ponty writes half of his book as if he were still a Marxist,
the other half as if he no longer were . . ." (*Marxism and the Existentialists*, 78). Merleau-
Ponty succinctly presents this same deep understanding and apparent sympathy for Marxism alongside a fundamental critique of it in "The Yalta Papers," *Signs*, trans. Richard
McCleary (Evanston, Ill., 1964), 274–77.

45. For a discussion of the evolution of Merleau-Ponty's politics and an excellent critique of *Adventures* see Sonia Kruks, *The Political Philosophy of Merleau-Ponty* (Brighton, Sus-
sex, 1981).

46. For a discussion of the vitality and revolutionary character of Western Marxism see
Jacoby, *Dialectic of Defeat*.

47. See note 24 above.

Ponty's argument. Having learned his Marxist realism well,[48] Merleau-Ponty rejects defeated versions of Marxism precisely because history has made them into "ideas without historical equivalents" (204). For him, the only historically substantive Marxist dialectic is the victorious one, embodied in Stalinism.[49] Western Marxism's distance from power is the very token of its political irrelevance.

Thus the changing locus of Merleau-Ponty's argument: whatever may be its philosophical insufficiencies, Marxism has been invalidated by *history* itself. As a result, "there is no longer much more reason to preserve these perspectives and to force the facts into them than there is to place the facts into the context of Plato's *Republic*."[50] Merleau-Ponty decisively ends the "wait-and-see Marxism" he announced a decade earlier. Because of the way events have evolved, there is no longer any reason to wait.[51]

Critique of Sartre

Atop this already complex argument Merleau-Ponty now seeks to build another of equal complexity, namely that Sartre's efforts to replace the obsolete philosophy with his own reveal the inadequacy both of Communist politics and of Sartrean thought. Merleau-Ponty is writing this, of course, in 1953 and 1954, after Sartre has declared his alignment with the PCF in *The Communists and Peace*. There Sartre tries "to declare my agreement with the Communists on certain precise and limited subjects, reasoning from *my* principles and not from *theirs*."[52] He has performed only a single study that might be called Marxist, an analysis (in the third of these essays) of the bitter relations between the French bourgeoisie and proletariat since 1871. At the moment of Merleau-Ponty's critique, then, Sartre has politically identified himself with the PCF and has tried his hand at historical-materialist analysis, but he has not yet begun the philosophical rethinking that will eventuate in the *Critique*. In fact, Merleau-Ponty's attack will provide a powerful basis for this reflection.

48. For example, from the second thesis on Feuerbach, which ordains that practice is the criterion of truth.
49. See Jacoby, 11–36, for a provocative discussion of "conformist Marxism" and the cult of success.
50. *Adventures*, 93.
51. As I mentioned, he saw its sponsorship of the Korean War as a decisive indication that the Soviet Union was just another great power. He discusses this in *Adventures*, 228–30.
52. "Les Communistes et la paix," *Situations* VI (Paris, 1964); trans. Irene Clephane, *The Communists and Peace* (London, 1969), 62.

Merleau-Ponty alternately attacks Marxism and compares Sartre unfavorably with it in an argument that shifts rapidly between several frames of reference: Marxism and Merleau-Ponty's "post-Marxist" rendition/critique of it; Sartre's embracing of the French Communist Party and Merleau-Ponty's critical account of it; Sartre's ontology and Merleau-Ponty's critical rendering both of it and its relation to Sartre's politics. Merleau-Ponty attacks not only *The Communists and Peace* but *Psychology of the Imagination, Being and Nothingness,* and *What Is Literature?* arguing that Sartrean dualism has not changed over the twenty years spanning these works.[53] Sartre, his argument goes, lacks the subtle and sophisticated, if flawed, historical and social tools provided by Marxism and so has no way to ground his philosophy in the real world of proletariat and Party; as a result, he uses absurd conceptions to justify a politics which in any case can no longer be justified by its original starting points.

The first section makes a relatively simple point: for Sartre, political action is not rooted in social conditions, economic structures, or history, but is a creation *ex nihilo,* a "conversion," an "invention." If Merleau-Ponty criticized Sartre's "philosophy of the subject" ten years earlier, in *The Phenomenology of Perception,*[54] he now insists that Sartre the "ultra-Bolshevik" remains stuck there. "Sartre's entire theory of the Party and of class is derived from his philosophy of fact, of consciousness, and, beyond fact and consciousness, from his philosophy of time" (*Adventures,* 105). Through its lenses majority rule, minority rights, democracy, control by the rank and file over the leaders—all dissolve before the fact that the Party is, by definition, the power of the powerless.

Merleau-Ponty then compares what he regards as Marxism's overly objectivist conception of truth with Sartre's overly subjective one in which all "facts" must await the interpretation that gives them meaning. And yet, paradoxically, if Marxism's dogmatic sense of truth-in-being entails an exalted sense of the Party, so does Sartre's subjective basing of all truth on consciousness. It is "the answer of consciousness, all the more peremptory because the course of things is so indecisive" (117).

In addition to the Party, Sartre transmutes each of the other key Marxist themes into his own: praxis, revolution, history, the proletariat. And in doing so he reveals his totally subjective, individualistic, and ahistorical perspective based on being-for-itself and "its inevitable correlate: pure being-in-itself" (142). Sartre melodramatically reduces history to the personal choices and actions of specific individuals, such as Stalin.

53. This charge was the one that most angered de Beauvoir. See "Merleau-Ponty et le pseudo-Sartrisme."
54. Trans. Colin Smith (London, 1962), 434 ff.

Thus he rejects as absurd the idea that there can be a historical and social current such as Stalinism without the specific man, Stalin.

Merleau-Ponty now probes more deeply into Sartre's ontology, arguing that it fundamentally lacks the dimension of sociality. Inasmuch as the dialectic appears "only in that type of being in which a junction of subjects occurs," Sartre's individualism must reject it. For him, on the contrary, being is not a common residence, but "a spectacle that each subject presents to itself for its own benefit . . ." (204). His argument for the writer's commitment is based on the same philosophy of permanent revolution, a philosophy lacking mediations, lacking sociality, where consciousness encounters consciousness and everything must always be recreated from scratch. "Yesterday literature was the consciousness of the revolutionary society; today it is the Party which plays this role." And the root of these common themes? "What continues to distinguish Sartre from Marxism, even in recent times, is . . . his philosophy of the *cogito*" (158).

Merleau-Ponty acknowledges that Sartre's historical study of French capitalism and the French working class has a tone which "in some passages is fairly new. It is no longer a tone of urgency or ultimatum but rather one of history" (172). But even a Sartre who has authentically moved onto the terrain of history and politics faces shipwreck due to the contortions the Party demands of a fellow traveler who happens to be a writer. Merleau-Ponty mocks Sartre's commitment-from-a-distance, which refuses to criticize the Party. Sartre's "commitment is action at a distance, politics by proxy, a way of putting ourselves right with the world rather than entering it" (193)—all the natural product of a philosophy incapable of entering the world.

More genuine forms of commitment would begin with an *evaluation* both of the Soviet Union and the PCF, including asking whether revolution is "still the order of the day." Once we see Communism detached from the dialectic which proclaimed it as bringing an end to history, it becomes secularized, deprived of its privileged position in our thought, one system among others. "If there is no logic of history" (183), Communism must be judged by its actual results: and they are "not sufficient to prove that the proletarians' interests lie in this system" (182). It is impossible to prefer a system revealing "only the leaders' authority, manipulation of the masses, the rigging of congresses, the liquidation of minorities, the masquerading of majorities as unanimity . . ." (183).

Keeping his freedom to himself, Sartre does not undertake such a critical analysis, but rather transmutes Communism into Sartre. Instead of developing new categories and habits of thought upon encountering history and politics, Sartre's notion of commitment stems from "a conception of freedom that allows only for sudden interventions into the world, for camera shots and flash bulbs" (193). The root problem, once again, is Sartre's conception of consciousness: "a pure power of signifying, as a centrifugal movement without opacity or inertia, which casts history and the social outside, into the signified, reducing them to a series of instantaneous views, subordinating doing to seeing, and finally reducing action to 'demonstration' or 'sympathy.'" Missing in Sartre's thought is the entire "interworld which we call history, symbolism, truth-to-be-made"—the world of mediations between men and men, men and things (198, 200).

In the *Critique*, Sartre will attempt to discover these mediations and, indeed, will attempt to ground social theory on praxis rather than consciousness. Even before the *Critique*, in 1956 and 1957, we shall see Sartre display a political independence and critical evaluation of the Soviet Union that Merleau-Ponty thought impossible. Then, most remarkably, in volume two he will deal with virtually every one of these specific criticisms, showing Stalinism as a social current inseparable from the specific individuality of Joseph Stalin, tracing the evolution of Soviet socialism, and speculating on its possibilities for democratic revitalization.

What Remains of the Dialectic?

"But," Merleau-Ponty asks in moving toward a conclusion, "what remains of the dialectic if one must give up reading history and deciphering in it the becoming-true of society?" (205). Was it only a myth? Not at all. In the final pages Merleau-Ponty tries to rescue the dialectic for his project of liberal reform, by developing the thesis that there is indeed a dialectic of history and society, a movement of progress through the free play of oppositions. But the dialectic is not a revolutionary one pointing to an "end of history" and embodied in a specific class, such as the proletariat.

Revolutionary thought, in fact, is *not* truly dialectical, but utopian and dogmatic. After all, it projects a class that "will not be a new positive power which, after dispossessing the fallen classes, would in turn assert its own particularity; rather, it will be the last of all classes, the suppression of all classes and of itself as a class." The problem is that "there is no dialectic without opposition or freedom, and in a revolution opposition and freedom do not last long." Revolutionary power destroys the dialectic: "Precisely because it rules, the new ruling class tends to make itself autonomous" (210, 207, 209). To hope that the proletariat will be the last ruling class, and will suppress all classes *including itself,* is to project hopes and wishes that are not dialectical because they have no basis in fact.

In writing about the French Revolution, historian Daniel Guérin dreams of "an 'end of politics' out of which one is to make a politics. Like 'proletarian power,' it is a problem that presents itself as a solution, a question which is given as an answer, the transcendence of history in ideas" (218; translation changed). After all, revolutions must defend themselves, and in so doing create weapons against their enemies *and* their adherents. This means that "revolution and its failure are one and the same thing" (219). All revolutionary advances yield new ruling classes, and therefore a "permanent decadence." Because ruling classes resemble each other *insofar as they rule,* even the dictatorship of the proletariat will become "something like a bourgeoisie" (220). Proletarian revolution is thus not only a dream, but a dangerous one: the more we dogmatically assume that *this* class will cure history's basic problems, the more likely we are to erect a power beyond control.

As a result, Merleau-Ponty calls for a "new Left"—a genuinely independent non-Communist Left freed from "the pretension of terminating [the dialectic] in an end of history" (206) and capable of seeing the full complexity of society, social change, and the contest between the United States and the Soviet Union. This Left will make the dialectic its living principle only *by accepting parliamentary democracy,* "the only known institution that guarantees a minimum of opposition and truth" (226). The complex "effort of enlightenment" Merleau-Ponty calls for is *not* possible under Communism, but is possible in the West. And so he seeks an open-ended "new liberalism" which aligns itself with the proletariat but not with the Party, does not necessarily accept capitalism but certainly rejects the idea that social problems admit of "a solution the way a crossword puzzle does or an elementary problem of arithmetic" (227).

In 1946 he had described Marxism as follows: "It jammed [*s'est enrayée*] when the revolution was limited to an underdeveloped country, but one feels its presence in the French and Italian labor movements. Even if the Marxist dialectic did not take possession of our history, even if we have nowhere seen the advent of the proletariat as ruling class, the dialectic continues to gnaw at capitalist society, it retains its full value as negation: it remains true, it will always remain true, that a history in which the proletariat is nothing is not a human history" (228). Ten years later he renounces his earlier effort to separate Marxism as negation from the Marxist revolution that came to a halt in the Soviet Union. The disappearance of a neutral zone such as Czechoslovakia and the participation of the Soviet Union in the Korean War led Merleau-Ponty to conclude that, finally, the Marxist critique he had accepted yielded the Communist actions he had rejected. And so he began the exploration leading to renunciation: "There must be something in the critique itself that germinates the defects in the action" (231). That something was the Marxist dialectic itself, with its sweeping vision of a future classless society.

It is because they are heirs of Marx that Communists fail to see history as ambiguity and will, chance and choice, but rather pretend that Truth is lodged in the historical unfolding of being. The root problem is already present in the *Communist Manifesto* when it proclaims that Marx's theoretical conclusions "merely express . . . actual relations springing from an existing class struggle, from a historical movement going on under our very eyes" (130). In fact the Marxist dialectic is a grand projection beyond the boundaries of human knowledge, while the dialectic itself, chastened by such adventures, would still describe conflict and transcendence, but without any hope that grand solutions are at hand. And so Merleau-Ponty renounces being a revolutionary, without renouncing the right to struggle against injustice—in the name, we may say, of the dialectic.[55]

Merleau-Ponty's Challenge

Could this total critique demand any less than a total reply? Merleau-Ponty fundamentally challenged his former close colleague *at the very moment* Sartre was moving toward theoretical Marxism. This is not to say that Sartre's political-theoretical energy over the next few years would be explicitly dominated by the task of satisfying Merleau-Ponty's criticisms. But, occupied with intervening politically and revitalizing Marxism, Sartre carried out a project whose meaning can be described vis-à-vis his former colleague in the exact same terms we have seen him use to characterize *The Communists and Peace:* "a systematic refutation . . . opposing point by point, my views to his." In fact he would address virtually every significant issue Merleau-Ponty had posed, incorporating this powerful critique in seeking to go beyond it.[56] The result is a major effort at refashioning his own thought *and* Marxism as he assimilates the one to the other. Thus *Adventures of the Dialectic* forms an inevitable set of reference points in what will become Sartre's unique appropriation of Marxism.

---

55. That his commitment stayed alive, as well as his deep interest in Marxism and Communism, is amply evidenced in the second half of *Signs.*

56. Merleau-Ponty did not choose to reply to Sartre, even as Sartre reaffirmed his com-

The Ghost of Stalin

Sartre's first major response came in late 1956 and early 1957 in his famous articles in *Les Temps Modernes* denouncing the Soviet invasion of Hungary and the PCF's knee-jerk support for it, giving evidence of being the "completely new type of sympathizer"—independent, critical, able to say why he is *not* a Communist—Merleau-Ponty hoped but doubted he could become.[57] He analyzed the "neo-Stalinist" intervention from a non-Party Marxist point of view, one which rooted it in a detailed account of Soviet history. Yet in words owing a great deal to Merleau-Ponty's earlier formulations, Sartre also forcefully affirmed his commitment to the Communist project as the universal human project, in spite of its contradictions:

> For more than a century, under forms which change in the course of history, one movement alone has drawn the exploited on to lay claim, for themselves and for everybody, to the possibility of full and complete manhood; one movement alone has exposed in all its reality and defined the bourgeoisie as the exploiting class when all the rest treat it as the universal class; one alone produces through and by action an ideology which gives it understanding of itself as well as of others; that movement is the socialist movement taken in its entirety. This movement is the absolute judge of all the rest because, to the exploited, exploitation and the class struggle are their reality and the truth of bourgeois societies; it sees the deep meaning of working men and of operative processes because it cannot but tie them to the fundamental structure of history, because it is the movement of man in the process of developing himself.[58]

Above all, Sartre's premise explicitly rejected Merleau-Ponty's new position, in *L'Express* (drawn from the analyses we have just examined) that Communism must be seen relatively as one fact among others,

---

mitment to the PCF in the face of Merleau-Ponty's critique (in his "Réponse à Pierre Naville") and used Merleau-Ponty's original ideas against his newer ones (see below). Nor did Merleau-Ponty choose to publicly discuss the *Critique*, published in early 1960. (His revealing private notes will be mentioned in chapter eight.) Instead, he chose, in the introduction to *Signs*, completed in September 1960, to comment at length on why Sartre drew near to Communism when he did, referring to Sartre's essay on Paul Nizan, in *Situations* IV (also in Eisler trans., *Situations*).

57. *Adventures*, 187.

58. "*Le fantôme de Staline*," *Situations* VII; trans. Irene Clephane, *The Spectre of Stalin* (London, 1969), 4, translation changed. Compare with *Humanism and Terror*, 149–60, and "The U.S.S.R. and the Camps," *Signs*, 263–73.

"without privilege." "Its aim," Sartre says, "is to give justice and freedom to all men; this basic intention cannot snatch it from history since, on the contrary, it is in and through history that it will come true." Sartre rejects Merleau-Ponty's newfound "eagle's eyrie from which the evolution of people's regimes and of capitalist democracies could be jointly appraised."[59] On the contrary, this state, this movement, "in spite of everything that has happened . . . still carries within it the likelihood that it may lead to socialism."[60]

Likelihood? In a telling reference to Plato, which ironically builds on Merleau-Ponty's original realism while explicitly refuting his equation of Marxism with the *Republic*, Sartre emphasizes that this "bloody monster which itself tears itself to pieces" was indeed socialism. "That was socialism even in its primitive phase; there has been no other, except in Plato's heaven, and it must be desired as it is or not at all" (ibid., 61). *This reality*, with its weaknesses, remains an authentic path to the future free society—the *only* path we can see today.

> And I quite see, in fact, that Merleau-Ponty is not very indignant about the Soviet intervention: if the USSR is worth no more and no less than capitalist Britain, then, in fact, there is hardly anything else left for us to do except cultivate our gardens. To preserve hope, it is necessary to do the exact opposite: to recognize, in spite of the mistakes, the abominations, the crimes, the obvious privileges of the socialist camp, and to condemn with so much the more strength the policy which puts these privileges in danger. (Ibid., 91)

Thus does Sartre show signs of absorbing his mentor's lessons while trying to go beyond Merleau-Ponty's critique: he recognizes all the evils of Communism in 1956, but as one who still embraces its project and, indeed, who seeks to use Marxist tools to explain these evils.

Search for a Method

Sartre's next response, equally forceful and equally famous, appropriately follows Merleau-Ponty's own trajectory and moves onto the theoretical plane. Published in September and October 1957, *Search for a Method* explains, as Merleau-Ponty had demanded Sartre do,[61] why he is

59. *Spectre*, 89, 90. This is succinctly formulated in a post-Hungary essay collected in *Signs*, "On De-Stalinization" (303). Merleau-Ponty himself had criticized this stance ten years earlier, in *Humanism and Terror*, 185–86.

60. *Spectre*, 6.

61. *Adventures*, 165–70.

not wholly a Marxist (and by implication why he is not a Communist). But it does so in asserting that Marxism is the "only valid interpretation of history." [62] Marxism is, indeed, "the philosophy of our time" (*QM* 36; 29; *SM* 30). Because it is "simultaneously a totalization of knowledge, a method, a regulative Idea, an offensive weapon, and a community of language," it forms "the humus of every particular thought and the horizon of all culture." Merleau-Ponty's "post-Marxism" would thus have to be an illusion—either a veiled return to pre-Marxism or the rediscovery of ideas *already* contained in Marxism. One cannot go beyond living philosophies such as Marxism "so long as man has not gone beyond the historical moment which they express" (*QM* 21; 17; *SM* 6–7).

Then why does Sartre not simply convert to Marxism? Why keep existentialism alive, as a parasitic ideology on its margin? First, because "Marxism stopped" (*QM* 31; 25; *SM* 21). It was destined to be the unity of theory and practice, guide to reshaping society. But when it became dominant—in the Bolshevik Revolution—its normal course of development was frozen. In the besieged Soviet Union "the free process of truth, with all the discussions and all the conflicts which it involves" had to be curtailed. As a result, theory became separated from practice, "transforming the latter into an empiricism without principles; the former into a pure, fixed knowledge" (*QM* 31; 25; *SM* 22). Where Merleau-Ponty had spoken of Marxism eventuating in opportunism or terror because of its ontological starting point, Sartre argues on the contrary that the historical situation itself generated such alternatives. Under urgent conditions reality was violently assaulted, and theory became an absolute idealism.

Reality came to be understood through a network of a priori categories, as Marxism stopped paying attention to the specificity of individuals and events. "Men and things had to yield to ideas—a priori; experience, when it did not verify the predictions, could only be wrong" (*QM* 31; 25; *SM* 23). As a result, today's "lazy Marxists" render all events—the Hungarian Revolution, Valéry's poetry—through abstract ideas which pretend to explain but give us no knowledge at all. To correct this we need, within and alongside Marxism, an approach which can return us to Marx by respecting and studying individuals and events in all their specificity. Again and again Sartre insists: "What is necessary is simply to reject apriorism" (*QM* 44; 36; *SM* 42).

The second, and related, reason for Sartre's refusal to embrace contemporary Marxism is that he takes its ideas not as knowledge but "as guid-

62. *Questions de méthode*, 30 (1960, 24); *Search for a Method*, 21. Future references to this work will be denoted by *QM*, followed by the page numbers, respectively, of the 1985 and the 1960 editions, and to *SM*, with the page number of the Barnes translation.

ing principles, as indications of jobs to be done, as problems—not as concrete truths." Even after accepting Marxism, "everything remains to be done; we must find the method and constitute the science" (*QM* 40; 33; *SM* 35). While providing us with general keys, Marxism by itself does not allow us to understand, for example, how a specific individual of a specific class—such as Valéry the petit-bourgeois—chooses his specific individual path. Sartre uses precisely the theme, mediations, Merleau-Ponty had used in criticizing him. "Marxism lacks any hierarchy of mediations which would permit it to grasp the process which produces the person and his product inside a class and within a given society at a given historical moment" (*QM* 53; 44; *SM* 56). For example, Marxism avoids seeing the way in which the family operates as the key mediation between the individual and "the general movement of history" yet is lived by the child "as an absolute in the depth and opaqueness of childhood" (*QM* 57; 47; *SM* 62).

Next Sartre explores the ways in which mediations operate, especially through the family. Then, in the remainder of *Search for a Method*, he indicates his project of developing these mediations. He sketches the progressive-regressive method as the path to understanding how an individual internalizes the elements of his situation and then reexteriorizes them as his project. The specifics of these discussions need not occupy us here, but Sartre's general intent is decisive for appreciating the alternative he develops to Merleau-Ponty's abandonment of Marxism. We have seen Merleau-Ponty flatly oppose "Western Marxism" to "naturalistic Marxism," the subjective dialectic to the objective dialectic. He found the first to be a historical irrelevancy outside of great revolutionary moments, the other as accounting for history's weight and the urgency of social pressures but by lodging the dialectic in the facts themselves. When he concluded that the subjective dialectic led to an unrealizable fantasy and the objective dialectic to the oppressive reality of Soviet Communism, Merleau-Ponty left himself no choice but to abandon both.

Sartre, on the other hand, looked for the links between the two, the process whereby *each* created the other, as did Gramsci and the Frankfurt School. He rejected Merleau-Ponty's either/or, searching instead for the subjective roots of the objective alienations and the objective root of the subjective possibility—at one and the same time. There is no question, he insisted, of *adding* a method to Marxism. The dialectic itself must, and can, be developed to be adequate to the human beings who are its objects. In doing so, we will avoid opposing individuality to generality, chance to necessity. Sartre, for example—in opposition to Merleau-Ponty's claim that Stalinism is a general phenomenon separable from the personality of the individual[63]—wants to show that a historical situation does not demand general traits which can be met by a number of individuals but, rather, *creates* and *asks for* the very individual who pushes it forward (*QM* 70–71; 58–59; *SM* 83).[64] In seeking to create a Marxism which takes full account of the individual, Sartre seeks "not to reject Marxism in the name of a third path or of an idealist humanism, but to reconquer man within Marxism" (*QM* 71; 59; *SM* 83).

Merleau-Ponty had attacked Marxism, above all, for lifting the moving force of history out of human hands and lodging it in an apparently autonomous sociohistorical process; this is what he meant by his remarks that the truth and direction of history were inscribed in being. If the subjective dialectic was impotent, this objective dialectic had resulted in terror and the cult of the Party. In contrast, Sartre understands that an adequate Marxism—or social philosophy of any stamp—has to explain *both* the density and weight of history *and* the transforming activity of human subjects. Merleau-Ponty had seen both statically, as opposing camps, and so had not thought beyond them. As a result, he could not fail to regard each as equally incorrect. Sartre, on the contrary, now shows his full distance from Merleau-Ponty by looking forward to developing an analysis which takes account of each side in terms of the other:

> If one wants to grant to Marxist thought its full complexity, one would have to say that man in a period of exploitation is *at once both* the product of his own product and a historical agent who can under no circumstances be taken as a product . . . [As Engels said,] men make their history on the basis of real, prior conditions . . ., but it is *the men* who make it and not the prior conditions. Otherwise men would be merely the vehicles of inhuman forces which through them would govern the social world. To be sure, these conditions exist, and it is they, they alone, which can furnish a direction and a material reality to the changes which are in preparation; but the movement of human praxis goes beyond them while conserving them. (*QM* 73–74; 61; *SM* 87)

Until Marxism learns this lesson, existentialism will continue to exist as a philosophy, demanding that it "reintegrate man into itself as its foundation" (*QM* 131; 109; *SM* 179). How will this reintegration be accomplished? First, in a *critique of dialectical reason*, which performs its basic theoretical steps, and, secondly, by encouraging other work which, col-

---

63. *Adventures*, 144–45.
64. This prefigures Sartre's major discussion of Stalin, which will be explored below, in chapter six.

lectively, completes this task. "From the day that Marxist thought will have taken on the human dimension (that is, the existential project) as the foundation of anthropological knowledge, existentialism will no longer have any reason for being" (*QM* 132; 111; *SM* 181).

The Daunting Task

And so Sartre turns to create the *Critique*. If these two brief prefaces have already turned out to equal the entire length of Merleau-Ponty's *Adventures*, Sartre's effort has only begun. He will try to show that another Marxian dialectic exists than the one Merleau-Ponty has prematurely rejected, and that this dialectic *both* bears the weight of the world *and* is wholly produced by human beings. But to see the light of day this dialectic must be liberated from the "organicism" which sees society and history as moving on their own.

To set the dialectic straight and account for its deviation, especially in isolation from others who had been attempting the same task, was to be a daunting project of world-historical import. No wonder, then, Sartre worked as if a man possessed. De Beauvoir describes the fury with which he wrote: "For hours at a stretch he raced across sheet after sheet without re-reading them, as though absorbed by ideas that his pen, even at that speed, couldn't keep up with; to maintain this pace I could hear him crunching corydrame capsules, of which he managed to get through a tube a day."[65] And in the evenings, exhaustion, alcohol, more alcohol.

The result, even unfinished, was a manuscript separated into two volumes, *five times* the length of Merleau-Ponty's farewell to Marxism. In the process Sartre wrote an entirely new and original work, one which scarcely mentions Merleau-Ponty but bears the mark of his critique on every page.

The Critique as Theoretical Praxis

The *Critique*'s most general purposes absorb and frame the issues we have been exploring. We have seen Merleau-Ponty argue that Soviet Communism's weaknesses and brutality are rooted in historical materialism's philosophical weakness—that of inscribing the dialectic as rooted in being itself, as if *events themselves* unfolded toward Communism. The *Critique*'s very first section will respond by distinguishing "critical dialectic," which self-consciously traces the subjective-objective movement of history, from "dogmatic dialectic," which lifts history beyond the human beings

---

65. *Force of Circumstances*, 385.

who are its source. Thus the dialectic, which is "both a method *and* a movement in the object" (I, 140; 120; 20), *went astray* historically, in praxis itself, and at this moment calls for a critique to set it back on track. As "the living logic of action" (I, 156; 133; 38), it can only appear in its true light, as "the rationality of praxis" (I, 157; 134; 39) to one who performs the *Critique* "in the course of praxis as a necessary moment of it . . ." (I, 156; 133; 38). Sartre's praxis, more specifically, is to ascertain the limits of the dialectic after Stalinism: "the *abuses* which have obscured the very notion of dialectical rationality and produced a new divorce between praxis and the knowledge which elucidates it" (I, 166; 141; 50).

Such a critique makes sense only *after* the dialectic "was posited for itself in the philosophies of Hegel and Marx," then had become the algebra of twentieth-century socialist revolution, and then "Stalinist idealism had sclerosed both epistemological methods and practices. It could take place only as the intellectual expression of that re-ordering which characterizes, in this 'one world' of ours, the post-Stalinist period" (I, 166; 141; 50). If the "totalizing activity of the world" had led to a "divorce of blind unprincipled praxis and sclerosed thought, or in other words the obscuring of the dialectic," the movement of de-Stalinization now makes a critique of dialectical reason both possible and necessary, indeed urgent. Merleau-Ponty, then, had contemplated, but not seen beyond, this frozen "naturalism" that developed under the conditions faced by the Soviet Union after 1917: Sartre's project is not to reject the dialectic, but to *perform the intellectual labor necessary to free it from rigidification.*

The Critique as Political Praxis

Yet the full story is even more complex. Sartre himself had an unmatched record of political intervention from the early 1940s to virtually the end of his life. The *Critique* was framed by his sustained contribution to the Algerian struggle for independence, on the one hand, and his attempts to create sympathy for revolutionary Cuba menaced by the United States, on the other. Most readings of the first volume have grasped its formal and metatheoretical Marxist ambitions. But its imposed self-sufficiency, and a lack of comparison with Merleau-Ponty's critique, has forced them to miss the concrete political purpose which, for Sartre, lay at the heart of the project:[66] in the act of thawing the dialectic, to trace the praxis-process of its freezing.

If Merleau-Ponty was wrong to blame the dialectic itself for its sclerosis, a post-Stalinist Marxism urgently had to establish the real reasons,

66. The exceptional reading of the *Critique* confirms the rule: it is based on a study of volume two. See Anderson, *In the Tracks of Historical Materialism*, 70–72.

which lay in history and not in philosophy. Thus Sartre set *historical and political* tasks in volume two: to determine why the Bolshevik Revolution followed the course it did, and to explore the prospects of its evolving into a different socialism.

This had indeed been one of Sartre's great obsessions even before his formal adherence to Marxism, to be explored time and again in the ten years before beginning the *Critique* not only in *The Communists and Peace, The Spectre of Stalin*, and *Search for a Method* but also in the plays *Dirty Hands* and *The Devil and the Good Lord*. In fact, in the little-known screenplay *In the Mesh* (1946), Sartre traced the tragic course of a socialist revolution in a small Eastern European country rich with petroleum. Its dictator has betrayed the revolution's original goals, because of the threat of foreign intervention. He is overthrown by comrades who seek to realize the revolution's original goals: nationalization of the foreign-owned oil industry, freedom of speech and press, an elected parliament. Even though he has become progressively more corrupted by his own violence, the dictator alone knows that the powerful capitalist neighbor makes it impossible to fulfill the revolution's goal. Only an impending larger war will give the small country the space to carry out its revolution, and until then the revolutionary hopes must be forcibly restrained. As the deposed dictator is led to his death, the new revolutionary rulers learn the same grim lesson, submitting to the demands of the oil cartel and the foreign ambassador.[67]

In the *Critique* Sartre reflects on the very same theme—the revolutionary success-cum-deterioration of Bolshevism. He is spurred on by his own deep interest, as well as by Merleau-Ponty. In volume one we watch the group slowly formalize and institutionalize itself in order to survive, creating anew the seriality against which it originally formed. By volume two the Bolshevik Revolution's success through deviation becomes, remarkably, the central historical experience within and around which Sartrean social theory develops.

While his specific analysis in volume one begins with the storming of the Bastille, and most of his references are drawn from the French Revolution, the study of the passage from the group-in-fusion, to the Terror, to the institutionalization of the revolution, to bureaucracy and the cult of personality ends up by mentioning not Napoleon but Stalin (see I, 743–46; 628–31; 660–63). Considered by itself, volume one may not allow us to say confidently that in its central sections Sartre meant to understand the Russian Revolution through the French. But this impres-

67. *L'Engrenage* (Paris, 1948); trans. Mervyn Savill, *In the Mesh* (London, 1954).

sion is strengthened not only retrospectively, by the clearly anticipatory analyses of Communism in *The Communists' and Peace* and *The Spectre of Stalin*, but above all by the central pages of volume two.

There we shall see Sartre discuss first the general problem of the contradictions and opposition within a revolutionary group, then the Trotsky-Stalin conflict, then Stalin's political practice in the 1930s (including collectivization and industrialization), then the meaning of the "cult of personality," and the question of Stalin's antisemitism. This sustained work on the Soviet Union, nearly half of the 200,000-word book (177 of 390 pages), is both theoretical and political, finally asking—and answering—the question of questions: Why Stalin? In it Sartre's ambitions as historical and political thinker rival his ambitions as social philosopher, as he reflects not only on how the dialectic became "obscured" under Stalin but also on whether the Revolution's positive results can now be freed from its negative ones.

In these monumental analyses we shall see Sartre exerting intellect and commitment with all his considerable might in a decisive refutation of Merleau-Ponty, insisting not only on the dialectical character of the blockages of the dialectic, but also on the human praxis at the heart of some of the grimmest facts of the century. His is a pitched struggle on behalf of Marxism and socialism and against Merleau-Ponty's post-Marxism, as well as against all political and intellectual tendencies which would confirm human products as forces *beyond* human control (and reversal). On the one hand, as we shall see, Sartre here combats both bourgeois and Marxist outlooks that would separate our (however alienated) product from us and would impose it back upon us, inherent in being, as laws, Society, or fate. In the process he will also combat Merleau-Ponty's attempt to blame Marxism itself for its apparent default, proclaiming the dialectic itself as the only tool able to understand and free itself from its own rigidification. And he will project, but not complete, a description of history itself as a meaningful and comprehensible totalization resulting from the scattered and conflicting actions of its myriad agents.

We shall experience in these analyses—and through the retrospective light they throw on the entire *Critique*—a heroic, single-handed effort to move heaven and hell (indeed to expose both as human creations) in order to restore our ability to think about the world and its alienations as *ours* and changeable in decisive ways. How radical, then, how ambitious is the *Critique!* This sketch of its purposes in light of its second volume may enable us better to appreciate it, especially if we set it in light of the narrowing of hope indicated by *Adventures of the Dialectic*. A sense of how vast are Sartre's goals may help to explain why he wrote as a man obsessed, under the greatest strain, and why he abandoned the *Critique* without finishing it. And it may encourage forgiveness of the project's profound failings, its tortuous character, and the difficulty it imposes on the reader.

2 Totalization without a Totalizer?

We are ready to follow Sartre onto the daunting terrain of the *dialectic*. The very term serves to remind us of the deeper complexity lying within the relative simplicity and clarity of Sartre's project in volume two. Relative indeed: just to attack one of the key terms of dialectical reason, "totalization," in order to clarify Sartre's meaning, would require a massive essay necessarily exploring a number of other key terms, precious few of which could be defined succinctly at the outset. Why? Under the rubric of the dialectic, we are dealing with a process of ever more complex *self-development*. This means that the study's formal categories cannot be spelled out in advance, because they are intended as the emerging substance and structure of the study itself (and indeed of reality). And so they must bear a considerable weight of ambiguity, serving more than one purpose and often changing over time. This also means that no key term can be understood without the others, in an analysis destined for complexity and lack of analytical precision by its very focus on a region synonymous with "totalization" and the "truth of history."

Access to the zone of reality which Sartre seeks to describe—*the* dialectic, but as created by the multiplicity of *individual* praxes—requires persistent and often confusing acts of abstraction. Thus even volume two is not intended to lead us "to the absolute concrete, which can only be individual (*this* event at *this* date of *this* history), [but] at least to the absolute system of conditions for applying the determination '*concrete fact*' to the fact of *one* history" (I, 183; 157; 69).

In such a study, self-consciously seen as a process paralleling the self-development of human reality itself, the reader will be challenged to determine just what is at stake in any particular discussion. And indeed, once a moment of precision is attained, the next stage of discussion may necessitate shifting ground and require yet another act of self-situation before the reader is again sure of its direction—whereupon, once again, the ground may shift, forcing yet another retaking of bearings, far now from the original moment of clarity. Moreover, it should be evident that Sartre's agenda for volume two simultaneously contains, and may even confuse, a number of separable if interconnected purposes. If Sartre will indeed focus and narrow the direction of volume two at its outset, let us first establish its place in the *Critique* project, allowing the part and the whole to illuminate each other. Then we can observe him setting out on his first steps.

A Progressive-Regressive Study

Why, we may ask, does the central thrust of the *Critique* call for an attempt to decode both individual struggle and "the complex phenomenon which has to be described as a praxis-process and which sets classes in opposition to one another as circular totalizations of institutions, groups and serialities?" (I, 882; 745; 806). The most obvious part of the answer lies in Sartre's description of the halves of the *Critique* in the terms announced in *Search for a Method*, as a *regressive-progressive* project. *Critique I*, as the regressive component, has sought to deconstruct social reality into its abstract elements, categories, and processes, its synchronic structures, to demonstrate "the intelligibility of practical structures and the dialectical relation which interconnects the various forms of active multiplicities" (I, 894; 754; 817).

But with this achieved, "we are still at the level of synchronic totalization," and it is time for the progressive study, in which the researcher turns back toward reconstructing the concrete by considering "the diachronic depth of practical temporalization." Its "aim will be to rise up to the double synchronic and diachronic movement by which History constantly totalizes itself" (I, 894; 754–55; 817–18). In other words, having first revealed "the static conditions of the possibility of a totalization, that is to say, of a history," it is time to "progressively [recompose] the historical process on the basis of the shifting and contradictory relations of the formations in question" in order to learn whether the complex interactions, including struggles, reveal "an intelligible (and thus directed) totalizing movement" (I, 183; 155; 68).

One History

In asking about History with a capital *H*, Sartre is, however, pointing to another goal of the project's second part: "it will attempt to establish that there is *one* human history, with *one* truth and *one* intelligibility" (I, 184; 156; 69). One history? Althusser attacked the first volume precisely for its "historicist" reading of Marxism, dominated as it was by "the shade of Hegel."[1] For the Merleau-Ponty of 1946 this had been one of Marxism's most appealing features, discarded as he came to conclude that it was not becoming true in any positive sense. In the face of such agnosticism Sartre's unflinching purpose was indeed "to establish the dialectic as the universal method and universal law of anthropology" (I, 138; 117–18; 18).

From the very beginning he rejected the thought of a pluralism of approaches to human reality, insisting on the dialectic as the master logic. This strategy entailed establishing "the permanent necessity for man of totalizing and being totalized, and for the world of being an ever-broader, developing totalization" (I, 140; 120; 21). Marxism's Immanuel Kant would "explore the limits, the validity, and the extent of dialectical Reason," allowing it to "ground itself and to develop itself as a free critique of itself, at the same time as being the movement of History and of knowledge" (I, 141; 120; 21).

The dialectic: method, structure of reality, vision of universal history being unfolded through our acts. With a breathtaking Hegelian ambition and sweep, Sartre sought to lay the a priori basis for Marxism. He simultaneously claimed the dialectic as *the* method of any study of human reality and sought to "discover the basic signification of History and of dialectical rationality" (I, 894; 755; 818).

We Create the Dialectic

But besides accepting Marxism as providing the decisive keys to the meaning of history and the overarching logic by which that meaning is grasped—as well as illuminating and advancing the struggle by which the historical process advances—Sartre's project was to be shaped and driven forward by yet another commitment, also falling under the rubric of the dialectic. He criticized Hegel and Engels for dogmatically and one-sidedly making the dialectic external to, and imposing it on, the individuals who create it. This was what Merleau-Ponty had meant by complaining about a truth inscribed in being. Sartre's goal was to acknowledge that there was a genuine experience behind this common sense of an external dialectic without losing track of its ultimate human source.

> So, in a sense, man submits to the dialectic as to an enemy power; in another sense, he *creates it*; and if dialectical Reason is the Reason of History, this contradiction must itself be lived

1. Louis Althusser, *For Marx*, trans. Ben Brewster (London, 1977), 116.

dialectically, which means that man must be controlled by the dialectic insofar as he *creates it,* and *create* it insofar as he is controlled by it. Furthermore, it must be understood that there is no such thing as man; there are people, wholly defined by their society and by the historical movement which carries them along; if we do not wish the dialectic to become a divine law again, a metaphysical fate, it must proceed *from individuals* and not from some kind of supra-individual ensemble. Thus we encounter a new contradiction: the dialectic is the law of totalization which creates *several* collectivities, *several* societies, and *one* history—realities, that is, which impose themselves on individuals; but at the same time it must be woven out of millions of individual actions. We must show how it is possible for it to be both a *resultant,* though not a passive average, and a *totalizing force* though not a transcendent fate, and how it can continually bring about the unity of dispersive profusion and integration. (I, 154; 131; 35–36)

Paradoxically, then, while seeking the most general and abstract laws of self-unifying human social development—laws whose existence many thinkers, some Marxists among them, would deny—Sartre simultaneously insists on their origin in the activities of individuals:

Thus there is no *one* dialectic which imposes itself upon the facts, as the Kantian categories impose themselves on phenomena; but the dialectic, if it exists, is the individual career of its object. There can be no pre-established schema imposed on individual developments, neither in someone's head, nor in an intelligible heaven; if the dialectic exists, it is because certain regions of materiality are *structured* in such a way that it cannot not exist. In other words, the dialectical movement is not some powerful unitary force revealing itself behind History like the will of God. It is first and foremost a *resultant;* it is not the dialectic which forces historical men to live their history in terrible contradictions; it is men, as they are, dominated by scarcity and necessity, and confronting one another in circumstances which History or economics can inventory, but which only dialectical reason can explain. Before it can be a *motive force,* contradiction is a result; and, on the level of ontology, the dialectic appears as the only type of relation which individuals, situated and constituted in a certain way, and on account of their very constitution, can establish themselves. The dialectic, if it exists, can only be the totalization of concrete totalizations effected by a multiplicity of totalizing individualities. (I, 155–56; 132; 37).

Two Goals

Sartre seeks *the* dialectic, rooted in *individuals:* this is the path of Sartre's undogmatic Marxism. The striking originality of the *Critique* lies in his adherence to *both* poles and all they imply. It lies above all in his determination to see the individuals as the source of the dialectic: "it is no more than ourselves" (I, 157; 134; 39; translation changed). The reader can perhaps glimpse the immense scale of Sartre's ambition by considering that these twin commitments intend not merely to present, but to integrate, the most radical ontological and sociological individualism and the most sweeping sense of the oneness of human history. In short, Sartre seeks both to trace the dialectic back to its source in individual action and to view it, writ large, as the meaning of history. In doing so, Sartre is directly rebutting post-Marxism; less directly, he is undertaking the passage from his own subject-centered ontology. The two purposes become one as he takes his own starting point, individual praxis, to be the sole guarantor of a critical, rather than a dogmatic, dialectic.

Whatever its difficulties, and indeed whatever its subsequent weaknesses and structural improbabilities, Sartre pursues this ambition with a consistency, force, and honesty which mark it as a truly great intellectual adventure. The entirety of volume one is a remarkably bold and sustained effort to explain basic structures of social reality without recourse to the "hyper-organism" of *Society*, an independent being seen to move and act on its own—by demonstrating how each structure under consideration depends on a multiplicity of individual actions. The materiality thereby created—as product, as tool, as organizational structure of the producers themselves—absorbs the separate actions of the multiplicity, holds them in its inertia, and then in turn imposes itself as the given of future actions, redirecting and reorganizing them according to *its* logic. Indeed, this brilliant concept, the practico-inert, points to a socialized dimension of individual activity without conceding the existence of Society.

Toward Volume Two

Given these purposes, however, it will be in volume two that the wager is won or lost. In addition to its more genial formal purpose of allowing the structures adduced in volume one "to live freely, to oppose and to cooperate with one another" (I, 894; 755; 818), it bears the urgent substantive burden of establishing that the scattered and separate multiplicities do indeed produce a single history. It approaches "the problem of totalization itself, that is to say, of History in its development and of Truth in its becoming" (I, 15; 11; 824). Were he not to meet this challenge we would indeed be left viewing a series of elements with no sense of whether or how they combine, a sense of those focused and directed moments of historical rupture and their congealing into institutions, but no understanding of how separated and even hostile multiplicities combine to create *a* history. Lacking volume two, we have many histories, but no History. In Sartre's eyes this result would drain each history of its meaning, depriving the dialectic, totalization, and even Truth of their sense, destroying any hope of achieving *an* anthropology. Volume two, then, is more than fully half of the project—it is its destination, its culmination.

Volume two helps us place the most monumental aspect of the *Critique* in appropriate relief: its attempt to dissolve the frozen, fixed givens of social life in the process of their constitution. Sartre does not merely proclaim that "praxis creates the world" but sets out to *demonstrate* it, and the first volume shows ever more complex realities being built up from simpler ones, beginning with individual praxis. Indeed, his concern is to reveal how and under what conditions our products become forces beyond our control and in turn dominate the praxis which creates them. In a sense, nothing is given, all is created, even in its genielike escape from its creator's control—and by the end of the second volume this focus will be extended to the very meaning and direction of history itself. Volume one concerns itself only with the elements and first-level products of action, or with structures which, in one form or another, have been specifically intended. But absolutely essential for completing the map are the products intended by *no one*—on the first level, the results of class conflict, and at the furthest reaches of study, the direction of history itself.

Early on, Sartre himself had posed four questions which must be answered "if the dialectic is possible":

> (1) How can praxis in itself be an experience both of necessity and of freedom since neither of these, according to classical logic, can be grasped in an empirical process?
> (2) If dialectical rationality really is a logic of totalization, how can History—that swarm of individual destinies—appear as a totalizing movement, and how can one avoid the paradox that in order to totalize there must already be a unified principle, that is that only active totalities can totalize themselves?
> (3) If the dialectic is comprehension of the present through the past and through the future, how can there be a historical future?
> (4) If the dialectic is to be materialist, how are we to compre-

hend the materiality of praxis and its relation to other forms of
materiality? (I, 193; 165; 79)

Solutions to questions 2 and 3, it will be obvious, cannot even be attempted before the second volume. Problems 1 and 4 can be posed, but
the first can certainly not be completed without exploring and establishing the meaning of history as a joint production of necessity and freedom. Only the last question might have been answered—but was not—
in the first volume. In fact, Sartre will wait until the end of volume two to
deal with it. The point is that by the end of volume one we have understood certain elements of the dialectic, have seen the way they may combine, but have not yet observed them combine to form the irreversible
and large-scale entities which emerge in and seem to direct our history.
Accordingly, we must turn to its second volume.

The Purpose of Volume Two: Totalization without a Totalizer

Given that the *Critique*'s overall purpose is to philosophically anchor and
delimit the dialectic as method of comprehension, as meaning of history,
and as guide to political action, volume two must bear most of its bur-
dens. It must, to return to our first and simplest formulations, show how
and whether totalization does take place even at the heart of conflict,
which is to say, how history's positive direction takes shape and sustains itself even within negativity. If he agrees with Marx's famous dic-
tum that "the history of all hitherto existing society is the history of class
struggles,"[2] Sartre seeks to explain why these struggles yield human development, rather than—nothing at all.[3]

Sartre makes these questions more precise at the end of volume one,
and because of their great interest they are worth quoting even at the risk
of some repetition.

> We have seen how the mediation of the third party realizes the
> transcendent unity of positive reciprocities [that is, how indi-
> viduals each engaged in the same practice form themselves
> into a coherent single group-in-fusion through the mediation
> of a third person engaged in the same activity]. But is this
> unity still possible when each action is aimed at destroying
> that of the Other and when the observable results of this

2. Karl Marx and Frederick Engels, *The Communist Manifesto*, in *The Collected Works*
(London, 1976) 6:482.
3. This is a position he explored with considerable sympathy in *Cahiers pour une morale*
(Paris, 1983), 47–49.

double negation are nil or—as usually happens—when the
teleological significations which each adversary has inscribed
in it have been partly erased or transformed by the Other, so
that no trace of concerted activity is any longer to be seen? (I,
893; 754; 816–17)

Taking the example of individual combat, how are we to understand that
significant results are produced in a situation in which "each blow dealt
by the one is dodged or parried or blocked by the Other—but not completely, unless they differ greatly in strength or skill" (I, 893; 754; 817). In
the face of the complex totalization which is history, we are left trying to
understand efforts which "have to be comprehended not as the realization of a project, but in terms of how the action of each group (and
also of chance, accident, etc.) prevented them from realizing that of the
Other, that is to say, to the extent that they *are not* practical significations,
and that their mutilated, truncated meaning does not correspond to any
one's practical plan so that, in this sense, they fall short of being human"
(ibid.).

At stake in the next stage of analysis is nothing less than the nature
and meaning of history itself, seen as

the totalization of all practical multiplicities and of all their
struggles, the complex products of the conflicts and collabo-
rations of these very diverse multiplicities . . . This means
that History is intelligible if the different practices which can
be found and located at a given moment of the historical temporalization finally appear as partially totalizing and as connected and merged in their very oppositions and diversities
by an intelligible totalization from which there is no appeal. It
is by seeking the conditions for the intelligibility of historical
vestiges and results that we shall, for the first time, reach the
problem of totalization without a totalizer and of the very
foundation of this totalization, that is to say, of its motive-
forces and of its non-circular direction. (I, 893–94; 754; 817)

Volume Two: Epicenters in Conflict

And so we come, after a pause, to volume two. In a step-by-step introductory discussion, Sartre both indicates what volume two is *not* about
and deepens our sense of its tasks and importance.

If the task is to understand *contradiction,* at the outset Sartre indicates
and dismisses the kinds of contradictions he does not have in mind:
those arising "at each moment of action" (II, 12) in a single, coherent

praxis as, for example, it inevitably opposes this or that section of a practical field to the others, or as it necessarily seeks to go beyond its initial results and limits. Indeed, "contradiction" may well be used in an a priori fashion to assimilate two opposing sides—a "double praxis of antagonistic reciprocity"—as "a given moment of totalization." But wherein lies the unity? Dialectical intelligibility, after all, starts with totalization; and totalization is the product of a unifying praxis. A given region is intelligible *when* and *because* human intentionality itself shapes its structures and history. But when two men fight against each other, *conflicting* intentionalities are at play:

> In fact there is, if one wishes, a single movement of these two bodies but this movement is the result of *two* enterprises which oppose each other. It belongs at the same time to two practical systems, but, precisely because of this, it escapes in its concrete reality—at least partially—each of them; if the plurality of the epicenters is a real condition of *two* opposed intelligibilities (insofar as there is a comprehensive intelligibility in each system and starting with each praxis), how could there be *one* dialectical intelligibility of the ongoing process? (II, 13)

We may certainly regard a boxing match as a *fight, an object* to appreciate, to find tickets for, to remember, "but this unity is imposed *from the outside on an event*" (II, 14). The point demands closer attention:

> An object for individuals, groups, collectives, defined as totality by language, by the press and the organs of information, and then subsequently, in the past, designated as a unity of its being-past by memory ("It was *the day of the* Carpentier-Dempsey *fight*"), the fight, in itself, appears as one of those mathematical symbols which designate an ensemble of operations to carry out, and which figure as such in the series of algebraic equivalences without the mathematician's ever troubling to really carry out the indicated operations. It is an object to be constituted, to be utilized, to be contemplated, to be designated; in other words, it plays a role as such in the activities of others; but no one is concerned to know whether this reality—the noematic and unified correspondent of individual and collective praxis—is in *itself*, as internal operation to be carried out by two individuals in a state of antagonistic reciprocity, a real unity or an irreducible duality. (II, 14)

Sartre admits without hesitation that *the* match exists, for many people and for many purposes; his goal is "to know if *as struggle*, as objective fact of reciprocal and negative totalization, it possesses the conditions of dialectical intelligibility" (II, 15). Does the struggle itself create the unity?

Appreciating this question as relevant, legitimate, and important is critical to grasping Sartre's purpose. We see here, on the level of struggle (but not yet class struggle), *the* questions of the progressive synthesis: How do separate, antagonistic actions yield *a* history? How do individual totalizations lead to Totalization (and also progress, the direction of history, its truth and meaning)? From the outset, in posing the very questions themselves, Sartre is rejecting the dualism—either history is inscribed in being or it has no direction at all—which led Merleau-Ponty to abandon Marxism. First, his questions affirm that there are meaningful paths, leading to a single meaningful path, of human development. Second, Sartre presupposes that individuals do more than carry out the will of History, and in fact are the very bases and agents of any larger syntheses. Here more than anywhere in his *oeuvre* Sartre directly and unflinchingly approaches the master problem of the passage from Descartes to Marx, from cogito to society, from individual praxis to collective membership.

Dialectical versus Analytical Reason

But before continuing to approach it directly, Sartre introduces another main line of *Critique II*. He embarks on a lengthy methodological reflection whose purpose is to distinguish the dialectical analysis of struggle from the examination of battles usually undertaken by analytical reason, for example in military schools. His goal is to define his terrain of study further.

Rationally and in a systematic manner, the instructing officer "again goes over all *possible* maneuvers in the situation at hand in order to determine whether the one which was done in reality is indeed the *best possible one*, as it should and claims to be" (II, 15). The point is that this approach does not give us the whole *as struggle* but rather as a "complex whole of n^x possibilities, which are rigorously interlinked" (II, 16). Whatever its utility for practical purposes, an approach that concentrates on "a multiplicity of relationships between possibles" (II, 16) has abandoned the plane of dialectical reason. This is the gravamen of Sartre's criticism of analytical or positivistic reason: it evades "the scandal of irreducible antagonism in order to fall into conditionings in exteriority" (II, 16).

As *Critique II* develops, we shall observe a sustained and ever-deepening attack on all forms of analytical, positivist, or sociological reason. So much so that Sartre repeatedly clarifies the dialectic by contrasting it with its antagonist—which, in the end, we shall see him assign a lesser and technical role, *managed by* dialectical reason (see chapter seven). In initiating this major strand of volume two, Sartre tries to stress that there are two radically different ways of viewing combat: on the one hand, from the outside, and on the other, from the point of view of the antagonists. Why does one deserve the privileged designation, dialectical, and the other the pejorative one, analytical?

Because even if necessary for practical purposes—anticipating all possible responses to a given maneuver, for example, and developing an answer for each response—analytical reason is unable to grasp the "historical reality and temporal individuality" of a given conflict. It is an abstract and external understanding carrying us "far from what could be called the irreducible singularity of the epicenters" (II, 17). The military instructor, we have seen, studies every conceivable maneuver in a given battle or campaign in analyzing whether the actual one was really "*the best possible*" one. "These *possibles* have never had real existence, but they have been placed in relief, most often, by a hundred years of discussion in the military schools" (II, 15). Certainly in his ability to see all the interconnected possibilities he is superior to the actual combatants: he knows a good deal about *both* armies, as well as what maneuvers were chosen on each side and who won the battle. He is free from all urgencies, except as further external considerations: "Ignorance, material difficulties, specific interests, and the play of passions which actually confronted the armies in their historical singularity are factors that he considers abstractly but that remain foreign to him" (II, 16).

And so the actual conflict disappears "into a formal theory, into a quasi-mathematical calculus of possibles" (II, 16). Sartre points out that such theorizing is used in developing airborne machine guns which seek the enemy's probable position and, if mistaken, correct their aim automatically. Today we might note that nuclear war theory operates in the same way, as an analytical calculus of possibilities.

Dialectical, on the other hand, applies to an understanding which would center itself *within* the perspective of either of the combatants— rather than claiming a necessarily external neutrality—and illuminate the individual situation of that combatant. Nothing could be further from the military schools' abstract calculus of possibilities than the "blind and passionate" combatant who actually does battle, under threat, urgently forced to respond.

> A real combatant is a violent and passionate man, sometimes
> desperate, sometimes ready to seek death, who risks every-

thing to destroy the adversary but who maneuvers in a time that is measured for him by the rhythm of the other's attacks (and by a hundred other factors of every order), in having at his disposal (for example) a limited number of men and arms (which forbids certain operations), and who struggles in a variable but always profound ignorance (ignorance of the enemy's real intentions, of the real relationship of forces, of the real position of reinforcements—for the adversary and for him, etc., which obliges him to take risks, to decide upon the most probable without having the necessary elements for being able to calculate it, to invent the maneuvers which take account of several eventualities (if the enemy is disposed in such a fashion, the operation will take place in such fashion or such manner; if it is discovered in the course of action that he is otherwise disposed, the operation is conceived to be able to be instantaneously modified, etc.). It is this blind and passionate inventor who gambles in uncertainty in trying to limit risks, and whose every action is conditioned by external and interiorized scarcity, it is this man we call a fighter. (II, 17–18)

This man is the center and source of the dialectic. His ignorance, urgency, blindness, and passion—all driven by scarcity—may be obstacles to an analytical reconstruction of the map of possibilities. But a dialectical understanding grasps our action "*in its insufficiency, in its imperfection, in its mistakes* beginning with the negative determinations which it conserves in transcending them" (II, 18). It is of the essence of real history that no action can be seen as the best possible one, "since the best possible solution can only be found if one possesses every element of the situation, all the time necessary to gather them into a synthesis which transcends them, all the calm and objectivity necessary for self-criticism" (II, 18). In reality, adversaries in combat miss much of what is going on, because they see only from their own point of view. In short, a dialectical understanding of a struggle, the genuinely historical one, is constructed not in spite of, but *in terms of*, these various negativities. Unlike the military schools' study it takes place "at the very level of the concrete" (II, 18).[4]

Contradiction and Antilabor Introduced

Sartre, we may notice, has shifted back and forth between the mode of comprehension and its object. The dialectic seeks the historical individu-

---

4. It is thus no accident that Sartre chooses Stalin—driven by every conceivable negativity—as the main actor of his historical study.

als, in their actual situation, with their actual confusions and urgencies. But, as we saw before the digression, the dialectic seeks more: it seeks the larger wholes created by their praxis in conflict with each other. Obviously it makes no sense to posit the whole as if it somehow exists on its own: this habit is precisely what drove Merleau-Ponty from orthodox Marxism. The question is: What justifies our assimilating "a battle to a contradiction and its adversaries to the terms of the ongoing contradiction" (II, 19)? In abstracting from concrete history, volume one explored how a single praxis could be said to create larger unities, but if history itself is totalizing, this is only through a unique praxis-process in which "the process is here defined as the deterioration of one praxis by the other" (II, 19).

The common dialectical term for this praxis-process of conflict which builds larger unities is *contradiction*. If this is a meaningful term it implies that we can regard individuals, common individuals, or subgroups in conflict (no doubt en route to regarding classes or nations in the same way) "as the transitory determinations of a more ample and more profound group of which their conflict supposedly actualizes one of its present contradictions . . ." (II, 19). It also implies that in conflict itself the group manages to transcend this "pitiless struggle toward a new synthetic reunification of its practical field and an internal reorganization of its structures" (II, 19). In a sense, no matter how bitterly opposed might be the adversaries, the real secret of their struggle would be *the group's* self-development. If this is so, each struggle would have three characteristics: to express a contradiction, to particularize it, and to totalize the group. To see if this indeed happens is the first "essential problem" of dialectical understanding.[5]

The second essential problem will later be described under the theme of "antilabor."[6] It focuses on the products of conflict, the "residues of the struggle," these apparently "incomprehensible objects." These "ambiguous and insufficiently developed" events become "the factors and conditions of further history" (II, 20). A certain intention—to create the Ateliers Nationaux (National Workshops) in 1848—may have been conceived to meet a social need of the moment, but was generated by, and became the object of, intense class struggle.[7] Inaccessible to the clearly deline-

5. Sartre will return to this theme at length in the first half of chapter four.
6. This will be developed at length in the second half of chapter four.
7. In theory the Ateliers Nationaux, associated with moderate socialist leader Louis Blanc, were to be efficient cooperatives of producers, aided by the state, which would guarantee work and compete favorably with capitalism. With the workers of Paris having just overthrown the July monarchy, the Provisional Government, of which Blanc was a member, immediately decreed that the workshops be established. But in reality they became as much a scheme for controlling and depoliticizing workers as for satisfying them. Sartre

ated categories of analytical reason (the object's traits become grasped as
rooted in one side's action, the other's reaction), before dialectical reason
the products of such struggles appear as *aporias*, matters which put us at
a loss. At one and the same time they seem to be "results of a common
enterprise" to testify that "this enterprise has never existed, unless as
the inhuman inverse of two opposed actions each one of which aims to
destroy the other" (II, 20). No one's original intention has been met, yet
"in spite of the deviations and partial annulments something remains of
the original project and the enterprise conserves a confused efficacy
which leads to unforeseen results" (II, 20–21).

Struggle as Collaboration

These two themes, contradiction and antilabor, focus the problem. If we
are to make sense of history as totalization (and thus to see each struggle
in turn as *a* totalization), we must be able to grasp "individuals or groups
in struggle as collaborating in fact in a common enterprise. And as the
enterprise is perpetually given, as residue of the struggle—be it the dev-
astation of a battlefield, insofar as one could consider the two adversaries
as having together burned and sacked the fields and woods—one must
be able to grasp it as the objectification of a group at work, itself formed
of two antagonistic groups" (II, 21). Not as achieved by their concerted
praxes, but as in the case of the Ateliers Nationaux, having indeed become "historical realities only to the degree that they do not conform to
any of the projects that have achieved them in reciprocal antagonism"
(II, 21). Although Sartre does not explain why this is so, the answer is
given in the Marxian notion framing the entire *Critique:* insofar as history is class struggle, *its development and its products* will most often occur
precisely as did the Ateliers Nationaux. Remarkably, then, social objects
born from a struggle are historical to the degree that, made by men, they
escape from their makers—"to the degree, in short, that they deviate
from every route one wants to assign them, themselves taking an unforeseen route and producing results that could not be guessed" (II, 21).
They deviate not because of the externality of materiality as such, nor
because of seriality or alienation, but rather because each person "steals
his act from the other" (II, 21) in a history based on a plurality of epicenters in conflict.

---

will return to them later in his extended analysis of antilabor, and appropriately so: much
of the history of the period between February and June 1848 can be written around the
struggle over, and deformation of, the Ateliers Nationaux.

Social objects formed in such processes and bequeathed to future generations would thus "contain as internal structure the double negation of themselves and of each component by the other" (II, 22). Every social whole contains "a certain aporia": "the apparent unities and partial syntheses cover over lacerations of all orders and sizes. From a distance the society seems to hold all by itself; from up close it is riddled with holes" (II, 22).

Scarcity

But these struggles are "never and nowhere accidents of human history: they represent the very manner in which men live scarcity in their perpetual movement to transcend it" (II, 22). Or, to put it yet more strongly, the struggles themselves *are* scarcity, lived as a human relationship.

> By this we mark a fundamental link of man to himself through the interiorization of the relationship of man to the non-human object: the practical and technical relationship of man to the universe as field of scarcity is transformed in and by labor; and these transformations are interiorized necessarily (alienation) as objective transformations of interhuman relationships, insofar as they translate scarcity. Insofar as abundance as new relationship of man to the universe will not have replaced scarcity, the displacements of scarcity (scarcity of the product, becoming scarcity of the tool or scarcity of man, etc.) are interiorized and transcended as displacements of human struggles. It is the permanent existence of these struggles which creates classes at a certain level of the technical development of production, although it is classes, by their opposition, which create struggle. (II, 22)[8]

In penetrating beneath struggle to its source, Sartre has laid the basis for the entire analysis to follow: there are human beings, there is scarcity, classes develop. Classes struggle and produce a larger totalization—which is this negative unity we know as history.[9] Some societies may

8. Sartre's manuscript of the last clause here quoted reads: "bien que ce soient les classes, par leur opposition, qui créent la lutte" (ms. page 22). The editor has rendered it as "*loin* que ce soient les classes, par leur *apparition*, qui créent la lutte" (emphasis added).

9. Sartre leaves out another dimension: prior to or alongside the struggle, there is a common or collective human interaction to combat scarcity. Therefore classes in struggle also cooperate, as do boxers in the ring. Sartre leaves out this equally a priori basis for totalization, as we shall see, and thus deprives himself of a powerful key for explaining *why* the totalization can take place on the basis of struggle. After all, its basis is not struggle alone, but struggle *and* cooperation. See chapter eight for an extended discussion.

transform original scarcity through "rigorous systems of mediations-compensations" and thus "correct chance by a redistribution of certain goods" (II, 22). But then, even if they prohibit conflict, it remains present as tension and as latent conflict, the malaise of the entire society.

Still, the necessity and universality of scarcity is no more demonstrable a priori than that of history. No one can say "that every practical ensemble should secrete a history, nor even that all possible histories should be conditioned by scarcity" (II, 23). Sartre limits his claims by insisting that such developments "arise with all the contingent richness of a *singularity*" (II, 23). It happens that *our* history, internalizing *our* scarcity, has been one of class struggle: "in the framework of scarcity, the constitutive relationships are fundamentally antagonistic; from the point of view of their temporal development they come in the form of this event which is struggle" (II, 23).

The Question of Questions

Sartre has reached the definition of the historical process whose intelligibility he pursues. First, its strange products "will become the material circumstances which will have to be transcended by other generations torn by other conflicts" (II, 23). Second, these products refer us "wholly and from every point of view" to the conflicting praxes in which they originated; but third, the product "overflows the adversaries and because of them becomes other than what each one projects" (II, 24).

In studying history, Marxism remains guided by two theses, which now seem contradictory: that history is driven by class struggle, and that it develops dialectically. Marx was well aware of this "formal contradiction" between conflict and unification but, seeking concrete analyses and practical results, did not devote himself to answering it. Insofar as he dealt with it, "he always refused—and rightly so—to give a reality to this verbal entity that one calls Society.[10] He saw there only one form of alienation among others" (II, 24). Indeed, we have seen this habit of orthodox Marxists to be one source of Merleau-Ponty's theoretical break with Marxism. Sartre, on the contrary, hopes to "totalize struggling classes" and to discover "the synthetic unity of a society totally torn apart" (II, 24).

And so Sartre poses the question of questions: "Is there a unity of different classes which sustains and produces their irreducible conflicts" (II, 24)? Is there, he has asked at the end of volume one, a totalization

10. *Société* is capitalized in the ms. and rendered in the lower case by the editor.

without a totalizer? As I suggested in chapter one, when Sartre asks this he recurs to *the conceptualization used by Merleau-Ponty* to explain his renunciation of Marxism: it is today "at the very moment when the machine seems jammed [*semble coincée*] that it is fitting to clear up the formal difficulties which have hitherto been neglected" (II, 20). In *Adventures of the Dialectic* we have seen Merleau-Ponty describe how, "just after the war," his *attentisme marxiste* was based on the very same fact: the Marxist dialectic "jammed [*s'est enrayée*] when the revolution was limited to an undeveloped country . . ." (*Adventures*, 228).

The remarkable parallel emphasizes the remarkable fact: Merleau-Ponty's reason for rejecting Marxism becomes Sartre's opportunity. It is time, today, to inquire whether struggles are totalizing or detotalizing—that is, whether they create a larger, meaningful, and developing whole or whether, as Merleau-Ponty had concluded, they amount to nothing at all or indeed dissolve previous totalizations.[11] Sartre does not assume the answer in advance, and thus, as he indicates in this trenchant summary, Marxism itself is at stake:

> Marxism is rigorously true if history is totalization; it is no longer so if human history is decomposed into a plurality of particular histories. Or if in any case, within the relationship of immanence that characterizes struggle, the negation of each adversary by the other is on principle *detotalizing*. Certainly, we have neither the intention nor the possibility of showing here the full truth of dialectical materialism—something we will no doubt attempt elsewhere, in a book devoted to anthropology, which is to say to the concrete as such. Our only goal is to establish whether in a practical ensemble torn by antagonism (whether there are multiple conflicts or they are reduced to only one) the breaks themselves are totalizing and carried along by the totalizing movement of the ensemble. But if in fact we establish this abstract principle, then the materialist dialectic, as movement of history and of historical knowledge, need only prove itself by the facts it illuminates or, if one prefers, need only discover itself as a fact and through other facts. (II, 25)

But if such a totalizing movement exists, "it occurs everywhere"—leading Sartre to the important new idea, central to what follows, "that

11. "At the same time that there is historical progress, there is, therefore, a consolidation, a destruction, a trampling of history; and at the same time as a permanent revolution, there is a permanent decadence which overtakes the ruling class in proportion as it rules and endures, for by ruling it abdicates what had made it 'progressive,' loses its rallying power, and is reduced to the protection of private interests" (*Adventures*, 220).

each singular event totalizes in itself this whole—be it planetary or indeed were it to become interplanetary—in the infinite richness of its singularity" (II, 26). If there is a totality, then, each particular struggle may itself be seen as a "totalization of every struggle." Before asking, later, about the nature of history or its truth, we must first seek to comprehend a single irreducible conflict, such as the boxing match, "as totalization of the whole of contemporary irreducibilities and splits . . ." (II, 21). And so, in the next paragraphs, Sartre launches into his analysis of a particular conflict, a boxing match, for which his introductory discussion has carefully prepared us. The study proper begins. By now its question has been given precision, its outer limits and internal structure shaped, and its significance indicated. We now know what we must look for and why.

3   Boxing and Incarnation

The first concrete study of volume two, over thirty pages, focuses on boxing. Philosophically exploring such unlikely terrain is, of course, common practice for Sartre. Here he investigates the links and interactions between the specific projects of single individuals and the social world which gives them meaning and identity. In so doing, Sartre courageously heads into the eye of the storm, subjecting to close analysis the relations between both poles of his thought, his original individualism and his more recent Marxist sense of historical totality. The question is, how does the praxis of opposed individuals gain shape from, and in turn shape, a larger social and historical totalization?

His task, of course, is to explain social entities and the historical process while insisting that their source is the praxis of individuals and not the movement of some "hyperorganism" acting on its own. At the same time he seeks to show precisely how these social realms shape the individuals who create them, right down to the most intimate personal details. In developing the theme of *incarnation* to do this, Sartre undertakes a major reflection on the hoary question of the universal and the particular.

The World of Boxing

Why boxing? At the very beginning of volume two, Sartre speaks of two wrestlers who, as they roll about on the canvas, appear to be "a single beast of eight limbs, struggling against an unknown danger" (II, 13). Thus does Sartre, before he changes to study two boxers, suggest a comparison with Roland Barthes's moral and esthetic analysis of the symbolism of the grandiloquent spectacle of wrestling.[1] At first it might seem Sartre is simply pursuing the suggestions that Barthes has offered, namely to sketch boxing as a real event, unfolding in time, where—

1. "The World of Wrestling," *Mythologies*, trans. Annette Lavers (New York, 1972).

unlike wrestling—the actual result is in suspense. The point he will develop as he switches to boxing is that even if we see a single movement, this movement results from *two* separate projects, struggling against each other. Sartre will study individual parties in conflict precisely in order to see whether and how their struggle leads to a larger unity, perhaps in spite of themselves. If he can demonstrate this, Sartre will have begun, in dissecting a specific, simple conflict, to lay the foundation for understanding history as resulting from a multiplicity of individual praxes.[2] As it unfolds, his analysis moves further from Barthes in its Marxian and dialectical attention to the entire historical and social world incarnated in boxing.

Sartre launches into the problem by declaring that "the deep truth of each particular fight is the competition for titles" (II, 26). This is most obviously reflected in the arrangement of the program. "The evening is hierarchical (double hierarchy, building toward the big fight at the beginning of the second part, descending again to a final fight) and this hierarchy is lived in *tension* by the spectator . . ." (II, 27). The evening's first fight, "synthetically unified to the others as the first moment of an unfolding process" (II, 27), will contain the less skillful fighters and will be missed by many spectators who, knowing this, arrive late. For them it is only the *beginning*, "the temporal equivalent of the *first rungs* of the ladder" (II, 28) of the world of boxing. After the fight, winner and loser may wind up at other rungs, the one rising and the other falling.

Does the hierarchy determine the boxers themselves, or is Sartre talking about the boxers as seen from the outside, by the audience, managers, promoters, etc.? Dialectical comprehension, after all, is supposed to distinguish itself from the far more limited analytical understanding by virtue of its *internal* grasp of a given praxis. In a title fight, Sartre insists, the hierarchy has been interiorized by the fighters as their own experience. "These two men very much at ease (in appearance) who climb into the ring in the midst of applause, in vividly colored trunks, these are in themselves 'common' (individuals), they contain in themselves the opponents they have already defeated and, by this mediation, the whole universe of boxing" (II, 28).

The reference to common individuals leads back, of course, to volume one, where Sartre is not speaking symbolically. Each boxer appears where he does on the card according to his actual place in the synchronic hierarchy. "Thus the movement of the evening reproduces the movement of their life; and the preceding matches reproduce the history of their own

2. Or, alternately, to show how class struggle, one truth of Marxism, generates what he regards as another, the progressive unity of history.

fights, the descent toward oblivion of nearly all those they have beaten"
(II, 29). This fight, then, between these boxers, can be deciphered only
through all fights, and indeed through boxing as a whole—which it in
turn retotalizes by virtue of the fact that its outcome alters or reconfirms
the hierarchy with which the evening began and which the program reflected. In this sense, and in others Sartre will now indicate,

> *all of boxing* is present at each moment of the fight as sport and
> as technique, with all the human qualities and all the mate-
> rial conditioning (training, health conditions, etc.) that it de-
> mands. By this we must understand first[3] that the public has
> come to see and that the organizers have arranged (well or
> poorly) to give them *good boxing*. And this signifies a practice
> of fighting (on the part of the opponents) which transcends a
> learned technique while completely realizing it at each in-
> stant. The movement itself will be *invention:* choice to hit an
> opponent on the left side, who has let his guard drop, per-
> haps by design, risks assumed in ignorance, etc. But all this
> cannot even be tried without a set of technical acquisitions—
> speed, punching, etc.—and, more profoundly still, without
> the habit of putting (without losing equilibrium) the entire
> weight of his body in each punch. Boxing is there as *exis*,[4] as
> *technique* and as always new invention of each one of them.
> (II, 29)

Hierarchy, techniques, training, promoters, receipts, national and international organizations, rules: the whole world of boxing is present
within the specific confrontation between two social beings produced in
and by this world. "Thus each fight is boxing as a whole" (II, 30).

It appears, then, not only in the boxers' place on the card but, more
internally, in the art they learn. They seek to transcend this art in their
acceptance of its rules, and they seek to be measured in it. This remains
so even when they box badly: "It determines the limits and the capacities
of the two opponents; it defines their future place in the hierarchy, their
career—through the demands and protests in the auditorium, registered
by the organizers and managers. One comes to sense its thick presence,
the very degree that it dominates the fighters without their being able to
transcend it . . ." (II, 30).

3. The editor leaves out "1°," which I have translated as "first."
4. The editor of the English edition of *Critique I*, Jonathan Rée, defines *exis* as "an inert,
stable condition opposed to *praxis*" (828). We shall see that *exis*, for Sartre, becomes that
which is produced in praxis and has assumed a stable, structured state—characterized by
its *being*, its *thereness*. The Greek term, *hexis*, remains characteristically Sartrean by its implication of a *habit* assumed by prior action.

Incarnation

What is the "it"? By this point, it is clear, Sartre has effectively argued that the two individuals become who they are through the social whole, boxing, and in turn sustain and redefine that social whole in *their* fight. *Each* boxer *is* a boxer through this world which produces him, and, win or lose, *his* activity retotalizes the social whole. But what, we might ask, is the precise status and nature of this world of boxing? This unique event of two singular individuals simultaneously puts "*boxing as a whole*" into play. To further explore this relationship Sartre introduces the key term of this section of the *Critique, incarnation:*

> In each fight, boxing *is incarnated,* is realized and slips away in being realized; in each fight it is there, fixed and totalizing as the milieu which produces *in itself* as a growing legend,[5] *the fight of these two singular people.* Nobody can comprehend the passion of the spectators—and, indeed, often of the boxers themselves—without recognizing this double dimension of the match, as well as the double presence of boxing. This brawl would be of no interest if it *did not totalize* in its concrete temporalization this fixed and abstract world which retotalizes it; but this totalization would remain schematic and formal (which is the case when a boxer and his sparring partner give a "demonstration" without hitting each other) if it were not incarnated in the singularity of a "doubtful fight," that is to say, one which contains an inexhaustible richness and an at least partial unpredictability. (II, 31)

The "it" is a "fixed and abstract world" which comes to life only in *this* match and yet gives it its meaning. By itself "it" is "schematic and formal"—unless *these* fighters incarnate it here. In using *incarner,* "to give flesh to," Sartre is stressing the abstract, timeless, and empty quality of the "it" before these fighters go to work, embodying it in the here and now.

Sartre's first use of the term *incarnation,* in *Being and Nothingness,* took place within a now classical discussion of the provoking of sexual desire. As a for-itself I am a being who seems to be essentially consciousness, but I "make myself flesh" in order to seduce the Other to do the same. "Thus the revelation of the Other's flesh is made through my own flesh; in desire and in the caress which expresses desire, I incarnate myself in

---

5. The word is not clear in the ms. I read it as "*légende,*" the editor as "*lézarde.*"

order to realize the incarnation of the Other. The caress by realizing the Other's incarnation reveals to me my own incarnation . . ." Possession, the result of this interplay, is a "double reciprocal incarnation." But I may *use* my flesh to attract, manipulate and control the Other *without* incarnating myself in it. Indeed, in sadism the for-itself "enjoys its own non-incarnation." [6]

The term itself, *incarner*, derived directly from the Latin *carnalis* for flesh, suggests, as it always did in the Christian tradition, a dualism between spirit and flesh, as well as a priority of spirit. Sartre's first use of *incarnation* evokes this tradition by virtue of his own dualism of for-itself and in-itself. The for-itself passes into the flesh, em-bodies itself, through its own act. It may indeed, in the case of sadism, manipulate "its own" flesh *without* incarnating it, the better to degrade the Other.

Whether or not this passage of the immaterial being *into* the material remains a presumption behind Sartre's use of the term in *Critique I*, he does retain the notion of passing from one state to another. In shifting from his earlier use in suggesting the idea of a relationship between the two, and in making the first a broader and more general entity and the second a resolutely individual one, Sartre has in mind a striking new purpose. He seeks to describe the group's effort to stabilize and strengthen itself by institutionalizing its common-being in the person of a sovereign individual. In this sense, sovereignty itself is incarnation:[7] "the production of the group by the group in the form of *this* particular person, with *these* individual characteristics, *these* ailments, *this* irreducible physiognomy, and of *this* particular age . . ." We shall see this effort of the group lead to the cult of personality by a "condensation of the *common* by means of an immense pressure which is liable to translate it into *idiosyncrasy.*" The spirit, or for-itself, does not pass to flesh, or in-itself, in this process: the deteriorating group—which is nonetheless a *general* reality—seeks to be "reborn, materialized, concretized . . . *by the flesh*, re-created through the virility of one individual," who becomes its integrating organ (I, 707; 598; 622). He incarnates the group, condensing its unity in his very particularity.

In the second volume, of course, the boxer does the same as he incarnates the world of boxing. The development of this idea, to extend over the next thirty pages, is suddenly complicated as Sartre adds a new argument. He asserts that, in an immediate way, "the match is the public incarnation of *all conflict.*"

6. *L'Etre et le Néant* (Paris, 1943), 460, 469; trans. Hazel Barnes, *Being and Nothingness* (New York, 1956), 391, 399.
7. In the English edition of *Critique I*, it is translated as "embodiment."

What do we see? Men assembled together who passionately
follow a particular duel. But we already know that this duel is
the present incarnation of a certain species of regulated violence called boxing. Now the set of rules and technical imperatives which constitute this "art" draw their origin from a
systematic and continuous perfecting of the most immediate
and naked violence: that of unarmed men who are their own
instrument of combat. All social groups that we know today
are armed—rudimentary as may be their technique. But in
each is the possibility, for individuals set one against the other
by anger, to return to a mode of combat which seems to be *the
original struggle* although one cannot demonstrate that this is
in fact the first confrontation of individuals situated in a field
of scarcity. What is certain is that, in each brawl, the profound
origin is always scarcity. (II, 32)

We may be puzzled about whether the "world of boxing" incarnated
here and now by this fight is, on the one hand, an instance of a yet-
undefined general entity or, on the other, the aggregate of a thousand
and one individual particularities which make it up. Sartre will "resolve"
this later, by attacking the crudest formulations of conceptualism and absorbing, unclarified, the universal plane of experience into his discussion of incarnation. And still later, as we will see in chapter six, he will
attack the very plane of universality itself, replacing it with a radical particularism. Rather than exploring this problem now, Sartre has moved to
a very different, but dazzling, line of reflection: the "world of boxing"
incarnates "original violence," whose roots in turn lie in scarcity.

Violence and Scarcity

Beginning there, Sartre describes how urgent and fundamental violence, rooted in scarcity, becomes socially purified so as to be posed as
"a disinterested virtue, before a violent public" (II, 32). "In cutting every
link with immediate interests, in imposing the mediation of the entire
group, in making of the 'purse' a kind of prize of merit and victory (except in the case of a KO), of a deliberate decision of competent witnesses, violence loses its extreme urgency, it strips itself of the significations which materialize with it, which mix with it and which refer to
motivations" (II, 32). Undertaken with precautions such as gloves, rules,
and professional technique, it becomes transformed into violence for
"*recompense* rather than *conquest*" (II, 40).

As naked conflict in this way becomes *spectacle*, it takes on a social value: "In the Manicheism of scarcity, violence is in the service of Good, it is Good itself; the individual (and the group just as well) assimilates its sense of the dignity of man and of the counterviolence which sustains it" (II, 33). Violence becomes *strength:* "The man of good should be strong; strength is the proof of his right" (II, 33). After all, if he is defeated, the other becomes right.

The Spectacle Is Real

As violence becomes spectacle, it does not thereby become less real. Sartre's very careful and detailed early studies of the imagination— central to his formation—have provided him with the conceptual basis for indicating the slightest degree of derealization discovered in the audience's relationship to the boxing match.[8] He insists that it would be incorrect to suggest that the boxers engage in imaginary violence only, that their purpose is to present it to the audience. "They are too occupied in fighting, above all if the struggle is hard and risks becoming fatal" (II, 34). Once more Sartre attempts to capture the proper relationship by using "incarnation": public combat incarnates "fundamental violence before everyone" (II, 34).

The fact that this is real gives us the key both to the event's status and to its relationship to the audience. Barthes's analysis of wrestling treats it as a species of drama, of "Human Comedy" or pantomime.[9] Sartre insists that if boxing were imaginary I would remain passive and impotent, due to the "unbridgeable distance" separating me, as in the theater, from the fictional characters or their fictional violence.

> But the spectator of this purified brawl is actor because it takes place before him. He encourages the boxers or blames them, he shouts: it seems to him that he is creating the event as it is unfolding: his violence is totally present and he tries to communicate it to the fighters to provoke movement of the fight. This violence, moreover, is not limited to objectively taking part in the effort of each opponent: it would not be violence without favoring, without preferring, without choosing to be partial . . . (II, 35)

Siding with one of the opponents, the spectator will ignore the punches he has taken, will encourage him. His identification is so great that "he

8. See *L'Imaginaire: Psychologie phénoménologique de l'imagination* (Paris, 1939), translated as *The Psychology of Imagination* (New York, 1949); and my discussion in *Jean-Paul Sartre,* 37–63.
9. "The World of Wrestling," 16–19.

fights through him: he is himself the incarnation of violence, occasionally to the point of hitting his neighbor . . ." (II, 35). In fact, a brawl can
always break out among the audience of partisans. But in both boxer and
audience this anger is only "awakened" at the start of the fight. In the fan
it is "the incarnation of a preexisting violence which draws its origin
from [his] very situation and which maintains itself in him—outside of
those moments where it can be interiorized—as malaise, nervous tension, sometimes even as sad passivity" (II, 35).

The spectators' violence enters the boxers, animates and sustains
them: they incarnate this violence in their match. "The public *produces the
boxers*" (II, 36), then, not only by its encouragement and blame, but
equally because it financially supports "the immense operation that can
be called world boxing. Thus each spectator's consciousness, of himself
being the living force of the fight and of inspiring it in his favorite, is not
false: it translates a practical truth into particular attitudes; and these attitudes (enthusiasm, howls, whistles) enclose the implicit comprehension of this truth: if the witnesses let themselves shout, storm, insult, *it
is because they have paid*" (II, 36).

The source of our violence, latent until the boxers step into the ring,
can only be the deep structure of our own lives: social constraints, oppression, alienation, exploitation, overwork—all displacements of original scarcity. Sartre captures this marvelously: "The two boxers gather
into themselves, and reexteriorize by the blows they give each other, the
whole of the tension, the open and masked struggles that characterize
the regime in which we live and which has made us violent to the softest
of our caresses" (II, 36).

Incarnation Is Totalization

We have seen Sartre begin to characterize incarnation by insisting that
the process is real, not symbolic, and one in which the spectators' own
violence appears before them in the boxers. By pointing to scarcity as
the source of our violence Sartre is also taking a further step of definition: other violence, born elsewhere, becomes expressed here. In fact,
all violence is in *this* fight. Incarnation, in other words, is a form of
totalization.

Why "totalization"? Sartre's goal is to describe the large unities of human history as the largely unintended result of specific conflicts and
struggles. In keeping with this, "all" violence would mean not violence
as some kind of generality but *every specific act* of violence. If so, the process whereby they are gathered together, unified in a single incarnation,

and projected outward as a single individual's praxis is quite precisely a totalization.

Dispersed and latent, the many forms and layers of the spectators' violence are unified and made explicit in *this* fight. Its content "is the ensemble, totalized or in the process of totalization. And by this we do not mean that it is the symbol or expression of it but that it is realized very really and practically *as the totality producing itself here and now*. Every boxing match incarnates all boxing as incarnation of all fundamental violence" (II, 36). Incarnation means that

> the fight envelops fundamental violence in itself as its real substance and as its practical efficacy. It is immediately here and everywhere in the hall, it is the very stuff of the movement of temporalization as production of the fight by the spectators and as unification (and reciprocal confrontation) of the spectators by the fight. And the reason for this incarnation is not mysterious since it is the scattered violence of each spectator that is retotalized, from organizations and groups that have been constituted to furnish it the occasions to be retotalized. (II, 36–37)

To insist therefore that fundamental violence is completely present *in person* does not mean that it does not exist elsewhere, "but simply, we will discover that this violence is always *whole* everywhere it exists" (II, 37). Sartre's claim seems extravagant or, at best, puzzling until we look more closely. Let us contrast his way of conceiving the problem with the approach of analytical reason, which seeks to dissolve a given act into its components. Sartre seeks the integrity and "unicity" of an intentional act, which reexteriorizes that which has been interiorized. His insight stems from his standpoint: the dialectic is the logic of praxis itself as a synthetic activity. Sartre does not seek pressures or factors "reducible, in the best of cases, to a common denominator," but a subject's unifying act.

But why take the further step of insisting that a given violent act is always *all* violence? Sartre's point is to distinguish his description not only from any that would analyze violence into its various forms and sources but from any attempt to separate its far-flung manifestations from each other. He insists, rather, on the fundamental interconnectedness of every violent act *and* the displacement of violence from one plane of experience to the next. Violence is a praxis, rooted in scarcity. To call a given act *all* violence is to see it as "reexteriorization of interiorized scarcity; but this scarcity is never an abstract principle external to the social whole: it is at every moment a synthetic relation of all men with nonhuman materiality and of all men with each other via this materiality, insofar as the whole of techniques of the relations of production give to this relationship its determination and unity" (II, 37). Sartre unflinchingly and persuasively concretizes this startling claim: "It suffices to see what the act of a drunken father who strikes a child gathers into itself of oppression, alienation, and poverty to comprehend that all the social violence of our regime has made this man and his present fury" (II, 37).

Sartre against the Concept

Incarnation means that any individual act of violence interiorizes the general, social violence. It means that "the totalization is *individuated:* this fundamental violence explodes here and now, but with all the characteristics of a here and now, that is, with the opaque richness and negative determinations of the concrete" (II, 37). If two individuals, one from the north and one from Marseilles, are fighting at a given time and place in Paris, their fight is all violence but "it can only exist as its particular determination" (II, 38).

Does this way of framing the relationship of the singular and the general imply that Sartre has in mind the individual and the concept? No, Sartre argues, the concept is a schema of analytical reason. "Even if the concept is discovered, in the course of experience, in the individual object and as its essential structure" (II, 38), it is postulated as being transcendent as an abiding, abstract, and already-given rule. It is already conceived as separate from and independent of its particular determinations. Second, the concept, as an allegedly given and stable entity, would not be created or understood by action but would, rather, be presented to contemplative reason. And third, the individual object's empirical characteristics would fall "outside of the concept" and be manifested in relationship to it "as simple accidents." "This evidently implies that the ensemble of determinations, in the interior of the concept, are linked by relationships of exteriority . . ." (II, 38).

Thus does Sartre seek to dispose of the possibility that a quasi-Platonic world of universals exists in any way independently of this particular world of countless singularities, that their general meanings are accessible independently of action, and that singularities have a lesser status than, or can be understood as external to, their general "essence." His first arguments in fact bear a striking resemblance to Aristotle's critique of Plato's theory of ideas.[10] Notice, however, that Sartre does not prove,

10. Aristotle, *Metaphysics*, trans. Richard Hope (Ann Arbor, 1960), 19–29.

any more than did Aristotle, the nonexistence of universals but only that there are no static, external, and privileged universals. Sartre does not deny that a general plane exists: he simply denies it any explicit ontological or epistemological status. There is indeed a "world of boxing" but it is both a material totality and is present *in* each event, comprehensible by active reason, and is internally related to every singularization. Sartre does not use these arguments to *redefine* the notion of the concept in, say, a more Aristotelian fashion.[11] Rather, under the heading of *incarnation*, he explores the relations between singularities and these unclarified totalities/universals.

Living an Absolute Conflict

Incarnation means neither "the exemplification of the concept" nor the "conceptualization of experience." Perhaps above all, the relationship of incarnation must never be seen as contemplative: "it is praxis or praxis-process" (II, 39). In watching and cheering on this life-and-death match, we *create* it. First, no one *observes* an act of violence, from the outside, "having witnessed the action without participating in it" (II, 39). Indeed, most legal codes recognize this, calling for penalties against people guilty of "nonassistance." *Complicity*—witnessing without intervening—is itself a praxis, an internal and not external relationship to the violent act. "*Therefore* not witnesses to violence but only participants; nonviolence, even and above all when it is erected into a maxim, is a choice of complicity" (II, 39).[12] Our relationship to this reality, therefore, is not primarily cognitive or contemplative, but *lived* as an action unfolding in time.

Second, the participants in violence "live an absolute," a real life-and-death conflict. Every violent event is lived, by every participant and from every angle, as *the absolute* because it risks death "as untranscendable and menacing term of each life. . . . Thus, in conflict, life is revealed in its precious unicity, in its irreversibility, in its fragility, and in its fierce affirmation of itself, through the alternative: kill or be killed" (II, 40).

This is not a conceptual or general truth but a concrete and existential one, no less "profound and fundamental" for that. When watching the fight, screaming for a knockout, the audience seeks "a public realization of death. *Symbolic* realization? No: the man collapses and dies; it is the

11. Aristotle treated *ousia* (primary being) as being simultaneously the physical object, its essence, and its *telos* or "goal." Thus he sought to do justice both to the undeniable fact of a universal plane of the world of experience *and* to its material specificity.

12. "There are, however, subversives who are 'nonviolent'" (II, 52, Sartre's footnote).

end of the fight. Whether he revives or not in the dressing room, the spectator has taken the battle to its extreme end, that is, to that ambiguous moment when its completion and its disappearance are produced each by the other and simultaneously" (II, 41).

Since the boxer is not really dead, and the audience knows this for all its cries of "kill him!" we might expect Sartre to moderate his claim that the match is intended as a life-and-death struggle. Rather, he continues to sharpen it, arguing against treating the fight and the phenomenon of incarnation as being at any remove from reality. Incarnation clearly involves a displacement of the audience's original violence, but it is a displacement which in no way softens it. Every spectator puts himself into play *as killer* because he lives as one who is physically liquidated: "by compulsory overwork, by poverty artifically maintained by a social choice, by the violence, always possible, of the 'forces of the law' or, if he makes common cause with oppression, by the violence of a revolutionary movement" (II, 41). If, outside of the auditorium, he kills and is killed, here this same reality comes into play:

> Not at all a conceptual or merely verbal signification: what makes of these lives the incarnation of life is quite simply the passionate seriousness of the praxis of each participant, their present impossibility of turning away from the match, which they prefer to everything *for the moment,* all the while knowing that they have cares of another importance as if, all together, there had never been an *outside,* as if behind these closed doors nothing existed, neither city plunged into night nor country surrounding the city, as if all humanity were no more than this handful of men producing this struggle to the death as the incarnation of their destiny and as if, on the contrary, two billion men remained outside, lost in serial dispersion and impotence, but totalized and fused together in this major and unique struggle, whose stakes were nothing other than the fate of humanity. (II, 41–42)

Sartre does not pause to analyze his own qualification: "as if." Instead, he treats this act of incarnation as a wholly real, material process, one that is neither conceptual nor symbolic. In it the latent becomes explicit, the scattered becomes unified, specific individuals provoke, draw together, and realize, in their praxis, the intentions of hundreds and thousands of others who sustain them.

In other words, incarnation does not have a diminished ontological status: it is totalization. This match is one such totalization. Sartre continues to leave open the central question of whether an all-embracing totalization of envelopment can exist—and furnish the meaning and truth of history, the basis of its very intelligibility. Nevertheless, he insists that the positive content of "all practical and concrete reality" is nothing other than the totalized whole "of all the totalizations in course"—in other words, that the very meaning and substance of this match, here, can only be the vast progressive totalization which is history itself.

His main point, however, continues to be that the "incarnated totalization" is not one that is *named* or *thought*, but *lived* and *produced* by its participants. To emphasize this he describes his own experience in Havana in 1949, in which the cockfights he attended became "a grid, a synthetic schema" through which he grasped *Cuba* without its being expressed by any idea. At the other extreme one may seek to "reduce the match to its character as a strictly individualized event" (II, 43), as managers and organizers do, while still locating this match as a "small local event in the interior of the total world of boxing" (II, 43). Each extreme is a totalization, in which general and specific, social whole and individual event, are given not as essences (or concept) and accidents but together. *This* fight is three things, at one and the same time: "the specific fight of a young boxer from Martinique and a Parisian boxer, boxing itself, produced in common by all the participants, and human violence exploding publicly" (II, 44).

But what are the larger entities he is speaking about? What is the status of the "human violence" and "boxing itself" that *these* boxers incarnate? They are indeed "concrete universals." To continue exploring the process of incarnation and the relationship of the planes, constituents, or dimensions making up the "incarnated total," Sartre now turns to examine "the relations of the singularities of the fight with the concrete universals that it totalizes" (II, 44). Sartre leaves the terrain of *immediate* totalization to treat "the problem of mediated totalization"—to sketch the meaning and role of boxing in capitalist society. In doing so Sartre will now explore a concrete universal, looking closely at *what* is being incarnated and *how*.

Violence against One's Own Class

Sartre seeks to describe a "new totalization" whose participants are the same as before, and so to sketch "the ensemble of mediations through which these boxers, this boxing match, these organizers, and these spectators have been reciprocally produced" (II, 45). We have seen him raise the issue of mediations in *Search for a Method*, inquiring precisely about the links between a specific individual, Valéry or Flaubert, and the larger social world in which he takes shape. Thus, by turning to *mediations* Sartre seeks social structures and institutions. The earlier "immediate" analysis showed a direct encounter/interchange between the audience and its violence and the boxers and theirs. His new goal, he cautions, is not to undertake a historical or dialectical interpretation of boxing but only "to indicate what order of research should allow marking the process of incarnation in its real limits" (II, 45).

Boxing as we know it is, first of all, an institution of bourgeois societies, with their structures of exploitation. "At this level, we shall indicate that boxing is an economic enterprise and that the entrepreneurs recruit workers among the exploited in order to subject them to another type of exploitation" (II, 45). Most boxers, after all, come from the working class. "These young people, formed by violence they have undergone, are suitable for inflicting violence: what they will incarnate in their fights is the very violence which the dominant class exercises over the working classes" (II, 45). This is the "fundamental and singularized" violence of scarcity, but it "appeared, in its historical form, as *the violence of our society*" (II, 45).

But it can be redirected to its structural source. If reabsorbed collectively by revolutionary parties and unions, it "becomes completely absorbed in social praxis and becomes the *common* stimulus of class actions" (II, 45), instead of being wasted as individual violence. "He has become violent at the level of organized communities, as *common individual*: in socializing his anger, in making him into a receptacle of it so that he is responsible for it to his class, workers' organizations release him, permit him—as free practical organism—to choose from other sources all the forms of positive reciprocity toward his circle" (II, 45).

On the other hand, in becoming a professional boxer, the young man tries "to tear himself from his class." Like his comrades, he has been subjected since birth to the violence of oppression and exploitation and has interiorized it. If this structural, social violence demands a *collective* response which would attack its structural, social source, any other response of the would-be boxer indicates a diversion and defeat. For example, isolated because of his personal history, he does not reexteriorize the violence collectively, in a combat group, but rather turns it against his own class.

The poor fight each other, just as Fanon has spoken of colonial natives fighting each other, when they have not yet become revolutionary. Similarly, sometimes victims of bourgeois oppression will become organized in right-wing paramilitary groups. Their oppressors will capture the violence "in each isolated one and through him return it against his class of origin" (II, 46). All individualized explosions are a transcendence of the original situation but, however obscurely, are also the project of escaping from his class of origin. Indeed, the young man's teachers are pleased to see in him the "*individual* violence of a desire to escape his condition" (II, 46).

Physical and psychological personal traits, training, skill—the entire process in which "boxing produces its man"—lead us to the *contractual moment*. Here, in the decisive instant of incarnation, we see confirmed the

> deliberate project of making his violence a commodity for leaving his class for the one, a project of buying this violence and of making it the source of his profits for the other, as if it were the *labor power of a worker* . . . In inventing being treated as a commodity in order to transcend the status of his class, all of whose members are commodities, in alienating his violence, in selling it, to conserve it, to henceforth be socially designated by it alone, the young man reinvents boxing as the transcendence toward the universal which will conserve his particularities and as the chosen transposition of his original alienation. (II, 46–47)

The Necessity of Contingency

Sartre describes how the boxer's individual qualities become central to the process, in an analysis which fulfills the promise of *Search for a Method* to integrate specific and general in a single discussion. The sport demands that one particular person, with his physique, his character, his past, even his shortcomings, be pitted against another "because the combatant must be an individual, with this synthetic whole which reveals his practice and which unites in each movement somatic structures and history (history recapturing these somatic structures); positive and negative qualities, tactics, the past and the future unveiled as destiny" (II, 48). Individual peculiarities are not inessential accidents, then, but are their required starting points, to be conserved and transcended by the techniques they impose:

> Between these two middleweights, the difference of height, reach, musculature is considerable. The one is tall, with impressive arm development, but a *relatively* undeveloped musculature, the other is of medium height, with a reach inferior to that of the first, but he is strongly muscled. From the beginning we know that these temporal structures are transcended

and conserved by the techniques they impose and which are ceaselessly reinvented. We know that the first counts on his quickness, on his legwork, that he wants to win points with his left while keeping as far as possible from the opponent, and that the other, his head sunk in his shoulders, blocking blows with his gloves, walking more than dancing, ceaselessly advancing, seeks to penetrate the opponent's guard and to work close to his body in a clinch. Everything is written in advance on these bodies and on these faces: for neither one is any other tactic possible; but each circumstance of the match demands the reinvention of all experience in a fake, a dodge, a lightning punch, a correct appreciation of distances and risks; and this reinvention is operated precisely as the synthetic actualization of each individual history: courage, *sang-froid*, skill, etc.—which will probably decide the final outcome; it is the very life of each one as style of practice. (II, 48–49)

Even contingent differences—such as hair color, good looks—which have nothing to do with boxing, are necessary because they *signify* each individual to the audience. The blond champion may not owe his victory to his hair color, but it will concretize his victory for the audience and the wider public. Boxing demands that each man's life be incarnated in his face.

Far from opposing contingency to necessity, Sartre is insisting through his description of the process of incarnation on their internal connection, on "the dialectical intelligibility of chance." Dialectical understanding seeks not to eliminate or abstract from contingency or necessity, but rather to see how they became "enveloped, unified, and transcended by a human practice that singularizes them and which, as praxis and as all praxis, is itself the other side [*l'au-delà*] of every singularity" (II, 49–50). Each invention is rigorously specific to *this* boxer, yet it is also *a* beautiful fake. Incarnation unites both into *the concrete universal*, according to which *a* punch "is indissolubly singular and universal." The very necessity of the accidental "*is* produced and grasped by the participants in the very individuality of the fight and as its character of absolute event: in this singularity, all boxing and all violence are singularized and the lived singular reveals their singularity" (II, 50).

What Is Being Singularized?

The main purpose of Sartre's discussion of incarnation, both in his specific analyses of boxing and in his general theoretical reflections, has been to make clear how the social, the universal, the general are *singularized*. Inasmuch as the balance of his discussion has been skewed in this direction, the reader is likely to emerge with considerable insight into how these dimensions of experience become individualized, but to be little or no clearer about *what it is* that is being individualized. The world of boxing, fundamental violence, oppression, the structures of capitalism, the art of boxing—Sartre has assumed their existence but has not yet asked what *are* these universals, incarnated in this particular fight. Yet his analysis everywhere depends on a bedrock sense of their reality and importance. How else to suggest, for example, that the young man had somehow *mis*directed his violence by becoming a boxer rather than joining others in his class to attack the social system? Without explicitly posing the problem in these terms, Sartre's final step of theoretical reflection on incarnation will now clearly suggest his way of characterizing these generalities.

Returning to the contractual moment in which a young worker becomes a boxer, Sartre describes *boxing*, this "quasi-institutional whole of international organization," as being in turn a unity of fights, each of which controls the others. It is therefore itself a singularity. Sartre explains this by once again taking the general as the *concept*, and by regarding it ("individual man," "man in society") as the "exemplification of *possible man*." From the totalizing or dialectical point of view, in other words, the possible is an abstract and general "structure of the real." But the real itself is primary. "This relativity of the possible to being . . . makes the abstract universal a secondary structure of concrete totalization" (II, 50). Possibilities are not the Aristotelian *telos*, which underlie and drive the process forward and thus lay claim to being primary being, but rather are "practical determinations of the social field; they are defined as margins of objective choices and depend on the singular totality in course of totalization as well as on each historical agent." In other words, the singular totality or concrete totalization is primary. "Thus the enormous singularity which is temporalized by each one of us as the history of humanity can never be anything than an incarnation deciding concretely the possibilities it engenders in itself" (II, 51).

In these brief and undeveloped comments, Sartre's point is not to open the question of possibilities but to dissolve the realm of the general into it, giving both a secondary status to the specific individual. Then he insists on the irreducible particularity of our world and our human adventure. After speculating on the possibility of other worlds (which would then make ours into a particular case of something more general), he goes on to conclude: "But *in the human adventure* the particular case does not exist as such and every reality internal to this adventure must be

conceived *with its possibles* as a full incarnation of the totalization in progress" (II, 51). We might again ask about how Sartre conceives the totalization in course which is incarnated here. Isn't this a concrete universal needing to be understood as such, as both concrete *and* universal?
Sartre's answer is clear enough, though it leaves key problems unresolved such as the meaning of the universal plane he himself brings into
the discussion: even if our adventure could be shown to be part of a still
larger and more general one, it would be just another singular incarnation, another individual.

The Boxer as Worker

Sartre now turns from the methodological and metatheoretical issues
surrounding incarnation to the boxer *as worker*, in order to resume his
analysis of the boxer's violence as mediated by institutions of capitalist
society. However successful a few champions may be, we should not forget that most boxers are little more than workers, often living even more
precariously. They too sell their labor-power, rendering more hours of
work than their salary costs. They become a means for entrepreneurs to
make profits and so to live from their labor. While in training, they are
"treated, indeed, as a machine to be built and then maintained, and
everything is calculated as a function of this objective: taking into account their possibilities, give them and preserve in them the greatest destructive effectiveness" (II, 52). Which of course leads to an alienation of
the fighter from his own body, as all his needs and activities are subordi-
nated to making it over into this destructive instrument. It may be possible to reduce the number of fights allowed each boxer annually, and so
to minimize the destructive physical effects of boxing, but the demands
of the market and the boxers' own desire to make a name for themselves
tend to increase their overwork and exploitation.

> The alienation is total. The adolescent placed his value and his
> freedom in his individual violence. He refused to believe that
> he was accountable for it to his comrades, to his class, in the
> name of this ethics of force and domination, to escape the
> common destiny of the oppressed in which he discovers and
> detests his own poverty, which is that of a victim. He sells his
> strength, his agility, his courage, he sells this very fury which
> makes his combativeness. Now *it is no longer his*, it is taken
> from him: the affirmation of his sovereignty becomes his
> means of living . . . (II, 52–53)

He develops a new personality as he is taught to save his aggressiveness
for the day of the fight. Outside of the ring, he is courteous and soft,

inside it his violence is used to make his living, losing its liberating character. Once it was the "explosive and blind reaction to exploitation of a solitary person" (II, 53); now it serves the bourgeoisie, and the boxer tries to move out of his class. "In fact, the movement [*le passage*] has not really happened (except for a very tiny minority): he sells his violence, remains an exploited person, and rediscovers in the marketplace of boxing the competitive antagonisms which oppose workers in the labor market" (II, 54).

At least workers have, through years of collective struggle, reduced their competition and developed class solidarity. Our boxer, on the contrary, has produced "this competition, he is subjected to it, and he lives it in each of his fights" (II, 54). In fighting his "enemy brothers" a transformation of his violence takes place: "it was originally the very violence which goes from the oppressors to the oppressed" (II, 54) and is returned from the one to the other in class struggle. This violence, in forms appropriate to industrial societies, is the incarnation of scarcity. "But in buying it, the bourgeoisie recovers and transforms it: alienated, this aggressiveness of the oppressed is changed into competitive antagonism . . ." (II, 54). In this inversion, the better fighter-commodity will sell himself dearer in the next fight; worked matter is no longer mediation between men, but men themselves are worked matter.

Potentially liberating violence appears "only to be yet further alienated. The event, closed in on itself, constitutes for the spectators both a participation in fundamental violence and a localization, a distancing, of this violence, which in being channeled and contained in a singular fight, is itself manifested as an exterior, finished, dated event" (II, 55). This event "*incarnates* an always-true aspect of regimes of oppression and exploitation: the alienation of the violence of the oppressed" (II, 55).

Boxing develops in a period of great struggles, when the proletariats have grown conscious of their class violence. Certainly they experience this force as impotence during times of retreat, but this is only temporarily so, even if mystified into some inherent "plebeian impotence" by bourgeois propaganda. Insofar as the temporary can be successfully made to seem permanent, violence becomes derealized. The boxing match incarnates this very mystification, as the conflict "will find its solution *in boxing* but *boxing is not a solution* . . . The participants' violence breaks out and is derealized all at once; it becomes spectacle without ceasing to be lived in its explosive force . . ." (II, 56).

In involving its audience-participants, the fight draws them back to the reality, already transcended by labor unions, of the antagonisms between the sellers of labor-power in the competitive market. The fight shows two of them, fully products of capitalism, opposed by their interests, acting out the sentence capitalism has imposed on them—when in fact workers have forged instruments of unity and struggle against it. Once again Sartre insists that the public watches not the *image* or the *symbol* of competition within the working class but a "very real episode" and a "present incarnation." Yet derealized, the violence of the oppressed changes its original nature as revolt, appearing to everyone through the structure of the bourgeois competitive market as a highly profitable organized conflict between two individuals.

The same event thus contains a fundamental ambiguity, "a multiplicity of incompatible meanings but without these badly clarified incompatibilities' being able to be specified into contradictions" (II, 58). This confused multiplicity becomes part of the enveloping totalization: it contains all our violence, rooted in scarcity and so sustained by fundamental violence.

> Everything is given in the slightest punch, from the history of him who makes it to the material and collective circumstances of this history, from the general process of capitalist society to the singular determination of this process by the merchants of boxing, from the fundamental violence of the oppressed to the singular and alienating objectification of this violence in and by each one of the participants. And if everything were not present and transcended, the singular invention, the unique and concrete reality that is *this* punch, made on *this* day, in *this* auditorium, in the midst of *this* public would not even be possible. (II, 58)

Incarnation Summarized

How, we must ask, can "everything" be given in this punch? Incarnation is inconceivable "unless as totalization of everything" and is irreducible to the abstract: "its concrete reality is, indeed, to be an oriented totalization" (II, 58). In it a "multiplicity of antagonistic actions" overflow every singular human intention and yet singularize "*all the circumstances* of the social whole in movement," thus incarnating the "totalization of envelopment which is the historical process" (II, 58). To be sure, Sartre insists that the very existence of such a process must be demonstrated, but for now he seeks only to underscore that "*this* match envelops every match" and each match in turn "envelops *this* match in its objective reality" (II, 59).

From this point of view, Sartre tells us, moving toward a summary of the entire discussion of incarnation, there are two possible paths of dialectical understanding. The first, the "approach of decompressive expansion," moves away from the object to arrive at the whole. A visitor to a boxing match from another planet would certainly require explanations by relations which transcend the particular facts: "the simple spectacle of individuals queuing at the box office and exchanging banknotes for tickets could not be understood without being referred to the contemporary monetary system and finally to the entire present economy . . ." (II, 59). But Sartre's purpose in this discussion has been to reverse this approach, insisting that each and every such "elementary and fundamental" structure is "gathered directly into the event itself" and contributes to *singularizing* it.

Sartre echoes *Search for a Method* by attacking the practice of other Marxists. The discussion of incarnation, he now indicates, carries further his hope for a Marxism adequate to individual experience.

> The first step, indeed, which is, unfortunately, that to which Marxist "analyses" too often are limited, dissolves the event in the ensemble of mediations as concrete *nonsingularized* totalities; the second—which alone is capable of grasping the dialectical intelligibility of an event—tries to discover within the event itself the interactions that constitute the singularity of the process from the singularization of circumstances. It is *by the project* which condenses them, indeed, that the mediating fields receive a new status of effectiveness. (II, 59)

Sartre argues that the first approach employs the concept as its central tool, the second shows rather a sensitivity to the praxis-process of incarnation. Under the concept, " 'interior' determinations are united by links of exteriority"; general rules and categories are applied from the outside, much as labels, without interest in the specific character of the object or event. In the preferred approach, all determinations are *concrete*, and they are united by a link of *immanence*—that is, the "general" defining traits become absorbed into and part of the specificity of the event, and connected with each other through its internal development.

A Critical Comment: Sartre and Universals

Why this animus against the general? An entire analysis of Sartre's career could be written from the point of view of his negative attitude toward, and brilliant use of, the general, universal, or conceptual planes of experience.[13] More to the point in the *Critique* is his quarrel with

---

13. This unresolved tension would probably be found at the root of Sartre's inability to complete an *Ethics*—which, after all, would sooner or later have to formulate general principles of conduct.

Merleau-Ponty on the one hand and "today's Marxists" on the other. After Merleau-Ponty, any effort to validate Marxism—which task remains, after all, one of the *Critique's* main goals—must free it from the "dogmatic dialectic" that unfolds independently of human will.

Sartre finds the greatest offenders to be those who take Marxism's general categories as providing ready-made knowledge about every and any situation, without taking the trouble to study the specific event or person being discussed. In often sounding like Aristotle's critique of Plato's theory of ideas, his Marxism develops in opposition to those who impose their concepts as substitutes for reality, seeking to respect it by studying it *in its specificity.*

But Sartre's attack on other Marxists and his effort to repair the damage done by overgeneralization or hypostatization of the general leans so far in the other direction as to undermine itself. His specific studies, such as that of the boxer as oppressed and totally alienated worker, depend heavily on the general, structural plane of experience and show its interpenetration with the most idiosyncratic individual plane in the concrete individual. At work in specific analyses, he operates as if there is indeed no individual as such, any more than there is a universal as such: he always moves toward defining his objects of study as *both*, in the most intimate union. And yet, when he formulates philosophical pronouncements, he first stakes out his goal as the "concrete universal" and then champions particular *over* universal. He writes as if individual could be added to individual until a whole plurality—the world of boxing—is assembled without ever crossing the epistemological or ontological threshold of the general.

In his actual studies Sartre remains close to Aristotle, who knew, even as he criticized Plato, that the general is real in some way even if it is not Reality. The notion of the "concrete universal" suggests that it is impossible to singularize something which is not also given *as* general—such as "the world of boxing." Sartre's utterances make use of implicit references to universals without which speech and thought themselves would be impossible.

Incarnation, in this sense, has a central role. It suggests a passage from one plane to another even while denying that they are separate planes. In a sense it becomes Sartre's device for remaining faithful to experience within a theoretical approach that distorts it, for preserving what he has just conjured away. Thus, for example, we have seen Sartre speak of how boxing incarnates "the alienation of the violence of the oppressed." What kind of "always-true aspect" of oppressive and violent societies is this if not a *general* rule? And where does it stem from if not from their social-structural properties, which allow Sartre to make such a deduction without examining every particular case? And is not this particular kind of incarnation the specification of a general realm whose existence Sartre has just denied?

Unity in Struggle?

Sartre now turns back to social wholes as such, reminding us that *each* struggle incarnates *all* the others, and explaining this once again with reference to fundamental scarcity and the forms it takes in contemporary society. Yet at the present level of analysis it seems that conflict is a kind of impassable barrier to any totalizing effort. It seems difficult to conceive of "the historical unity of a society cut up [*tronçonnée*] by class struggles." "*Tronçonner*," Sartre emphasizes, suggests a preexisting unity. Whether or not this has been true in the distant past, "we would waste our time wanting to relate the divisions of all history to this lost paradise of intelligible unities" (II, 60). If unity is to be found in our history, it will only be found in conflict: "it is within the very core of the struggle that synchronic totalization should be able to take place if history should be dialectically intelligible" (II, 60). And so it must be sought "in the thick of conflict."

As we have seen, volume two began with a brief reflection on whether or not class struggle might be considered a *contradiction*, with Sartre suggesting that this formulation implied a larger societal whole whose existence and status remained to be discovered. He now, at the end of volume two's first study, returns to the question, still insisting that "we do not yet dispose over the knowledge and instruments which would permit us to unveil this totalization, that is, for example, to decide whether *national unities* exist or whether the nation is only a collective if individuals are only linked by the mediation of worked matter (by the soil or subsoil insofar as they are exploited, by the whole of geophysical and geopolitical conditions, by the heritage of prior generations, etc.)" (II, 61). This problem cannot yet be approached. First, it is necessary to study an easier one, namely a conflict breaking out within an integrated community. Are subgroups fighting each other within an organized group to be seen as "simple agents of destruction" or as agents of a *contradiction*, somehow contributing to the development of the group and thus serving the dialectic?

Sartre's Achievement

The reader may be surprised, at the end of this lengthy exploration, to encounter there the very question with which it began. What, then, has the analysis accomplished if we have not seen the boxers create a larger unity?

Sartre's purpose in these pages lies in furthering the project announced in *Search for a Method*, grasping the individualization of social wholes—a project carried out most fully in *The Family Idiot*. Volume one of the *Critique* had investigated the processes whereby certain social realities come into being: the practico-inert, a whole variety of collectivities from the series to the group to social class. But Sartre now recognizes the need to see how—or whether—groups in conflict create a larger whole.

The particular whole just studied, *boxing*, cohered under a dominant organizing framework: the set of arrangements and relationships known as the capitalist system. Within this framework each boxer operates a totalization—absorbs the whole and advances it. Sartre's intention now is to examine events whose frameworks themselves are unstable and contested, to see how conflict itself can act as a "totalization without a totalizer." We have already seen that, in discussing boxing within a capitalist framework, Sartre has implied, but not sought to clarify, the governing social dimension through which all individual totalizations operate. Now, rather than moving to a new area of study, would not a sustained Sartrean reflection on the social wholes and their status—What, methodologically speaking, *is* capitalism?—better answer his own question?

Strangely enough, we have seen the question of *universals* turn out to be the major problem area of this part of the *Critique*. While Sartre has extended our understanding of the individual, we do not yet know what is the universal pole of the concrete universal that is being incarnated. Moreover, Sartre is kept from clarifying this by his stance toward the *concept* and its employment. From Aristotle to Hegel, not to mention Marxist studies of history and economics available to Sartre in 1958, the complex relations between universal and particular have been far better appreciated than he suggests. Sartre's hypothetical opponent is after all a straw man, his own argument distortively one-sided.

Critical comments, however, must not lose sight of the fact that Sartre never indicated that he regarded these pages as complete. And that even as unfinished they are a brilliant achievement. We have seen that the purpose of *incarnation* is to indicate, with the specific event and individuals at the center, a relationship to larger human realities and social wholes: scarcity, violence, life and death, capitalism, boxing. By contrast, Barthes's semiology treats "the world of wrestling" as a morality play in which Good struggles against Evil, but refers to no other social layers.

Even while leaving key issues unresolved, Sartre's analysis begins with scarcity and shows its displacement, preservation, and transformation from level to level. He insists on the reality of the praxis-process, on the active participation of all concerned, on the presence of *all* violence at each stage, on its totalization in this match—so that it is gathered in, clarified, and made explicit. At the same time he insists that all of history is the real meaning of each fight, that even while it is individuation of greater social wholes it may nonetheless be a diversion, performed under the hegemony of the dominant class, from the real source of everyone's rage. And, perhaps above all, Sartre emphasizes the singular character of this real event, right down to the color of the boxers' hair, as well as the singularity of our human world.

Perhaps the greatest contribution of Sartre's discussion of boxing is its pursuit of violence, from its origins in scarcity through its various displacements, transpositions, and transformations, to the audience shouting "kill him" on behalf of one or the other boxer. It is a classic Sartrean analysis. His discussion of this bizarre spectacle provides us with important keys for unlocking its mysteries and, by extension, for understanding other social phenomena. And it is constructed around a profound commitment to seek the true source of socialized violence and to illuminate the conditions of releasing it for human liberation.

4 Antilabor and Contradiction:

Antagonistic Subgroups and Their Unintended Product

Having studied how individuals fighting in a match produced by a larger social whole incarnate that social whole, we are now prepared to move toward the central problem of volume two: How do two groups in struggle "collaborate on a common work"? Sartre's purpose is to explain how classes in conflict collaborate to create a movement of history which carries them along even as they battle bitterly against each other. At stake is the intelligibility not only of class struggle but also of the dialectic itself.

To take another step toward this goal, Sartre now examines two subgroups in conflict within an organized group. Are they "agents of destruction" attacking the collective unity, or do they rather give vent to a contradiction which, expressed and transcended, furthers the group's development? If so, what is a "contradiction"? The next seventy pages (chapters three and four in the published text) first explore the general logic of contradiction between subgroups of an already-integrated group and then focus specifically on the Stalin-Trotsky conflict to show how such conflicts may eventuate in an "antilabor" (*contre-travail*), producing such products as the slogan "socialism in a single country": product of two antagonists but intended at first by neither.

Subgroups in Volume One

The *group-in-fusion*,[1] of course, was the original unity, produced—as the serially isolated individuals' response to mortal danger—to achieve immediate, urgent goals. Having accomplished those goals only provisionally or partially, still under threat (even if only in the long term), the group has set to work on itself, first by imposing the pledge on its mem-

---

1. *Groupe en fusion* is rendered as "fused group" by Alan Sheridan-Smith, which misses the sense of continuous creation so essential to Sartre.

bers, then by organizing and differentiating them according to functions (I, 484–574; 410–86; 382–479).

In its self-differentiation the group creates "specialized apparatuses" or subgroups. Both individual and subgroup receive their meanings within the organized group: each belongs to the group *only* insofar as it carries out a specific task (I, 547; 463; 449). Each function, determined as necessary for the group's survival or well-being, "is the reciprocal counterpart of the others (I, 568; 481; 472). Function is thus a prohibition against doing anything else and a right to carry out this particular duty. Furthermore, it is a right to receive, in the case of a specific common individual, "the necessary subsistence and training, etc., to enable him completely to fulfill the requirements of his job" (I, 548; 464; 451).

As we shall see, it is because of such differentiation that subgroups enter into conflict with each other. In volume one, Sartre already took the first few steps in this analysis, in a discussion that he clearly keeps in mind in volume two. He spoke of "disagreements within the organizing group," which in turn reflect "objective structures of the practical problem that has to be resolved" (I, 617–18; 522; 525). His example is the problem of city traffic, needing to be solved within a framework of scarcity, and giving rise to conflict between proponents of one or another term of the contradiction. One solution ignores the scarcity of resources by proposing that wider roads be built; another restricts parking and thus the use of cars, attacking the interests of the auto industry; a third ignores the needs of traffic flow. All fail, because "the contradiction is in the object; it manifests itself spontaneously and it explodes in the final synthesis all the more violently if the synthesis neglects one term in favor of an other" (I, 618; 523; 526). As the problem is structured, some interests can be served while others are neglected—and this is precisely what each proponent's "solution" tries to do.

In preparing for his examination of class struggle in volume two, Sartre now looks between subgroups rather than within a single one; he explores rather than presupposes the meaning of contradiction; and he presents a close study of how a genuine resolution is arrived at.

An Objective Contradiction

The question is, as Sartre now rejoins the group in the process of becoming institutionalized, How does it enter into contradiction *with itself?* Denying that contradictions exist as substantive absolutes which produce their agents a priori, Sartre nevertheless insists that members of a group "only enter into struggle in actualizing a contradiction in the process of development" (II, 61). What then is a contradiction?

First, as we have just seen him say in volume one, it is rooted in objective realities of the group's life rather than in subjective differences. A conflict within an integrated group "can never be born from differences (individual or collective) anterior or exterior to the group's constitution . . ." (II, 61). Certainly, different individuals, of different origins and dispositions, may personally incline toward different orientations of group praxis. But when subgroups fall out among themselves, their conflict "can *reveal* differences of character and rest on them, be reinforced by them, but it cannot be born from them . . ." (II, 62). On the contrary, when the differences between those whose past leads them to be "hards" and "softs" become *antagonistic*, it is due to objective and structural rather than subjective and historical factors: "the circumstances of the common struggle." The point is that "no conflict is even possible in an integrated community if it is not the actualization by men of an objective contradiction" (II, 63).

Indetermination

But to see it as objective does not mean that the contradiction may be found lodged in the group's structure, in a latent form, like an essence, prior to its violent actualization. Sartre strenuously seeks to avoid any sense that praxis is merely the agent of structures which preexist and somehow *drive* it.

In the "banal" example of two subgroups each seeking to assert its competence over a particular piece of group business, rather, "we find at the origin of the debate a real but relative indetermination of respective competencies" (II, 63). Perhaps at an earlier and cruder stage of the group's life, each subgroup operated with greater autonomy over a wider area, but now improved communications put them into relationship with each other and enable them to contemplate a wider scene of activity. Or perhaps group praxis as a whole has created new and unforeseen internal events over which no one has authority. In either case, until the group refashions itself to deal with its new situation, subgroups may fight over their respective spheres of competence. The point is that this indetermination, leading to conflict over who is the best qualified and most appropriate group agent, is not likely to have been latent in or prestructured into the group or its praxis. Rather, it is "the development of common praxis [that] has created this indetermination by introducing unforeseen changes in internal relations" (II, 63–64).

Structures versus Praxis

It should be clear that we are dealing with a very specific practico-inert result of praxis reaching back upon its very source, the group. Group praxis has created a new situation, and demands for a fresh response, to which more than one subgroup may lay claim even while none are specifically adapted to it. It is not just that the structured subgroups, as functions, are not adequate to their tasks or their object. The indetermination "goes retroactively from the object to the [original] functions because it is the object as new consequence of the action that makes the functions obsolete and disqualifies them" (II, 64).

Does this suggest a structural basis for conflict within the group? Indeed the historian may later be able to throw light on the indetermination by comparing the "objective meaning of the event to the organizational or institutional definition of the functions" (II, 64). Sartre's point is, however, that this approach remains wholly abstract. The new, undetermined, and potentially conflictual relationship "is only realized *practically* through the activities of subgroups, it is *brought to life* as hesitation or, if one prefers, it has had practical reality only in and by its interiorization. Otherwise put, although one could externally throw light on it as *structure*, it is first manifested concretely as behavior" (II, 65). Sartre's subsequent analysis will emphasize what he obviously regards as the most rudimentary principle of the dialectic of contradiction: contradiction is objective, not subjective, in origin, but it "is not explicit before being assumed by praxis" (II, 64).

But is it in some sense *given*, even if by a prior praxis, leading us to search for its structural side? We can better grasp Sartre's perplexing formulation if we see it as continuing his animus against all who might minimize the role of praxis and maximize that of structures, be they structuralists or Marxists. After all, we face one of the most characteristic and consistent of Sartrean themes, one that takes us all the way back to his first theoretical work, *Transcendence of the Ego*, which not only attacked the notion of an Ego standing behind our acts but, as we saw earlier, fleetingly criticized historical materialism. There as here, Sartre attacks structures which may be said to determine action. They would represent, he now insists, a transcendent and perhaps autonomous plane which individual action is limited to "realizing" or "carrying out." This would make structures (like concepts) more real than concrete reality itself. Praxis, Sartre is insisting, is autonomous, original, and determinative, and not simply the carrying out of a preexisting hyperorganic reality—or, as we saw earlier, the embodiment of a concept.

Sartre sustains this particular philosophical battle all the way through the *Critique*. Volume one contains extended comment on Lévi-Strauss's study of

> those strange internal realities which are both organized and organizing, both synthetic products of a practical totalization and objects always susceptible of rigorous analytical study, both the lines of force of a praxis for every common individual and the fixed links between this individual and the group, through perpetual changes of both of them, both inorganic ossature and everyone's definite powers over everyone else, in short, both fact and right, mechanical elements and, at the same time, expressions of a living integration into a unitary praxis of those contradictory tensions of freedom and inertia which are known as *structures.* (I, 576; 462; 480)

Sartre argues that structures are the passive syntheses sustained by the group in its praxis of survival and that their roots are the pledge and collective praxis. They are seen as inert skeletons, only from outside the praxis or by a native who is "simply creating an inert object which presents in exteriority, to a man from the exterior, a set of passive characteristics which retain only the inertia of these structures and which, indeed, falsify this inertia by presenting it as an elementary, suffered condition (whereas in fact it is produced by the pledge)" (I, 597; 505; 503).

The forms of analysis which locate structures, tendencies, and causes often seem to give them theoretical—and then political—primacy over the concrete humans and acts through which and in which they appear.[2] In volume one, Sartre yields the ground he absolutely must, indicating that the structure seems to be "both an inert relation and a living praxis" (I, 575; 487; 480). Then, in volume two, even after acknowledging a structural *side* to the entire process, Sartre returns to praxis as source and preserves its centrality. It may be, as he says in an interview given a decade later, that at the least what remains is "the small movement which makes of a totally conditioned social being someone who does not render back completely what his conditioning has given him."[3] Here we are not yet reduced to the *least:* the integrated group is only beginning to experience contradictions, generated by the practico-inert product of its own activity, and that conflict manifests itself only as praxis.

<hr/>

2. See, for example, "Contradiction and Overdetermination" and "On the Materialist Dialectic," in Althusser, *For Marx.*

3. "Itinerary of a Thought," *From Existentialism to Marxism,* trans. John Mathews (London, 1974), 35.

From Indetermination to Conflict to Contradiction

How does this disagreement over competency and authority become a conflict and, indeed, a contradiction, with that term's overtones of a deeply structured, objective irreconcilability which can only be resolved through violent struggle? Sartre's "banal" example is, indeed, remote in drama and significance from the monumental Jacobin-Girondin or Trotsky-Stalin conflicts to which he will return. Yet there is a logic to his presentation: he seeks to move in slow and definite steps from the "show" conflict of boxing organized by one and the same hierarchy to classes in open conflict moderated by no mediating authority. Each step has its conclusions for, and contributions to make to, the next stage of analysis.[4] Indeed, the almost totally abstract character of this "study" of subgroups in conflict only strengthens our sense that this is a deliberately structured series of logical steps building toward an ultimate goal (rather than conclusions drawn from a study of real cases). Competency over what? we may ask. But Sartre never answers. The purpose of this "example," it seems, is to build the larger argument by revealing the logic of the *first stages* of a contradiction within a group, and so to reveal the origin of certain decisive processes and structures.

The conflict of competence is spontaneous. At first it does not oppose vital policy directions to each other. It is a more-or-less "friendly" conflict within an integrated group, in which appeal can still be made to the group's unity, its traditions, its governing processes, and its members. Both sides, fully integrated into the group, are composed of *common* individuals, thinking and acting *for* the group. *As* group members, they find it appropriate that this matter be handled by their subgroup. At the same time, however—and this is the point Sartre now insists upon—when this minimal conflict crosses a certain threshold, it becomes a *contradiction*.

How is this fateful step taken? By itself, the initial indetermination is obviously not contradiction: the terms and subgroups have not yet been determined *as* opposing. Nor are they when both subgroups take initiative toward claiming the same business in question. They cross the threshold "at the precise moment when *the same matter* is claimed by each subgroup *against the other*" (II, 65). That is, this matter is *ours* to deal with and not *yours*. When "common praxis has created organs (similar or different) which both claim the undetermined object, objective con-

4. See the anonymous introduction to the section translated in *New Left Review* (note 14 below) for a statement of some of the stages. I have drawn on this excellent discussion in what follows.

tradiction becomes the meaning of their conflict. And this contradiction
is nothing other than the impossibility for two internal structures of the
group to temporalize themselves together in this moment of the global
temporalization" (II, 65–66). Their two putative praxes, in other words,
cannot both take place, because each one preempts the other. At this
moment of the group's history its tasks "objectively and simultaneously
determine the two [sub]groups to realize [this impossibility] practically.
And the practical realization of an impossible coexistence is precisely the
conflict" (II, 66).

Yet why must each subgroup claim the matter at hand, rather (for example) than one of them yielding authority, perhaps temporarily, to the
other? Why does each one *have to* so insist? And why can't the business
at hand be shared? As Sartre has already made clear in volume one, "an
individual belongs to the group insofar as he carries out a certain task
and *only that task*" (I, 547; 463; 449). Thus his function is his "right to
carry out his particular duty," as well as a prohibition against carrying
out any other. To have its function now claimed by another subgroup is
to simultaneously be challenged, in its very existence as a part of the
group, as well as (in its own eyes) to threaten the very well-being of a
group *depending on it* to carry out such-and-such a function.

Sartre will now make these points more precise as he turns to clarify the individual biographical and anecdotal dimension, the way in
which the practico-inert gives rise to the conflict, and the structuring of
contradiction.

The Individual and Anecdotal Dimension

Sartre stresses the *anecdotal* beginning of the conflict, its seemingly contingent and individual origins in which members of the group find themselves deepening a quarrel they would prefer to stop. But its individual
features and misunderstandings, indeed, the quarrel itself, will "vanish
at once if they are not *in themselves* a function of totalizing incarnation,
that is, if through them the coexistence of subgroups does not reveal its
impossibility" (II, 66). We know that the term "incarnation" indicates that
individual actions embody a larger, more fundamental conflict, that of
the group. With the best will in the world, the two subgroups are ir-
reconcilable *because of this logic*. For example, a specific incident in which
the Girondins opposed Robespierre's invocation of "Providence" manifests a more fundamental conflict between two sets of revolutionaries: "a
de-Christianized bourgeoisie which scorns the people and its 'supersti-

tions' [and] a group of petit-bourgeois whose politics seek above all to make the revolution for the people and, as a consequence, to spare popular beliefs" (II, 66).

Specific groups decide their coexistence is impossible, and they do so *"in singular circumstances,"* believing in the very "contingency of the conflict itself" and believing that "in consequence, it is always possible to put an end to it" (II, 67). But this is an illusion fostered by the "free transcendings" carried out by free practical organisms in conflict. In reality, each of the transcendings "is at the service of an untranscendable [*indépassable*] sworn inertia" (II, 67). In our example of a conflict over indetermination, this inertia, "the material product of a free oath," in fact stems from the group's self-structuring into subgroups. Each subgroup has taken on the inertia of the pledge, being sworn to respond to such-and-such situations, but now faces "this other inertia which is, for example, the indetermination of powers." When an unanticipated situation occurs, both subgroups find themselves sworn to respond to it. Indeed, in their very being as group members they *must* respond to it. They act freely, but through and in relation to a double inertia: the inertia of pledged subgroups and that of their specific indetermination vis-à-vis an unanticipated demand on them.

Doesn't this emphasis on inertia undermine Sartre's earlier antistructuralist insistence that contradictions are not due to preexisting structures? And doesn't he now suggest that group members are agents of the larger process which their actions incarnate? In keeping with his critique of Lévi-Strauss, Sartre insists on necessity *and* freedom, the one created by the other: "the absolute necessity of this contradiction, as objective and interior structure of the group, comes from an opposition of inertias *constituted by the subgroups themselves in their free practical movement"* (II, 67).

Sartre's point is that, while the conflict stems from prior group praxis, it does not emerge from it immediately and directly: "it requires the mediation of the practico-inert" (II, 68). The practico-inert does not simply impose itself "as in a decompressed social whole and without integration," but rather depends on being "reassumed and reanimated by a practice." If contradiction can indeed be seen as structural, this can be so *only* in the most intimate and mutually conditioning union with the praxis that brings it to light. "In the framework of destiny, transcendence gives to the transcended its own untranscendability" (II, 68). There is a practico-inert—indeed, we may even say structural—incompatibility of two subgroups. But it is realized as an untranscendable inertia of the group only insofar as the free praxis of each subgroup finds itself opposed by that of the other. "Everything is act, in short" (II, 69), as he will say.

But the act interiorizes and reexteriorizes an inertia (however active its source) which forces it into opposition with itself. Sartre's chosen task in the next ten pages, describing the transformation of praxis into a praxis-process, is a Herculean undertaking: How does action, perhaps especially when successful,[5] create the conditions for its own contradiction? Sartre argues both that it is free, transcending group praxis that creates its own contradictions, and that it cannot help but do so even while remaining free.

A Conflict

Two subgroups enter into conflict, for example, because they both lay claim to the same matter after the group praxis of internal reorganization has *improved* its functioning, including that of the subgroups; "they are better informed, for example: the questions they ask, the reports they send to the central organisms no longer remain unanswered or indeed the answers come back more rapidly, etc." (II, 69). In this "global enrichment of powers and knowledge," subgroup A, now placed into relation with subgroup B, can now also perceive that both seem "to exercise the same functions." An improvement in communications within the group and consequently between the subgroups makes it "necessary that one of the two be reabsorbed or that it be liquidated" or that they both be merged. Although the two may merge "by spontaneous accord," the group's praxis may have already evolved to the point where subgroups are posed for themselves, as identifiable entities having their own self-interest. If so, they will be threatened by seeing *their own* functions claimed by an other.

The Threat to the Subgroup

They may look and see an opposition which cannot possibly be interiorized. It is in this sense that improvement leads to indetermination, which leads to contradiction. In a highly structured group, well advanced along the road to serialization, the inertia of tradition may keep both subgroups intact: "there is no struggle, matters go indifferently to

5. "If we again take up one of the chosen examples, that of the two [sub]groups in conflict, following the relative indetermination of their respective functions, we will notice indeed that counterfinality only manifests itself as *inverse* of positive results" (II, 68).

this one or that, or indeed each subgroup sends them to the other and, finally, everything is engulfed in the circularity of impotence: each one of the two organs becomes *other* and is no longer anything but *the other of the other*" (II, 71). But in a group in an earlier stage of development, one in full activity and fully alive, this indetermination presents a serious problem (even if later it can be recognized as objective structure). Appearing as "negative action," it seems to one subgroup "as attack on its very existence, that is to say, on its function and its right to exercise it" (II, 71).

Members can address themselves to *either* subgroup, according to convenience or preference. Simply because it exists, the action of subgroup B is "constituted in spite of itself as violation of the rights of the other . . ." (II, 71). Sartre stresses that it is the objectively structured indetermination which makes this act a threat, but that this tends to be hidden. He points to the tendency of all praxis to ignore its own material circumstances and see itself as "practice and translucidity through and through . . ." (II, 72).

While he usually attacks the tendency to reify structures and material determinants to the disadvantage of praxis, Sartre now attacks the reification of *praxis*. Within groups the negative tends to be seen "as full and destructive activity: a blunder and even an accident for which no one is responsible appears as sabotage, as attack; at a certain degree of urgency in the climate of fraternity-terror, all opposition, as Merleau-Ponty has said, is treason" (II, 72).[6] The other subgroup's acts are experienced as *enemy praxis*, regardless of their objective effect or subjective intent. Such situations are governed by this dialectical law: "in a fully active group, every common individual is objectively produced as radically active, and everything he produces is interpreted necessarily in terms of action" (II, 72).

The Threat to the Group

Does the conflict represent a genuine threat to the group? Having indicated the basis of the subjective need to speak in terms of treason, Sartre now argues for its objective basis: indetermination is indeed "a danger of internal rupture." The problem is rooted in the character of group membership. Each subgroup "*incarnates* the entire group, as the part incarnates the whole; this means in particular that, for its part, it produces and it claims *unity*, that is to say, the maximal integration of the group

6. Sartre is referring to *Humanism and Terror*, 34.

insofar as common action must realize it, in the name of the goal to achieve" (II, 72). As Sartre has explained when describing *function* in volume one, each subgroup's action is, by definition, the group's *common* action *over here* (I, 542–59; 459–73; 445–63). Under a division of labor, no subgroup is troubled by its differences with others, because each one "realizes in itself the totality but under a specific form and through a particular action, that is to say, a particular determination of the total action" (II, 73).

But the present situation of indetermination is different: the fact that two subgroups have "*the same attributes,* when one alone between them must suffice to fulfill them, puts practical unity in danger by the introduction of a *dualism of identity*" (II, 73). At earlier stages of a group's life, each separate part is desired as both incarnation and particularization of the whole. But when, in an organized group, one subgroup sees itself as identical to another, it cannot help seeing itself and the group as menaced by the other—especially if the other wants to integrate *it* into the total unity:

> the identical *is the Other,* in a milieu *where there are no Others.* But it is an Other who is particularly hateful and dangerous: each subgroup, insofar as it is identical to an Other, discovers this Other as its own reality which has become foreign praxis. And the practical existence of this Other is a danger *not only for the identical and opposed subgroup,* insofar as the identity contests the unicity of its relationship to the totality in course of totalization, but also for the *totalization of envelopment,* that is to say, for the entire group, for its efficacy, for its objectives. (II, 74)

At the very least, we may conclude, the group is threatened by the confusion and loss of efficiency entailed in a duplication of functions. Thus, when each contending subgroup seeks to liquidate the "extra" subgroup, it may well be serving its own self-interest, but each one also genuinely wants this for the benefit of the larger group. Sartre now turns away from the main argment to insist that self-interest is not merely subjective, that in a group-in-fusion self-interest or "ambition" cannot be separated from policies pursued or "program."[7] Stalin as a historical phenomenon can be reduced neither to the "will to rule" nor to the "simple incarnation of the historical process"—that is, to personal ambition *or* the larger totalization. In a rapid preview of the discussion to come, Sartre speaks of the historical process itself being uniquely made

---

7. He equally insists that this can be so under conditions of bourgeois parliamentarism.

by *and* giving scope for Stalin's will of steel: "the historical process supports and carries the man who makes it" (II, 75).

The Struggle

The threat to the group goes deeper yet. Speaking structurally, the indetermination makes each common individual of the group "the member of two equivalent organisms one of which is a supernumerary" (II, 75). Each subgroup sees its opponent as a *traitor* because the other threatens *the group's unity* by deliberately usurping the other subgroup's functions. As a result, the entire conflict is dominated by the goal of restoring the group's absolutely vital condition, its unity. By liquidating its opponent, or reducing it to impotence, or reintegrating it elsewhere in the group, each subgroup seeks both its own advantage *and* "to reconstitute this broken or menaced unity" (II, 75).

What, then, is the logic of contradiction, understood as a group praxis-process? Originally, we may recall, asking about contradiction meant, for Sartre, appealing to a larger unity of which the antagonists were opposing terms. At the outset he argued that because the existence of this larger unity was precisely what was in question, much preparation was necessary before seriously examining the theme. Is he now returning to it prematurely? In the first place, the theme of incarnation has yielded considerable reflection on the individual act in its relation to the larger unity, which is now absorbed into the discussion of subgroup and group, part and whole. In the second place, Sartre does not yet ascend to the plane of class struggles and history, but here confines himself to the organized group. Many steps remain before exploring two opposing classes, each of which struggles independently of such commitments or frameworks.

Sartre is being rigorous and completely consistent: *contradiction* still refers to opposing terms/structures/subpraxes of a *larger* praxis, the group's. He now insists on the "profound reality" and the "reason" of the conflict between subgroups: "In each subgroup, it is the group which fights to preserve or reconquer its unity. And, in truth, it is really the group which opposes itself to itself" (II, 76). In this conflict *the group* enters into contradiction *with itself*. "Each one of the antagonistic subgroups, indeed, really produces itself as incarnation of the group, and in truth each one incarnates it . . ." (II, 76).

To say this does not mean idealizing contradiction, just as it does not mean appealing to a hyperorganism which produces the acts of its members. To speak loosely of the "action" of the whole "producing itself" in its members is to speak metaphorically: *they* act, *it* does not. But they act *as* group members. "Totalization is incarnated in and by their particular activity and in their antagonistic practices" (II, 76). Central to this, as we know from volume one, is the pledge, which "ontologically" produced the group in and for each individual (I, 516–42; 437–59; 417–44).

Sartre now steers through difficult terrain, struggling to do justice both to individual praxis and to the larger social-historical processes which, without reifying them, he is determined to explain and advance. *Unity* and *contradiction* must now be shown *both* as products of individual praxis *and* as having their own logics and imposing their own demands. The key to the explanation lies in the pledge, which has given the group a solidity and presence in each and every individual, as further explained by the concept of incarnation.

Each subgroup legitimately sees itself as "the center of this totalization whose center is everywhere'" (II, 76). Over here, the group exists *as* this subgroup; over there, it exists *as* that contending subgroup. It is the *entire group's* development—its lack of differentiation to this point *and* its doubling of epicenters (the incarnation of this in the subgroups)—that places the subgroups in conflict. At the same time, each has developed rights and obligations *as* member of the group, which are now jeopardized by the other's threatening to usurp *its* place. If this results in conflict, it is *the group itself*, "through each subgroup," that "tends to tighten its unity by violence . . ." (II, 77). It is the group's evolution that has put its own unity into question in this situation; the group endangers itself, and meeting the danger becomes its own "most immediate internal demand." The subgroups fight each other *as group members.*

Its unity thus threatened, *the group is in danger:* this palpable and undeniable fact seems all the more threatening because of the group's origins and history, its roots in the life-and-death danger to the once-serial individuals who, in self-defense, organized themselves. Each contender appeals to that sense of danger and its overcoming in the group's history, to the group's objectives and structures and members. Each one, in short, *correctly* claims to incarnate the group even if its very existence threatens the group's unity. At first those members remaining outside the conflict accept both claims and seek, however futilely, some reintegrative settlement of the dispute—for example, to mediate the "misunderstanding."

How is it possible both to call the conflict a *contradiction* and thus a specification of a larger structure's logic, *and* to avoid seeing that structure as hyperorganism? It should now be clear that the group's unity is the secret motor force of the conflict: not only because the struggle's eventual ferocity seeks to restore that unity, perceived on all sides as

mortally threatened, but also because that unity renders the conflict possible in the first place and is its very meaning. Why does one subgroup
fight against another, after all, if not to defend the group, to reunify it?
The unity engenders the duality *and* the demand to transcend it. And it
is also the meaning of the "liquidating violence" of each subgroup toward the other. "Thus the conflict would not even be possible if unity did
not stand up against itself. Far from struggle, when it appears, being
itself rupture of unity, it is unity that renders it possible; not only does
this unity represent the profound link of each part of the group, but, in
addition, it constitutes the *meaning* of the antagonistic relationship itself" (II, 77).

But the unity is not a structure, imposed on group members from the
outside, that somehow perpetuates *itself*. The group's unity is "never
anything other, indeed, than the permanent practice of reunification" of
its pledged members (II, 78). We observe "a complex reality, one of
whose faces is the praxis of struggle and the other the inert demand
of the moment . . ." (II, 78).

Opposition is a "synthetic, internal determination" of the group which
in fact has come from "worked matter, insofar as this inscribes its determinations in the framework of pledged inertia" (II, 78). This can be a
contradiction, however, only as the inert determination becomes *motive
force*, which is precisely what happens when each subgroup excludes the
other, in conflict.

What Is Unity?

It is now possible to understand contradiction, as action which realizes a
practico-inert opposition but does so only as a movement of reunification. The conflict indeed takes place "as if" unity itself unfolded "its
own difficulties and accentuated them in contradictions to better specify
them and to finally smash their limits" (II, 81). But, Sartre reminds us,
this "unity is practical: it is perpetually maintained and reserved[8] by and
for the global action" (II, 81). It is maintained by the praxes of group
members in their functions as group members. Contradiction does proceed from the larger unity, the totalization. But if we took this unity as a
substantial reality, we could never understand why it would choose to
split apart. Rather, contradiction is based on the antagonistic activity of
pledged common individuals.

Have the practico-inert divergences of the larger unity engendered the

---

8. "*Réservée.*" The editor has rendered it as "*resserrée*" (constricted).

conflict? Is the unity the larger reality, the substance, and the disunion its accident? Sartre insists, rather, that only by entering into *conflict* do the opponents cross that point of no return we recognize as a contradiction. If unity *is not a substantive unity*, it is rather the "common project in each one, here and everywhere in the group" (II, 81). In other words, the project of each individual, as group member, is to further the total development of group praxis. In doing precisely this, here, in their way, these members enter into conflict with the subgroup, there, simultaneously threatening that subgroup's position in the group *and* the group's unity. It is in the framework of the larger praxis shared by all group members that their particular incarnation of it, here, becomes contradictory of another, there.

Mediation

Sartre has already mentioned the situation where a crisis is avoided by effective organs of mediation, in order to "better show the movement of totalization at the very heart of the conflict" (II, 81)—by oscillating between the praxis which realizes a contradiction and the unity which is its secret. The mediator, to be sure, is an organ of the group entrusted with a totalizing function: to liquidate the divergences before they threaten the group's unity. A synthesis of opposed "points of view" often tries to make antagonisms vanish by suppressing them with a view to the group's future unity, denying that they have any meaning or substance. But "this Hegelian conception could only have meaning if the dialectic was a transcendent reality, a suprahuman development" (II, 80).

If his analysis of contradiction suggests that mediation—"as praxis of dialectical unification by invention of the solution to the problems" (II, 82)—*must* triumph, Sartre immediately dashes such "idealistic optimism." In so doing he modulates toward the central issue: the intelligibility of struggles which have no overarching and controlling totalizer. Frequently one subgroup triumphs by liquidating the other; a mediator may favor one of the adversaries rather than producing "a synthetic transcendence" of the two; he may do violence to both subgroups and refuse to consider "the partial truth which each one represents" (II, 81); he may not even understand the need to adapt the subgroups to the new situation of the group. Ineffective mediation perpetuates, whether in its original form or as displaced elsewhere, the unsolved problem of internal reorganization. And so failure is a distinct, and thus intelligible, possibility, showing as it does "the very difficulties of totalization."

Schism

When mediation fails, we are left with a nonmediated and relatively open-ended conflict. Sartre approaches it first by discussing the situation resulting in a *schism*, such as between Rome and Byzantium, where two new groups are formed. A schism stems from the impossibility of liquidating either of the opponents within the fragile group. Each subgroup experiences the explosion as *amputation*, but at the same time each reunifies itself by expelling the other.

Until the very end, the struggle of each, in the name of the group, was a unifying movement. Lacking mediation, each subgroup faced the antidialectical "non-sense of the struggle"—its inability to defeat the other and to reaffirm, in its victory, the group's hegemony over the antagonists. On a deeper level this suggests the "alienation of the fighters by the counterfinalities secreted by the struggle" (II, 84). At this moment the antagonistic dialectic *fails,* and is transcended by "the decision which transforms this inhuman mediation into two human rejections of any mediation" (II, 84)—two separate and distinct Roman Empires.

Liquidation

Having described the extremes of mediation and schism, Sartre now turns to the situation where one subgroup liquidates the other. He poses the question of transcendence, in terms closest to his goal of illuminating history as a totalization without a totalizer.

The risk of explosion is overcome by one side's victory, in the name of the larger group. The group's synthetic reunification casts new light on events, creating an orderly and structured sense of a "before" (the split) and an "after" (the new unity). At the same time, the victors take on new weight within the group. The group, reorganized by the conflict and victory, sees a new distribution of roles and tasks, including filling the functions carried out by the vanquished subgroup. Yet, most remarkably, the group absorbs into itself the subgroup it has just destroyed right down to some of the subgroup's individual members—"it necessarily inherits the attributes of the disappeared organism . . ." (II, 85).

The "necessarily" may give the reader pause: under Sartre's construction to this point the issue was the group's general indetermination insofar as the contesting subgroups were concerned. A "synthetic remaking of every office" and a reassignment of the subgroup's members would seemingly remove the structural basis for the old contradiction, and thus the subgroup's tendency to reappear would be vestigial (appealing to old memories, duties, privileges) but no longer situational or structural. Sartre, however, seems now to be thinking of subgroups engaged in principled political conflict—the left and right wings of a party, for example—rather than those, as in the original hypothesis, merely duplicating functions. Only thus would he seem able to insist that the dissolved community must be absorbed and *represented* in a new unity.

Indeed, his example confirms this: Communist parties in power have abolished both the extreme Left and Social Democratic parties. In this case each element represents real social forces and thus policy options which must be taken into account. And so the new party "must become both its own Right and its own Left . . ." (II, 85).

Suppressing all nonparty opposition, the Party finds an external void to its Right and Left. In reality, it has *interiorized* the opposition while subjecting it to iron rules of discipline and party unity. The needs of praxis now generate a sectarian Left, an opportunist Right, and a mediating Center which must "*conciliate* the extremes, exploit their divergences, use members of this extreme or that when praxis demands a change of personnel . . ." (II, 85). And so the Social Democrats reappear *within* the ruling Communist Party, and their opportunism now appears not in an organized faction but in attitudes and proposals projected in the name of the Communists' objectives.

Progress

In short, the victorious subgroup expands beyond its original orientation and composition by assuming, in the new unity, the tasks once carried out by the defeated. Will this mean bringing the group to an improved level of functioning? Returning to his original hypothesis that the group's formerly inadequate differentiation engendered the subgroups' conflict, Sartre now describes the conditions under which victory becomes progress: "the liquidation of one of the terms of the split unity by the other can itself be considered a transcendence only if, through it, the praxis of the whole group transcends itself toward a tighter moment of integration, of more elaborate differentiation, and of greater efficacy in relation to its principal objectives" (II, 87). Speaking dialectically, in other words, the resolution-victory is genuine progress only if it increases the group's effectiveness.

But does victory generally have this meaning? Does it always mark progress in the common project? Sartre now initiates a fascinating discussion, which will wind its way through twenty pages, on how, in advance, we might evaluate the possible outcomes of a struggle within a group. In one of the most important theoretical reflections of volume two, he will weave back and forth between a struggle's positive and negative outcomes, its foreseeable and unforeseeable ones, and its intelligible and unintelligible ones. He will seem at times to accept the notion of inevitable progress, only to reject it, en route to constructing sophisticated tools for evaluating the meaning of a contradiction. Then, in turning to the Trotsky-Stalin conflict, he will deploy these tools.

In using "progress," Sartre tries to avoid an external value judgment, having in mind the term's "simplest sense": an *"irreversible progression"* toward achieving the group's goals. He begins by suggesting that if the victory has a *meaning*, it is this kind of progress. But, at the outset, in this a priori study of the intelligibility of conflict within a group we must reject both optimism and pessimism as being dogmatic presuppositions.[9]

Having done so, however, we should not be deceived by the fact that even the necessities of a given struggle take "the form of contingency," and *must* do so. We must not miss the fact that within a group no victory is possible that is not the "internal and local incarnation of the totalization in course." In other words, victory is the "triumph of unity over the split . . . [and] can only fall to the subgroup that incarnates the true movement of praxis to reabsorb its internal duality" (II, 88).

We have already seen that struggle "is a mediated activity" whose outcome depends on the larger human milieu within which it takes place. But in this larger milieu, *who* decides the struggle? Every other subgroup mediates by individually totalizing the way the conflict develops; as does every common individual; as does the totalized totality of individuals and groups; as does the group itself and every human activity within it; as does every constituting and constituted dialectic.

When two military factions dispute their command in a besieged city, this struggle reveals the extent to which internal conflict is a function of the general situation and the group's common action. (The new case is not a conflict of competence, by the way, but a disagreement over strategy and tactics; it too spills over Sartre's original framework and points us toward his discussion of the Trotsky-Stalin conflict.) The conflict of the two factions takes place in and through the specific activities of and pressures on the group. The vicissitudes of the battle against the enemy, and the mistakes of the ruling faction pointed out by those who contest it, lead the common individuals and other subgroups of the group to decide against the ruling faction, and for its challengers.

They become mediators under this tension, giving victory to one sub-

9. "Pessimism, in the case which concerns us, is less the affirmation of Evil than of a disorder which allows Evil to triumph more often than Good. By Good must be understood the continuous progress of the enterprise; by Evil, its regression and involution" (II, 87).

group and, in the process, beginning a new reworking of the group as a whole. *The community* determines not only the victor but the form of its victory and, well before that, the nature of the conflict itself, in this case of siege not permitting schism, violence, or the destruction of either faction. Each faction seeks to win allies, in keeping with the group's structures and according to common functions, projects, and interests.

Thus "the mediation of all" decides the issue, and decides it in terms of *the group's vital goals*. The group's individuals decide *as* group members: only as the group's members become engaged is one subgroup allowed to emerge victorious, another to be defeated. In the first place no hyperorganism such as "the group" decides for the individuals, but they themselves decide as common individuals; in the second place, they seek to unify the group to better prepare it to meet the external threat.

Disadaptation

Does Sartre's argument suggest a reason for optimism about the outcome of such conflicts? Not at all. At stake, he emphasizes, are praxis and invention, which may indeed turn out to be *dis*adapted. He turns his attention to the possibility, and intelligibility, of disadaptation. Certainly the mistake was the leader's free praxis, "but this error of estimation gathers in itself, incarnates, and reproduces the total subgroup right up to its fundamental relationship to the group which has produced it; this is what renders it comprehensible" (II, 94). A subgroup, to continue the example, fails to seize its opportunity and is defeated because it missed its chance. Yet it has only "reproduced its original relationship to the group" insofar as it has been incompetent, has hesitated, has lacked self-confidence, or has behaved timidly before the ruling faction. Sartre presents a tight, closely determined relationship between individual act and the larger process it incarnates. This becomes a necessitarianism which, however qualified because it unfolds only as free praxis, becomes all-encompassing: the subgroup's defeat reflects on the group itself, which was "only able to be incarnated in it as incarnation defeated in advance . . ." (II, 94).

Perhaps, Sartre suggests in an analysis foreshadowing his Trotsky-Stalin discussion, the group had developed in such a way as to forbid all opposition as factionalizing, so that in its very first appearance the subgroup had already lost the common individuals' support. Later, if the group indeed turns toward the subgroup, its fatal hesitation only re-exteriorizes the group's earlier mistrust, and perhaps even reflects the group's continuing unwillingness to follow it in action. In short, the subgroup's current hesitation *incarnates* the group's confidence in the other, the ruling, faction. A larger process is always embodied, and works itself out, in this subgroup's individual acts and traits.

There remains, however, the slightest ghost of indetermination, a slippage which is itself intelligible: their opposition of yesterday draws the rest of the group toward the factionalizers today, but because of their original hesitation they (the opposition) "are not at the rendezvous." Diachronically, the group's history has produced *no other* oppositional subgroup, even though synchronically it might indeed be willing to follow a more decisive opposition were it somehow to appear. But this *opening of history* remains a dead possibility, because the winners are indeed "the strongest, the shrewdest, the best armed," and they draw these qualities from the mediation of the group. Or, more precisely, "they express its mode of recruitment, its history, the evolution of its structures, and its fundamental relationship to all" (II, 96).

A Dual Commitment

The individual act, Sartre is saying, embodies the group's history and structures through and through, and seems to do so with a force of necessity which allows no discernible space for indetermination. Indeed, even the apparent indeterminations—a subgroup's hesitation—are produced by the group itself. We can scarcely imagine a stronger argument that individual acts and traits are shaped by larger and more general entities. Sartre, however, is not flirting with Plato's theory of ideas, which gives the particular individual a decidedly secondary ontological status, or the Platonic-Marxist approach which sees Valéry as no more than a petit-bourgeois (*QM* 51–57; 43–47; *SM* 52–56). At each step of the analysis he is firmly aware of his other commitment, however far he has gone in a universalizing and necessitarian direction,[10] however much he sounds like the greatest apostles of rationalism. His entire analysis not only denies any greater ontological status to the larger and more general entities, but is firmly anchored in free individual praxis. The group exists, to be sure, but not on its own, independent of the plurality of individual praxes which, through countless mediations, sustain it and give it its force. Which is, of course, why the concept of mediations is decisive for Sartre's thought—it attempts to trace the passage from individual to larger entities and back.

---

10. I use "necessitarian" with full awareness that Sartre always emphasizes that the individual acts, even when his act cannot be otherwise.

Sartre tries to render their due both to the apparently deterministic and universalizing logic of incarnation and to the ontological primacy of individual praxis. Are these commitments self-contradictory? The emphasis on a larger logic usually denies the primacy of individual praxis and vice versa: Sartre seeks to combine the two. This accounts for the polar reversals we see through this section, as well as elsewhere in volume two. After forcefully arguing the first pole, Sartre always insists on the second in his attempt to do justice both to the specific individual and to the more structural and general social processes.

Progress Revisited

Sartre is aware that his discussion of conflict may be misunderstood as implying an optimistic outcome. Intelligibility is not progress, he cautions:

> It is true that victory comes to the victorious by the mediation of the entire group and that it incarnates a moment of the totalizing activity as praxis-process. But this does not mean that it realizes a progress of the group toward its own objectives: a priori we can decide nothing. The circumstances of praxis and the material givens alone can inform us. Nothing indeed shows that the liquidation of a subgroup will not reflect an involution of praxis; it disappears perhaps not because it arouses mistrust, not because it is sacrificed in the name of unity, but in the midst of general indifference, because the group members lose confidence in their common activity. (II, 97)

This remark is pregnant with consequences not only for the analysis of the Soviet Union to follow, but for the entire *Critique* project. Sartre, after all, is reviving a critical Marxian dialectic in the face of Merleau-Ponty's abandonment of orthodox Marxism. If his former political mentor rejected Marxism for inscribing a historical logic within being itself, Sartre's nondogmatic alternative is taking shape before us. Here, at the core of his most general reflections on conflicts within a group, he presents a remarkable agnosticism about their outcome. Certainly if no a priori tendency to progress appears *here*, in the praxis of the group, it would be even less likely to be forecast in class struggles, lacking a totalizer and lost amidst the vast and diverse practico-inert serialities of which real history is composed.

Sartre's subsequent comments go further in laying to rest any illusion that progress and improvement are more likely than corruption and decline.[11] Indeed, the group's support for a given subgroup may reflect and aggravate a kind of wandering [*égarement*]: "perhaps, by this tacit choice, the group has carried out a sentence on itself" (II, 98). In fact, neither of the subgroups *has to be* a lucid or legitimate product of the group's and their own history. In fact, the subgroups may find their vision blocked by these very histories. "Thus real and profound conflict can be expressed by abstract and scholastic oppositions; it can happen that one fights for myths and absurd 'opinions,' for articles of a dogma" (II, 98).

This decline is, of course, intelligible. A "collision of fetishized symbols" has its deeper meaning just as this very fetishization has its logic, but it incarnates a wandering, a diversion, an impoverishment. "One can get killed over the sex of angels: and that conveys a profound malaise of Byzantine society" (II, 98). For practical forces to become polarized around such symbols necessarily entails a partial loss of energy.

The Alienation of Every Struggle

Sartre now seeks a general explanation for this phenomenon and, in the process, makes a significant addition to his analysis. A transcendental dogmatism would make fetishes seem epiphenomenal, and thus would always guide us back to their "real," underlying meaning. But Sartre insists in a resolutely materialist spirit that the fetishes themselves are things: "determinations of matter, synthetic unifications of inert diversities . . ." (II, 99). If they are things, they have an autonomy and power to act on us. Sartre draws the explosive consequences within the same sentence, emphasizing "that these things will act *as things* on the adversaries; in other words struggle and victory are alienated in advance" (II, 99). Struggle and victory are alienated because they produce and turn on objects which cannot help but act on those who produce them. For Sartre this necessary alienation of every struggle only confirms historical materialism. In spite of the progressive coming-to-consciousness accompanying human struggles, such alienation is the essence of prehistory:

> Even revolutionary struggle produces its fetishes and alienates itself in them; even in the Communist Party one struggles over the sex of angels. That does not at all mean that history

11. Nor do his more abstract reflections, in the notes gathered in the *Annexe* at the end of the book, suggest any kind of necessary historical *logic* of progress. Progress can never be grasped from the outside, as signification, but is only a *meaning*, projected from within a praxis: "it is *lived* in interiority, practical organization of totalization. It is an *act*" (II, 411). On the other hand, the movement of science, because "it is exteriority itself, discovering itself everywhere" (II, 426), is therefore in a state of "continuous progress."

has no meaning (this fundamental problem, which we will touch upon later, can only be treated at this abstract and superficial level of our historical experience) but, most simply, that it is not a priori necessary in a conflict of subgroups within whatever group that one of the two opponents represents progress . . . nor that victory truly represents "one step forward." (II, 99)

Certainly in religious quarrels one side may well reflect greater rationality, but the existence of fetishes hides the interest of each subgroup and often gives the antagonistic regroupings a *monstrous* (*monstrueux*) character. This term, which will become central in what follows, here in its first use opens on to the Dreyfus affair. Sartre suggests that in fighting out other, deeper social battles, major forces in French life organized themselves around presumably "monstrous" themes such as antisemitism, the army's honor, or pure Justice. These are "monstrous" creations in that they hide the real issues yet become material social objects and bloody battlegrounds, all the while incarnating larger social forces and issues.

Deviating to Stay the Same

Such creations are the product of a consciousness which has begun to believe and live by its own myths. But, to return to the original example, even if the two subgroups remain lucid both about "common objectives and the real factors of the conflict," the process of liquidation still runs the risk "of *deviating* the common action" (II, 100). Sartre has already suggested that the original split reappears, under another form, in the victorious subgroup. The open struggle was originally intelligible to everyone; interiorized, it becomes ambiguous, obscure.

Sartre's first point, as earlier,[12] is that even if repressed and clandestine, practico-inert differences remain objective and internal, and will continue to reappear in new forms. His new point is that the fear of renewed conflict will create a distinct tension on victor and vanquished alike as they formulate and accept or reject new proposals. They will seek to avoid reopening the old conflict yet find its terms returning again and again. Having resolved the contradiction and reunified the group, the ruling subgroup now refuses to make them explicit and act on them. In so doing it acts "according to the principles, means, and in function of

---

12. Earlier he spoke of genuine political opposition as opposed to a conflict over functions, which presumably could be completely resolved by reworking the group.

the ends that it has assigned itself" (II, 101). Sartre seems to mean that *as* ruling subgroup it hides what is happening from itself and the rest of the group. Thus "the activity of the subgroup *deviates* because it wants to stay the same . . ." (II, 101). Sartre has in mind the Soviet leadership: "It changes because it stays the same, it doggedly tries to stay the same to not rupture the unity" (II, 101). Such deviation is enough, in certain situations, to draw the group's praxis to *other* goals, or to failure. Sartre will develop this in the next chapters as a central theme of Soviet history.

Degradation

But deviation is no likelier to happen than is continued progress. Sartre had said that pessimism *and* optimism must be rejected as a priori positions. Understanding the intelligibility of all possible contradictions means grasping two things: that the group's unity as unifying *project* "produces and sustains its own tears" and that all struggle incarnates the logic of the group. But this does not "prejudge in any way their development and their outcome: far from escaping comprehension, the deviations, errors, and setbacks are an integral part of it . . ." (II, 102). Indeed, it may even happen that, in certain cases, a slow degradation takes over a community "and ends up by hastening its total destruction" (II, 102).

The Grain of Sand

A marvelous discussion follows, amplifying the theme that even chance, as a significant historical factor, has its intelligibility in the praxis-process just described. What is the real meaning of the historical role ascribed to "Cleopatra's nose" or the "grain of sand" in Cromwell's urinary tract? "The 'grain of sand' is only important because Cromwell's regime cannot survive Cromwell, and this justly comes from the fact that it is not supported by the society which engendered it. In a word, it falls because of its own contradictions, which are the practico-inert oppositions of the base assumed by practical transcendence" (II, 103).

Plekhanov has argued, in his "inhuman and antihistorical dogmatism," that the historical result would be the same had Cromwell lived five years longer. This is not only wrong but misses the point, which turns on the role that chance is allowed to play by a particular group, by the circumstances of *its* development, *its* structures, *its* conflicts. "In a group which is durable, conscious, sustained by its base, strongly integrated, this margin is reduced to a minimum, it is as near as possible to zero . . ." (II, 104). Yes, illness and death remain present, "but they lose all historical efficacy: a system of replacement is already created, and the situation, in its urgency, imposes on the successors the continuation of the politics of those who have disappeared" (II, 104). Continuity may be assumed when the dead leader is replaced by one of his closest collaborators, for example someone who has aided him and shared the very same experience. And if such a death leads to a new political direction, it means that the role of the individual has already become important, and therefore the group's unity more precarious.

Which of the two situations characterized the Soviet Union at the death of Lenin? Sartre nowhere asks this haunting question[13] but, rather, concerns himself with the Bolshevik Revolution a generation later, at the death of Stalin. During his rule, as we shall see in chapter six, Stalin's person had incarnated the group's organic unity, and realized this through terror. His ascendency meant the sacrifice of every individual to the overall unity. Stalin's death, however, did not spell the end of the Soviet regime but of Stalinism. The development of Soviet society had reached the point where Stalin and Stalinism "had ceased being useful" (II, 104), as Sartre already described in *The Spectre of Stalin*. It was, in a deep sense, already de-Stalinized, because over his last five years it had undergone a "disadaptation of the leader to the situation his praxis produced . . ." (II, 105). The organized group's history was such that it gave chance little role to play beyond the exact moment of Stalin's death, "because the relationship of forces and the complexity of the struggle does not allow praxis to realize everything by itself . . ." (II, 105).

Chance

But can it be, we may ask, that chance, as "intervention of the practico-inert at the heart of the dialectic, only executes the sentence passed by praxis itself" (II, 105)? Hasn't Sartre just argued that the major feature of chance is to allow huge scope for individual praxis, such as Cromwell's, and that its exact extent depends on the group's relative retardation? Why then does Sartre now tie chance to the practico-inert?

After all, in some sense they are opposites. The paradox of the practico-inert is that it is produced by human praxis: the more developed the praxis, the more imperious its product. It is the "government of man by worked matter, rigorously proportional to the government of inanimate matter by man" (II, 287)—in other words, matter coming to dominate us

---

13. The most fascinating discussion of this question focuses on Lenin's efforts to avoid being succeeded by Stalin. See Moshe Lewin, *Lenin's Last Struggle* (New York, 1968).

insofar as we have succeeded in dominating it, not insofar as our poorly developed praxis has left space open for indetermination. In the discussions to follow, which form the heart of volume two, Sartre will explore in depth the phenomenon of deviation, in which praxis loses its way, its goals, its meaning, because of its efficacy.

Praxis seeks to limit the role of chance and indeed is successful in doing so. This leads Sartre to inquire, toward the manuscript's end, whether a praxis of "guided circularity" can temper the deviations. This scarcely developed side of Sartre's discussion of the practico-inert begins with the prospect that the more successful a group is, the more it has converted its praxis into *exis:* a practico-inert repository, effectively and uncontestedly inclining future practices and functions to serve the group's goals. The group's success creates a denser, more integrated network of structures and leaves less and less scope for free individual praxis. If so, I will suggest in chapters seven and eight, the role of group praxis might now be to continue and to improve the successful *exis*, further minimizing the role of future praxes and maximizing that of a well-disposed practico-inert complex.

In now talking about chance, Sartre does not seem to be consistent with either this positive sense or his usual negative sense of the practico-inert. Why does this fleeting remark ascribe *chance* to the practico-inert? If elsewhere the practico-inert is the product of concerted action, here it is the material effect of inaction or poorly developed action, giving scope to indetermination. Sartre will seem to return to this exact usage when discussing the Bolshevik project and when discussing peasant resistance to Bolshevik praxis: the Bolsheviks attacked the practico-inertia of backward Russia, specifically the Russian countryside (see chapter five). In these cases it seems that something other than the usual Sartrean practico-inert is at play, or that Sartre has simply made a mistake or is equivocating. However, when we see him discussing rural Russia below (II, 132) as the practico-inert negation of Bolshevik praxis, we will observe Sartre's analysis permitting clarification of what he means with regard to chance and Cromwell. Chance, we might now say, is given its role precisely by the praxis of the English Revolution. Without the revolution, the specific grain of sand that felled Cromwell would be meaningless. Instead, it becomes chance-within-praxis, the tragedy of the Revolution. The need for a specific individual, Cromwell, was a product of a specific praxis, and the praxis subjected England to the rule of chance inasmuch as his death would scuttle the project.

Antilabor

Sartre now passes to the final theme to be explored before he enters his study of the Soviet Union: that the two contending subgroups, in a kind of negative collaboration, produce a common *"antilabor"* originally intended by neither. If labor means "a material operation aiming at producing a certain object, as determination of the practical field and in view of a certain goal" (II, 105), antilabor is a *double* antagonistic activity in which each subgroup tries to deviate or destroy the object produced by the other.

The destructive efforts never succeed completely but, rather, create *new* realities at the center of the group. A violent conflict within a directing organ which leads to fundamental oppositions between two subgroups, for example, may be resolved by a conciliatory third project's being presented by a mediator. And this may in turn be modified by each subgroup. "The product of this revolving struggle bears in one way or another the mark of the three subgroups, but it no longer corresponds to the intentions of any of them" (II, 106).

Their activity remains a collaboration, but by negation, *in reverse*. The object so created is "a monstrous and deformed reflex" of the original project. Sartre returns to the example of the Ateliers Nationaux of 1848, amended until unrecognizable by the Assembly, then underhandedly but systematically sabotaged in being carried out. When such an object becomes no one's product, it is distorted, rendered half-effective, perhaps totally ineffective, turned counter to its original intentions. In making sense of it it would be absurd to look for the contributions of the separate contestants as more or less independent and irreducible layers. It is understandable, rather, as a strange and new unity, "the dialectical totalization of the two enemy tactics *in their irreducibility*" (II, 107). The final object consists of initial intentions only as successively deformed in these "acts of war."

The question is, how is this result intelligible? At first blush it is practico-inert, and thus alienated from the praxes of its antagonists: "as such it escapes intelligibility" (II, 107). But, as always, Sartre continues his analysis of such objects precisely to show their deeper logic. First of all, whatever their deformities, they are *used*, becoming "bad means for a free praxis." And, once we know this, their *negative* results—as in the case of the Ateliers Nationaux, which contributed to the insurrection of June 1848—may be foreseen, desired, awaited.

Antilabor thus creates a product which objectifies the conflict and negatively unifies the duality. This product is intelligible in the same way as any practico-inert object of any group praxis, undertaken by common agreement: it is a passive synthesis, waiting to be brought back to life by further action. Antilabor creates a product which acts on its producers and others within its field *"in spite of* its weaknesses of construction," and it lives *"in spite of* the malformations which render it unlivable . . ." (II, 108).

Furthermore, Sartre in conclusion suggests a deeper sense to the product of antilabor. Antilabor involves another type of "mediation of the group between the subgroups in conflict" (II, 109). The product of subgroups in conflict (the example of the Ateliers Nationaux reflects class conflict, not subgroups of a group) expresses the whole group "insofar as it is actualized by all the organs and by all the common individuals" (II, 109). The earlier analysis of the group's mediating role in resolving contradictions tells us that antilabor is produced by the entire group, and not merely the subgroups in conflict. As such it can be grasped by the dialectic but never by positivism. And now Sartre takes *as example of antilabor* (and its illumination by the dialectic), the ideological monstrosity, "socialism in a single country."

Socialism in One Country

"Socialism in one country"—first as slogan, then as practice—is an example of a monstrous object (one which is alienated, mystified, and deviated) created by the antilabor of subgroups in struggle. With this example, however, the tone, pace, and direction of *Critique II* change radically. The abstract a priori study of social philosophy now becomes a concrete historical examination of the vicissitudes of the Bolshevik Revolution—as the tools developed so far become employed over half of volume two (pp. 109–282) to understand Stalin's ascendancy and practice. Theoretically informed, penetrating, marked by detailed knowledge, Sartre's reflections confront some of the major interpretive questions concerning the Bolshevik Revolution, and do this so forcefully as to become one of the major interpretations of Stalinism.

At its first stage the discussion seeks to understand the Trotsky-Stalin conflict "not *for itself* but for the lessons we can learn from it" (II, 109)[14]

---

14. This section of the manuscript is the only one to have been published during Sartre's lifetime, in *New Left Review* (no. 100, November 1976–January 1977). I have used the *NLR*'s translation and will indicate its pagination following the page numbers of the published French edition. This quotation appears in *NLR* on p. 143. As in this case, I frequently alter the *NLR* translation in order to present Sartre's text as literally as possible. Minor changes have not been indicated in the parenthetical references.

about antilabor. The conflict erupted in the midst of the situation in which European revolution was "temporarily" on the wane,[15] and the Soviet Union was in *"mortal danger:* alone, surrounded by formidable and hostile powers . . ." (II, 109; *NLR* 144). If both leaders recognized the need to defend the Revolution and to construct socialism by the USSR's withdrawing into itself, they differed absolutely in their emphasis. Stalin took account of the threat by seeking to protect what had *already* been achieved, the Revolution itself in *this particular* country:

> He will make compromises in everything in order to preserve
> this fundamental basis; in order to save the nation that is
> building socialism, he will abandon the principle of nationali-
> ties. Collectivization? He will ensure that the towns will be
> fed. Industrialization? He will first hold it back; then, when
> he realizes it will be necessary, he will try to promote it at
> such a rapid pace that the targets of the early plans will not be
> fulfilled; and he does not hesitate to exact extra work from the
> workers, either directly by increasing norms, or indirectly by
> Stakhanovism and the restoration of piece-work. (II, 112; *NLR*
> 146; translation changed)

Trotsky as Abstract, Stalin as Concrete

Trotsky, on the contrary, would deal with the Bolshevik Revolution's vulnerability by risking its achievements: driving "deeper and deeper, transcending constantly its own objectives (radicalization); it had to spread progressively throughout the world (universalization)" (II, 111; *NLR* 145). Stalin, whose point of view Sartre emphasizes and largely accepts in this discussion, feared that "the Revolution might fail through trying to remain an abstract dialectic of the universal, just when it was being individualized by its incarnation" (II, 112; *NLR* 146). It is worth noting that Sartre frames the issue of consolidation at home versus revolution beyond Russia's borders—two highly specific emphases of ideological struggles within Bolshevism in the 1920s—in terms of the concrete incarnation versus the abstract universal. We have already seen him present the former general approach as being more adequate than the latter, and now the earlier epistemological and perhaps ontological discussion functions to tilt Sartre's historical analysis in favor of Stalin and against Trotsky, even if *both* are now shown to incarnate Marxism. Of course, we must not forget that historical judgment is not this discus-

15. Here Sartre seems to accept the Trotskyist perspective. Seventy years later, the waning hardly appears temporary.

sion's formal purpose: Sartre is describing antilabor. But the same is true over most of the remainder of the *Critique*.

Certainly, Sartre argues, biographical differences explain why each man took his particular direction, but they also reflect how each one incarnated revolutionary Marxism. Trotsky did so as theorist, as intellectual ("which means he always favored a *radical* course" [II, 110; *NLR* 144]) and as former émigré. On both counts Trotsky *lived* and *became* the revolution's internationalism, its universality, by interiorizing his exposure to the West and becoming "an abstract, universal man." Stalin, on the other hand, had always, in Russia, adapted the émigré leaders' Marxism "to the concrete situation and the actual people who were going to do the work" (II, 111; *NLR* 145). Sartre argues that Stalin, lacking the education and time to appreciate Marxism's theoretical side but close to the Russian masses, sought to carry out orders "*with the means at hand*" ("practical particularism"). Whatever Marxism's universalism may have meant to the exiles, Stalin had always to individualize it to fit *these* circumstances of Russia.

These differences between the two mattered insofar as they reflect contradictory praxes proposed by the stress of the objective situation. But they became differences not of the moment but of the most long-range objectives, and concerning "the very meaning of revolutionary praxis." As the conflict developed, *the very same policies* were advocated now by the one, now by the other, and so had different meanings—a fact which confounds analytical reason.

As urged by Trotsky, collectivization reflected his radicalism, to be sure, but "was a leap in the dark, the practical statement that the only possible defensive strategy was an all-out offensive" (II, 112; *NLR* 146). For Stalin, on the other hand, exactly the same measures "arose purely from concrete exigencies." What alarmed him in Trotsky was an a priori universalism, its goal being to *create* and project—which seemed to belie and threaten the specific reality that Stalin sought to save, consolidate, and then develop. This is why the conflict cannot be adequately conveyed as being among Left, Center, and Right (Bukharin). Although he first allied with it, Stalin saw the Right as being no less abstract then the Left in its faith in *evolution*. Stalin here appears as the genuinely creative Marxist, able to adapt Marxism to the circumstances while both Right and Left are mired in abstractions.

Sartre's appreciation of Stalin has special meaning when framed by Sartre's commitment, in writing the *Critique,* to develop an alternative to the "lazy Marxism" that looks at people and events by simply imposing a priori judgments on them. Attacking "today's Marxists" in *Search for a*

Method for their rejection of specificity ("Valéry is a petit-bourgeois intellectual"), Sartre proposes the very kind of Marxism he is here discovering in Stalin.[16] And later, shortly after laying aside the *Critique,* Sartre will visit revolutionary Cuba and celebrate its freedom from the bad habit of Marxist abstraction and universalism and its ability to do what *needs* to be done in each specific situation: Cuba's situation, not ideology, imposes socialism.[17]

I have elsewhere described Sartre's stance toward Cuban socialism as certainly anti-Marxist and also anti-intellectual.[18] Can we find the seeds of this direction here, in his analysis of Stalin and Trotsky? We have already seen indications of an affirmative answer in the discussion of incarnation—in Sartre's rejection of the concept and of universalizing thought. While the current discussion is marked by the same bias, Sartre seems more able to appreciate Stalin as having managed to *unite* theory and practice, Marxist generalities and Russian particularities.

The Monstrosity

"Socialism in a single country" was a monstrosity "to the extent that it says *more* than was necessary" (II, 114; *NLR* 147–48). It reflected, at one and the same time, the need to sustain the masses' revolutionary enthusiasm, Stalin's own particular policy orientation, his pointed rejection (and thus inverse incorporation) of Trotsky's orientation, and Stalin's successful tactics toward Trotsky.

> It falsified the specific exigencies of the situation, by giving them a synthetic unity whose motivations lie in the present and which pretends to operate on the basis of long-term objectives and of praxis as a whole in its future temporalization. It is a *manner* of saying "Let us rely on no one but ourselves"— but into this very manner enters a verbal formula that poses as a theoretical assessment of the possibilities of socialism and is really a maneuver designed to drive the minority into a corner. (II, 114; *NLR* 148; translation changed)

Sartre takes for granted that it was an absurd slogan, a monstrosity, "unintelligible as a verbal idea and theoretico-practical principle . . ."

---

16. How is it, we may ask, that Stalin, this truly creative Marxist, also "sclerosed" theory and practice during the period that bears his name? Sartre will never return to the theme of Stalin as theoretician, although it is vital to any understanding of how the dialectic became "obscured" under Stalinism and to Sartre's project of developing a critical as opposed to a dogmatic dialectic.

17. "Ideology and Revolution," *Sartre on Cuba* (New York, 1961), 148–50.

18. See *Jean-Paul Sartre,* 235–42.

(II, 123; *NLR* 156). The entire heritage of Marxist thinking about socialist revolution in a USSR tormented by Russian backwardness saw no possibility of socialism without a long prior period of bourgeois industrialization or massive assistance from more advanced socialist societies. Although Sartre does not specify this, he implies that the slogan's absurdity was to split what *had* to be unified—Soviet socialism and the Western proletariat—if the Revolution was to succeed. It amalgamated what *had* to be kept separate—*this* backward country and socialism—if the truth was to be told.

Why then such an absurdity? It was formulated by Stalin *so that* the Left could not adopt it—inasmuch as it meant a priori rejection of the interdependence of the proletariats of the world, and the submission of everything, most notably Central European workers' movements, to the needs of Soviet survival. It implied that the Soviet Communist Party was to exercise, for *Soviet* reasons, a dictatorship over European parties. The clever formula drove a wedge between *this* incarnation of Marxism and the Marxist internationalism and universalism without which the Revolution would have been inconceivable in the first place.

Accepting it meant that socialist revolution *had been* incarnated. Because it was really present *here*, it ceased to be an international ideal.

> But to acknowledge this precisely involved rejecting Westernism, universalism and the assumption that the proletariats of the large industrialized countries had achieved a greater degree of emancipation than the very recent proletariat of the USSR and, once they had taken power, would have such economic and technical strength that they would become the true animators of the international revolution. It meant relinquishing internationalism and "permanent revolution." (II, 114; *NLR* 148)

The formula presented the objective demands of the moment, which Trotsky accepted as well as Stalin, as a dogma with far-reaching implications. It was enshrined along with the choice of a particular future, determining propaganda and praxis, becoming indeed "the matrix of the institutionalization of the Russian Revolution . . ." (II, 115; *NLR* 148).

But how does this new object reflect the battle between Stalin and Trotsky when it is indeed *Stalin's* victorious formulation? Sartre's point is that its abandonment of Western revolution, its prioritizing of Soviet socialism were not necessary as a statement of the objective situation. They appear in the formulation *in order to* defeat Trotsky. Stalin is driven to incorporate Trotsky's revolutionary internationalism "as a rejected position." No, he might be saying, we reject "permanent revolution": we favor socialism in *one* country, the Soviet Union. His slogan makes sense only as product of Stalin's attempt to defeat Trotsky by answering his challenge. In this sense the formula is produced by the conflict, by *both* adversaries, as more and other than what each side alone would have claimed.

The Conflicts in Soviet Society as a Whole

If, as we have seen, conflict is a totalization of a *contradiction* in the group, what is the contradiction in the Party, and beyond the Party, in Soviet society as a whole?[19] Sartre insists that Soviet society's poverty and isolation between 1925 and 1930 were not *passively suffered*, but were *"products* of revolutionary praxis" (II, 115; *NLR* 149). Because they were consciously interiorized by Soviet leaders with a view to being transcended, poverty and isolation were produced and maintained by them as moments of their praxis. Mortal dangers for the Revolution, its poverty and isolation *"were also the Revolution itself* coming into being in a specific situation" (II, 115–16; *NLR* 149).

The Bolsheviks' acts *entailed* the civil war, economic blockade, and encirclement that befell the Revolution. Moreover, their revolutionary' praxis stimulated abortive revolutions and split proletariats elsewhere, and generated the bourgeois panic that drove it to violence and fascism. "In other words, Revolution incarnated in the center of the world, as a long-term praxis and determined by specific material circumstances, can not develop without producing—contrary to its leaders' project— impotence in foreign proletariats. In this sense, the incarnation of the Revolution directly contradicted its universalization" (II, 116; *NLR* 150).

Sartre's curious play between incarnation and universalization makes us wonder how the Revolution could have been universalized *without* being incarnated somewhere. Did Trotsky really intend this abstract process Sartre attributes to him? Obviously not. In Sartrean terms we might say that Trotsky sought a *different* incarnation, including the Western proletariats wherever possible. On the formal level Sartre is confusing properly epistemological and ontological questions with social and historical ones. Still, he does not lose the central contradiction behind the Trotsky-Stalin conflict: the event that *should have* aided proletarian emancipation outside the Soviet Union instead led to proletarian impotence. The Bolshevik response to this contradiction was inevitably insufficient:

19. Sartre reminds us that Soviet society, however, is not to be regarded as an institutional group. "It is torn by struggles, by practico-inert divisions, etc., etc. And, besides, we have not even begun the investigation of the experience of social unity. If there is such a thing, it must obviously be different from the unity of groups" (II, 115; *NLR* 149).

to aid proletariats everywhere without provoking Western intervention, which as often meant betraying them.

World Revolution Begins in Russia

"Socialism in one country" was a response to this contradictory situation. It prioritized building *this* socialism, without outside help. Unable to obtain such help, it thus "didn't need" it; and so the Soviet Union was freed from the burden of reciprocity with other proletariats. The Soviet Union would still help, out of "generosity," not obligation—when it could, but according to *its* vital survival interests. In this way, "the slogan *theorizes* the practical necessity" (II, 117; *NLR* 151) born out of the contradictory situation. Granted that the Trotskyist Left could not have adopted this slogan, Sartre argues that its actual policy would have had to be substantially the same as Stalin's. Its theoretical justification (its *idea* of itself)[20] would have expressed the *same contradiction*, but in reverse.

Why was Trotsky's older slogan, "permanent revolution," no longer adequate to the situation? Although Sartre does not analyze it, it is clear that by 1923 the German defeat had rendered it unthinkable for the tasks ahead. Russia had made her revolution, all the other attempts had failed: "permanent revolution" could not guide the construction of socialism in that exhausted country, in that situation of isolation.[21] A different possibility, mine not Sartre's, is: "world revolution begins in Russia."[22] Such a slogan meets Sartre's criteria: "It would have begun by affirming radicalization and universalization, but would then have imposed limits on them because of the situation" (II, 118; *NLR* 151; translation changed). Phrased provocatively, because of the conflict, such a Trotskyist formula might have shifted the threatening locus of "permanent revolution" back to the Soviet Union and thus domesticated it. It might have focused on the project of construction without abandoning the Revolution's internationalism. In a different conjuncture of power, it might have demanded acquiescence from Stalin or an admission of his betrayal of the (world) revolution.

I suggest this hypothetical slogan to indicate how far was the real Trotsky, in the actual situation after 1924, from being able to mount an

20. I, 406–9; 344–49; 300–306. Note that three pages of this text have been omitted from the 1985 edition.

21. See Edward Hallett Carr, *Socialism in One Country*, vol. 2 (Harmondsworth, 1970), 45–61.

22. I deliberately choose this over a slogan built on Trotsky's idea of uneven and combined development which is—characteristically, Sartre would say—more universalist in its orientation, assimilating Russia to worldwide development rather than vice versa.

effective campaign to wrest the leadership from Stalin. The actual conjuncture of power decisively favored Stalin, and his self-confident responsiveness to Russia's needs was inseparable from his political ascendancy. After all, when the controversy over "socialism in one country" broke out, Trotsky had just been politically defeated in the Politburo. On the defensive, Trotsky could hardly have been expected to assert a new and bold self-interpretation of a victorious but embattled revolution. The point is, to return to Sartre, that he does not discuss this one-sided conflict between Trotsky and Stalin as a *political* process which, indeed, was already far advanced by the time Stalin formulated "socialism in one country" in late 1924. Sartre's analysis may well be useful in explaining one side of why Stalin won and Trotsky lost, but it ignores the specific political struggle whereby Stalin came to dominate the Party and the Soviet Union.

Abstract Universality versus Particularized Incarnation

This was, continues Sartre, a conflict between people as *common individuals*, limited by their initial pledge. As such, their divisions were rooted in a past which produced a *historical* monstrosity: "an underdeveloped country moving without any transition from a feudal system to socialist forms of production and property" (II, 118–19; *NLR* 152). Living in what they saw as a backward nation (and thus a historical anomaly), Marxists in tsarist Russia had adapted universalizing Marxism. They particularized it, even while retaining its universalism, to guide their practice in a feudal society with a tiny proletariat.

> After the Revolution, it becomes the foundation of mass culture, and its systematic implantation into the Russian *people* is conditioned at once by education insofar as this was defined by the praxis of the leadership and by the steady growth of working-class concentrations—i.e., the absorption of peasants into the factories. These rough-hewn workers, so hastily created and still so close to country life, transform Marxism as they absorb it. It becomes *incarnated* as a national and popular culture, while in Europe it is still only the theoretico-practical movement of history. To adopt Hegelian terms—but their idealism is too blatant to be embarrassing—it is *the objective spirit of a people*. (II, 120; *NLR* 153; translation changed)

And precisely here we see the contradictory aspects, as Marxism became a dogma enabling "these mystified peasants to jettison all dogmas"; became vulgarized to make them more sophisticated; became alienated to set them free. On one level, then, the contradiction was that Marxism, universalist theory of revolutionary praxis, became ideology, justifier of this specific transformation. But this ideology, "socialism in one country," was also that of the only successful revolution, a fact that gave it pride of place over all other Marxisms and rendered them mere abstractions.

Thus victorious as incarnated here, in these ways, Marxism shaped Soviet man by reproducing all the contradictions in him: "the nationalism accepted and demanded through socialism, the particularism interiorized as an incarnation of the universal, and the combination of national pride . . . with a clear awareness of technical inferiority . . ." (II, 121; *NLR* 154). On the other hand, Marxism's abstract universalism was recreated through Trotskyism (appropriately, a movement in exile), in which revolutionary Europe sought to "escape from Soviet ascendancy." The original tension between émigré intellectuals and militants working at home thus draws its full meaning from, and leads appropriately to, this split between Marxism as abstract universality and as particularized incarnation.

The Absurd Idea Becomes the Solution

Sartre has insisted, of course, that the ideological conflict was a profoundly practical one. "Socialism in one country" *defines* Soviet man, as he was actually produced, and as he actually produced himself. It signified the process whereby "this still-traditionalist country, with its illiterate population, absorbs and assimilates at once the overthrow of its secular traditions; a traditional withdrawal into itself; and the acquisition of new traditions, through the gradual absorption of an internationalist and universalist ideology which helped the peasants sucked into industry to comprehend the transition from rural to factory labor" (II, 122; *NLR* 155; translation changed).

In other words, the unintelligible, absurd idea, inherently self-contradictory, becomes intelligible as a praxis which actually "holds together and unifies, in that specific moment of action, theory and practice; the universal and the particular; the traditionalist depths of a still alienated history and the movement of cultural emancipation; the negative movement of withdrawal and the positive movement of hope" (II, 123, *NLR* 156; translation changed). This does not suggest that the idea is correct or a scientific statement in keeping with Marxism; rather, it is an act of praxis, "going astray and becoming lost."[23] And, more specifically,

23. And, Sartre says, significantly, "only to find its way again in the end through its own contradictions, that is to say through conflicts between common individuals" (II, 123;

a product of two actions in conflict within a fundamental unity, trying to cancel each other—or as a weapon used by one subgroup to trap and destroy the other. They both struggle in the name of the common praxis, their conflict expressing the until-then implicit contradiction within *each* common individual facing objective difficulties. The monstrosity, the absurd and illogical solution, is supported by every common individual not because it is a "genuine synthesis and solution," but because it *presents itself* as being both a practical and intelligible transcendence of everyone's contradiction. For the group, it is, we might say, a "way out" of the intolerable situation. Interiorized, it is reexteriorized in a common undertaking which is seen not as absurd but as positive resolution of the contradiction. Given its members, given their formation and ideas, *they*—not the situation in the abstract—require the deformed object which is adopted as solution. The point, then, is not to determine abstractly what was the best possible solution, but to determine it concretely, to understand what these specific people would have accepted.

Correcting Thought and Reality

Sartre now makes one final specific point in his analysis of this example of antilabor: that the monstrosity becomes integrated into a newly reorganized project and a new theory. Insofar as the group grasps the monstrosity as a deviation, praxis reestablishes "its practical truth by correcting its own deviations, and the correction originated in the deviations themselves" (II, 125; *NLR* 158). An "enriching transcendence" preserves the deviation while "endowing it with truth, through an often quite complex system of additions, developments, compensations and transmutations" (II, 126; *NLR* 158).

"Socialism in one country" became clarified as the "socialism" that *precedes* communism, a transitory stage in Soviet evolution. Thus recognition was given to the proletarian seizure of power and social appropriation of the means of production, under the dictatorship of the proletariat exercised through the Soviet state. Contradictions existed, classes remained, struggles continued, as the basis was being constructed for a society of abundance. In short, the new formulation was used to theorize the new (and unanticipated) situation and to transcend the fundamental contradictions it presented to a Marxist outlook. "Thus the false formula becomes true, provided socialism is seen as a *praxis-process*,

---

NLR 156). This is neither a recurrence to an a priori optimism nor his evaluation of—or hope about—the outcome of the Bolshevik Revolution. Rather, Sartre's point is that praxis "finds its way" in a praxis and theory which takes account of, and corrects for, the deviation. See below, chapter seven.

building an order based on the fundamental socialization of land and machines, under emergency conditions and through continued sacrifice of *everything* to the most rapid possible increase in the rate of production" (II, 127–28; *NLR* 160). The contradiction reappeared: the process requiring several generations was taking place overnight. If the sense of *distant* objective was preserved, in the idea of communism as long-range goal, socialism had already accomplished the decisive economic and social transformations. "The consequence is that, in certain historical circumstances, it can be synonymous with *hell*" (II, 128; *NLR* 160).

Conclusions

With this notion of *correction*, Sartre's discussion of antilabor is complete. He has continued to avoid both optimism and pessimism by indicating the necessity of this kind of deviation *and* the group's response to correct it. The monstrosity has been produced, but it must be reintegrated back into the group's own sense of its project. Sartre does not indicate whether "socialism in one country" was the *best* response, but he does present its intelligibility. Yet in his account the historical logic, comprehensible only within the Bolshevik project, seems clearly to be on Stalin's side.

More important for Sartre's theoretical purposes, we must ask what his discussion of antilabor has established. First, revolutionary praxis *itself* has created its contradictory situation: the socialist revolution's impossibility of realizing socialism (poverty, isolation, decline of Western proletariats) is a practico-inert result of the Revolution itself. As a unified project, then, *it* has therefore engendered its own implicit contradiction, which becomes explicit in the conflict between Stalin and Trotsky.

Antilabor is obviously a major theoretical contribution, a central tool for showing how class conflict creates larger, unintended unities. Such an idea may make it possible to show how opposing actions might be said to create *one* history. Moreover, "socialism in one country" captures well the theme of antilabor and its products. It may be troubling that Sartre selects a slogan as his only example, but as he suggests, the idea itself became a decisive material reality in Soviet life—clarifying it, justifying it, reorganizing it.[24] As we shall soon see, Sartre's is a strategic choice, placing us in the early days of Soviet power after Lenin's death. In fact, it suggests the logic of Stalin's ascendancy. While fulfilling other formal purposes, Sartre's analysis of the Bolshevik Revolution's fate will continue as it takes us through to the death of Stalin.

---

24. Sartre returns to this theme in his 1961–62 reflections, indicating that "there is *a practico-inert of the idea.* Thus, the idea becomes a historical moment *of action,* as worked matter" (II, 433).

5 The Bolsheviks in Power

Sartre has succeeded in tracing the logic of contradiction within an already integrated group. He has done justice both to the enveloping totalization created by group praxis *and* the specific individuals who are its life—giving us insight into a larger logic which creates the individuals yet which they create even as "it" enters into contradiction with itself. The split, struggle, mediation, resolution, deviation—all enter into our understanding of antilabor, the "monstrous" object produced in this praxis-process. Yet Sartre has so far only described situations where synthetic unity *already* exists. Indeed, his study has made clear that it is the *unity itself*, not in some hyperorganic way but in the continuous action of common individuals under an oath to support the group, that engenders the contradiction *and* the struggle to overcome it, as well as the struggle's peculiarly deformed-yet-unified product. The group's unity is the fundamental premise of the analysis of contradiction and antilabor. The point is that everything we have studied so far owes its intelligibility to the activity of the human unifiers who are the group's members.

Group and Series in a Society

Sartre now seems prepared, and poised, to directly ask the second volume's central question: How does conflict unfold not within a group but in a *society*, whose structures "lack genuine unity"? Societies are characterized simultaneously by unity and by seriality. Even class struggle stops well before generating an organized group that liquidates seriality: it can only go so far as to unify one class against the other "as a practico-inert seriality." Two classes in struggle are not subgroups produced by struggling over, and sustaining, a greater unity of action: they unite themselves against each other and against "a seriality of impotence produced by a practico-inert process" (II, 131; *NLR* 163).

How is this struggle intelligible? This is the same as asking: How is history intelligible? Is it, as Merleau-Ponty might have concluded, "an ambiguous interpenetration of unity and plurality, of dialectic and anti-dialectic, of sense and non-sense" (II, 131; *NLR* 163)? Does it consist not of *one* totalization but of *several*? Does it actually lead to an ever-clearer meaning, or rather does it wait for a meaning to be assigned retro-spectively, by the historian?

This last would involve accepting human domination by the practico-inert, and this implies a kind of historical neopositivism, that is, a vision of history as made up of a plurality of discrete and separate events and histories, connected only from the outside. Sartre seeks more from his-tory than does neopositivism, namely a coherent, intelligible "move-ment of historialization" which moves from common praxis to an over-whelming practico-inert and back to a retotalized unity of praxis seeking to dissolve the practico-inert. In response, he reminds us that the prac-tico-inert, whose self-sufficient exteriority neopositivism takes at face value, "is produced by the counter-finalities of praxis precisely insofar as serialities of impotence, by making life impossible, give rise to the to-talizing unity that transcends them" (II, 131; *NLR* 163).

The specific serialities Sartre has in mind are human, leading him to now shift focus from the life of the group to that of a society "in all its diversity." He is modulating from the abstract level of the group (and its subgroups) to the concrete historical world where the dialectic has to be found if it has meaning.

But Sartre is not yet ready to study "a totalization without a total-izer"—to ask whether and how conflict can stem from or produce unity in a serialized society dominated by the practico-inert. In other words, he is not ready to study bourgeois society, the "most complex and most specious" example (II, 132). He will first make clear the relations be-tween the group's unifying praxis and the various types of practico-inert serialities of a society where revolutionary common praxis "transforms the society" and yet produces practico-inert results. There we shall see "the anti-social forces of the practico-inert impose a negative unity of self-destruction on the society, by usurping the unifying power of the praxis which produced them" (II, 131; *NLR* 163). And then "the de-totalized unity retotalizes itself in a common attempt to rediscover the objective by stripping it of counter-finalities" (II, 131; *NLR* 163).

To unravel this we must bear in mind Sartre's formal goal: to under-stand the dialectic as the logic of History with a capital *H* by seeing whether and how classes in conflict produce a larger reality. Having de-scribed contradiction within a group, Sartre must see if and how it exists in a *society*. But the *Critique*'s next step will be to study the relationships within a society dominated by a single coherent praxis—the Soviet Union in the 1920s and 1930s. Sartre will explore the relations between its unified groups and its serialities, in order to see how conflicting and partially serialized groups separated and dominated by the practico-inert may or may not function in ways similar to conflicting subgroups unified by and serving a common praxis. Then, we can assume, it will be possible to move on to a study which may describe "a totalization without a totalizer"—and then to the plane of history, with all its contending totalizations.

But alongside this formal goal appears another, more political one, which threatens to carry away his study. Clearly Sartre's description of the Trotsky-Stalin conflict is a highlight of *Critique II;* indeed it was the only part he allowed to be published during his lifetime. Having established some reasons for Stalin's victory over Trotsky, Sartre is now prepared for a full-scale study of the Soviet Union under Stalin. Rather than limiting himself to a brief formal analysis of relations between groups and series—the better to illuminate the question of a totalization of envelopment in a given society, then in history—Sartre in fact now plunges into 150 more pages about the Bolshevik Revolution, altogether making up almost half of volume two. Even as we must pay homage to this rich, brilliant, complex study, it will nonetheless leave us asking the question: Has Sartre wandered from his original purpose?

Bolshevik Goals, Soviet Realities

At first what I have called Sartre's theoretical and his political praxis—the *Critique's* formal and substantive goals—are indissolubly joined. The initial discussion focuses on the Bolshevik attempt to overcome the dominance of the practico-inert by submitting it to human control. We may recall that, in volume one, Sartre speculated on, without resolving, the "real problem" of the future: "To what extent will a socialist society do away with atomism *in all its forms?* To what extent will collective objects, the signs of our alienation, be dissolved into a true inter-subjective community in which the only real relations will be those between men, and to what extent will the necessity of every human society remaining a detotalized totality maintain recurrence, flights and therefore unity-objects as limits to true unification?" (I, 413; 349; 307). To the extent that we can gain insight from history, Sartre approaches the question in these analyses. We shall later (in chapter seven) see him return to wrestle with the question theoretically. In many ways, then, the discussion that follows is not only central to the *Critique* but is one of the most important studies in Sartre's entire body of work. For here alone does he study his major theme, the free alienation of freedom, in a specific historical analysis.

The Bolsheviks sought to create a society "where the worker will have permanent and integral control of the process of production" (II, 132).[1] Collective ownership of the instruments of production, the only possible means to achieve this, must be one of the Revolution's immediate goals. But Soviet history shows that for the workers actually to control the economic process presupposes a prior development of the means of production. Thus the Party's determination to intensify industrialization and collectivization "to the limit" was the only path to achieve "the suppression of antihuman mediations (by worked matter) and the liquidation of the practico-inert as field of human alienation" (II, 132).

This formulation is puzzling in light of Sartre's insistence that the practico-inert is an inevitable byproduct of praxis. Is he now suggesting that the Bolsheviks were too naive to see this? Was this revolutionary optimism the source of the disasters to follow? As I noted in chapter four, Sartre seems to equivocate when describing the practico-inert, sometimes referring to the "given" material facts of backwardness, including scarcity and social structures supporting it, sometimes referring to the material products of successful praxis. Yet here he emphasizes that the Bolsheviks hoped to substitute being dominated by underdevelopment and class society—domination of humans by humans and matter, or by matter through other humans—with human control over social and economic life. In so describing the Bolshevik project, Sartre does not seem critical or ironic. Indeed, he seems to accept the purpose of the entire enterprise: with the liquidation of the defeated class and the conquest of shortages, the state will gradually lose its functions and wither away. Such, Sartre argues, was the original goal of the Bolsheviks' praxis between 1917 and Stalin's death, seeking as it did "to give to the totality of collectives and disparate groups called Russia the means which will forge them into human unity, starting with a given historical situation" (II, 133).

The ruling group acted upon the society to transform it according to the Revolution's goals. Soviet citizens were seen to be unified by the future, not as hope or dream but as an abstract, distant, but absolute goal, not even conceivable "but rigorous," a goal "from which is organized the practical hierarchy of objectives that the sovereign assigns to the di-

---

1. Sartre's perception of the Bolsheviks on this point is of doubtful accuracy. After all, they had attacked proposals for workers' control as anarcho-syndicalist in inspiration. See Carmen Sirianni, *Workers Control and Socialist Democracy: The Soviet Experience* (London, 1983).

rected collectivity" (II, 133). To those workers who accept this project (and, we must remind ourselves, who are not part of the unified and directing sovereign group[2] but of the directed series), national unity appears as a future synthesis of millions of converging individual destinies. Their actions are produced both as loyal acts of free citizens *and* as "inflexible objective orientation" of their destinies. To promote this convergence means treating every one of the workers as *the same*, suppressing their past national particularities in anticipation of a future unity of Soviet peoples. *This* heroic nation, *the chosen people*, will in turn save all others from their national isolation. A new revolutionary national personality is to be created, and the Russian past reinterpreted as preparing the Revolution's present orientation and future goals.

This effort of sovereign praxis to forge "unity at the very level of serial dispersions and against them" (II, 134)—unity, that is, in a society—may be glimpsed in Soviet elections to this day. Their emphasis on unanimity seeks not merely to show popular support for government policy but above all to shape each impotent serial individual into a common individual by putting him or her into agreement with everyone else, while maintaining his or her impotent seriality. Thus the society is unified and integrated into a single praxis, which gives each "common individual" his or her specific role. To vote *yes* is, therefore, to integrate one's own practice into the single totalizing praxis which is the Soviet Union—as if, we might say, the original Revolution and its group praxis were still alive today.

But we know that the vast project of imposing unity will generate its own practico-inert counterfinality. In this united praxis of attacking the domination of people by the practico-inert, socialism has rejected the mediation of the market and insisted that the economy be *consciously*

2. We must not forget, in the entire discussion of Bolshevism and Stalinism to follow, Sartre's definition of sovereignty in Volume One: "By sovereignty, in effect, I mean the absolute practical power of the dialectical organism, that is to say, purely and simply its praxis as a developing synthesis of any given multiplicity in its practical field, whether inanimate objects, living things or men. This rearrangement—insofar as it is performed by the organic individual—is the starting-point and milieu of all action (whether successful or unsuccessful). I call it sovereignty because it is simply freedom itself as a project which transcends and unifies the material circumstances which gave rise to it and because the only way to deprive anyone of it, is to destroy the organism itself" (I, 666; 563–64; 578). This means that even under Stalin, the ultimate source of all sovereignty had to be *every single* individual: "In other words, sovereignty is man himself as action, as unifying labor, insofar as he has a purchase on the world and is able to change it. Man *is sovereign*" (I, 696; 588; 610). Here, in observing the developing bureaucracy as the sovereign group, we are en route to the displacement of all strands of sovereignty into the hands of the single, sovereign individual, Stalin. Yet as we shall soon see, each individual remains its ultimate source and must "retotalize" the sovereign individual's praxis for it to succeed.

managed: "socialist man is human because he governs things; every other regime is inhuman to the (variable) degree that things govern man" (II, 136).[3] Yet, on the one hand, the dangerous situation in which the Revolution found itself severely limited the Bolsheviks' efforts to pursue this goal. On the other, their interiorizing and transcending of the practico-inert sector led to "new practico-inert concretions and to new fissures" (II, 137). For example, by the time of Stalin's death the means of production remained collective, but they were totally controlled by the ruling bureaucracy, resulting in "the ownership *by everyone* of the instruments of labor, the direction *of everyone* by a relatively limited group . . ." (II, 137). This contradiction is itself a unity, "a passive synthesis taking its synthetic power from praxis itself and inscribing it on inert matter" (II, 137).

Deviation as Survival

Specifically, what praxis was demanded by the situation? First, it was necessary to *create* a working class, both because of these urgencies posed by Russia's backwardness and because the civil war and the exhausting period since had taken an enormous toll of the most advanced workers. Second, the shortages of needed technicians, and the difficulty of producing them, led managers to exercise decision-making power over wider and wider areas. In a reversal of Marxism, politics comes to dominate economics: politicians make *political* decisions about technical matters; the distribution of resources becomes a political rather than an economic question. The result? The famous Stalinist *voluntarism*,[4] product of a leadership which both demands everything of itself and demands everything from masses too passive to be granted the least responsibility.

The various economic sectors cannot be left to determine their own needs and possibilities but, rather, are centralized under an authority whose first concern is not what is possible but what *should* be done. But insofar as industry developed according to the common praxis (the Plan), it reacted back on the managerial layers "to stratify them and multiply the organs of direction" (II, 139). All large industry demands a pro-

3. This is an example of Sartre's equivocal use of "practico-inert" noted in chapter four. Compare with "Materialism and Revolution." There, the worker's freedom appears vis-à-vis things, but he is enslaved by men.

4. The phenomenon of voluntarism is perhaps best captured in the famous Stalinist motto (attributed to S. G. Strumilin, a leading economic planner): "We are bound by no laws. There are no fortresses which the Bolsheviks cannot storm." We can grasp the significance of this approach by contrasting it to Marxism as a *historical materialism,* insisting on the centrality of objective conditions in making possible social, economic and political changes.

liferation of administrative layers, and their grouping in a coherent organizational form. A form of worked matter based on pledged inertia, the
organization is produced by managerial praxis to serve the collective
praxis: it is "the skeleton indispensable to all transcendence but which
therefore rigorously limits the possibilities of inventing responses to
each situation" (II, 140). To fulfill the Revolution's goals, then, the directing layer needs, sediments, and makes use of a kind of inertial organization structure, which in turn will define and limit the process. In this
"petrifying repercussion of praxis on itself" the practico-inert, the original obstacle to collective control, reasserts itself at the heart of the project
to overcome it.

This is best seen in relation to the question of a salary spread. The
Revolution's principle of equality could not be preserved and the Revolution saved. But the Revolution's integrity would be lost if equality were
jettisoned. In fact "it is necessary to choose between the Revolution's
breakup and its *deviation*. Deviation is also detour" (II, 140).

To think in terms of *detour* is the Revolution's self-interpretation: it is
assumed that, later, future generations will be able to return to *our* original principles. But the revolutionaries do not see that these generations
will be produced by, and interiorize, the deviation.[5] They will have been
raised in a society whose goal is not to fulfill its principle of equality but,
by using differential salaries to raise the rate of production, to safeguard
itself. "Notice, here again, that the practical field they organize proposes
to them and often imposes on them the chosen solution" (II, 141).

The formerly revolutionary worker is now stripped of his right to control and direct,[6] and his destiny comes to him from outside: "his tasks
are fixed from statistical givens establishing the requirements of the
equipment to be produced, of armaments, of consumption, and it is
through the vulgarized summaries of the calculated givens that they are
communicated to him" (II, 142). In the late 1920s the general indifference
and lack of culture of a mushrooming and impoverished working class
made it unthinkable that the worker would collectively develop an interest in increasing production rates. His power and rights are not deliber-

5. At the same time, they may dispose over a cultural level and material conditions
which enable them to demand that the universal principles become operative. This, of
course, is one of the major lines for replying to Merleau-Ponty. But at the moment this is
not the issue.

6. Sartre is once again writing as if control by workers was an explicit Bolshevik goal.
More to the point, the worker was stripped of the Soviets, the councils created by revolutionary workers in 1905 and again in 1917, and which had become the basis for overthrowing
the Provisional Government. This new form of power gradually became powerless after the
October Revolution.

ately attacked by the leadership but they are set aside—by the growing gap between his own relative ignorance and the necessities of the entire economic organization.

The *Plan* now mediates between sovereign group and reified citizen: it is both a voluntarist political project of the leadership and a rigorous determination of the tasks to be fulfilled if socialism is to be saved. As under bourgeois liberalism, the worker obeys what appear to be physical laws, except that they are perceived as the laws of the apparatus erected to fulfill the Plan. Sartre once again emphasizes that the directors assume the producers' functions, which, in the situation, the latter "cannot exercise."

Creating a Soviet Working Class

Who were these workers incapable of fulfilling Marxism's vision? Doubling in number from ten to twenty million between 1928 and 1932, these newly urbanized peasants, illiterate or barely literate, underwent brutal changes, requiring a "long and difficult adaptation" to be able even to conceive of a workers' common interest. It has been argued that they were deprived of their rights. If these had been recognized, asks Sartre in reply, "How, with what instruments of thought, in the name of what unity would they have exercised them?" (II, 143). On the contrary, they would have quite rightly demanded less work and higher salaries. Such demands, if they could not be presented while the workers were controlling production and forming the Plan, could only be negative, and could only appear to management as a brake on industrialization. Therefore, the workers' minimum needs had to be met *in order to* avoid their resistance, and propaganda and education imposed on them to encourage producing for the common good. But, given the level of investment required to overcome backwardness, the workers' standard of living could not be allowed to reflect the industrial progress achieved by their backbreaking labor.

How then could the bureaucracy create a general interest in raising production while keeping consumption down and workers atomized? The answer was to induce competition between them. The leadership widened the salary differential and instituted production bonuses: Stakhanovism. While the general standard of living must be kept low, *everyone* would be given the opportunity to live better, in competition with everyone else. And so the bureaucracy would create a core of elite activist-workers, trying through a variety of honors and rewards to draw the others along.

Barred both from giving the workers power over the process and from using simple coercion, neither of which would achieve their end, the leadership had instead to choose the only available stimulus, "directed competition." Although it was not at all their purpose, an ever-growing system of "bonuses, distinctions, and privileged positions" was created which skimmed the masses and created "a voluntarist elite in the image of the managing groups . . ." (II, 145). Their individualism, which did indeed raise *their own* standard of living—"*against the mass*"—also wedded them to, and advanced, the common cause of building socialism.

What kind of socialism? They could not avoid equating their progressive rise with the progressive realization of socialism in a single country as an elitist voluntarism, directed by the ruling group. "The Plan creates the man of the Plan. But," Sartre reminds us, "the Plan is a praxis of men" (II, 145).

Creating Dignitaries

The directing group in turn "finds itself objectively modified by the hierarchical structures as determinations of the social field into which it is integrated . . ." (II, 145). Its power no longer results, as it once did, from its revolutionary praxis but more and more from its place at the top of the hierarchy it has created. Indeed, it cannot create a hierarchy without itself occupying its highest rung—not merely of power, but also of honor and salary. We are left to imagine the striking paradox "that a group of poor revolutionaries, without privileges, refusing every title—as was Lenin—could, for the needs of praxis, engender a society of dignitaries where merit is pompously rewarded" (II, 146).

Thus does revolutionary praxis develop, and become enveloped by, its own counterfinality: without intending to do so "it transforms its agents into *dignitaries*" in trying to save the Revolution. Stratification is produced as "*the process of praxis*" (II, 146).

Ontological Dualism or Historical Materialism?

This discussion of the evolving Soviet hierarchy has been informed by a characteristic theme, which Sartre now explicitly states. Two principles operate in history: "one is the action of men, which is both all and nothing and, without the inertia of things, would immediately disappear like a volatile spirit; the other is inert matter, in the agents themselves and outside of them, which supports and deviates the whole practical edifice at the same time as, it must be added, it has provoked its con-

struction . . ." (II, 147).[7] Every group action on inanimate matter—
and for this discussion it is important to note that the ruling group, the
Bolshevik Party, acts on the social collectivity, *the working class,* regarded
as inanimate matter no less than "a lump of coal"—necessarily results in
the interiorization of inertia in the group itself, transforming it. This
inertia "will deviate praxis at its source and will be reexteriorized as
deviated praxis" (II, 147).

Does this summary imply that the entire discussion has done no more
than newly express Sartre's original ontological dualism? This, of course,
was Merleau-Ponty's claim less than five years earlier, in *Adventures.*
Indeed, as I indicated in chapter four, Sartre leaves unclarified how a
situation of scarcity can be grasped as "the domination of man by the
practico-inert." Time and again, Sartre succumbs to his habit of opposing praxis the liberator to the practico-inert hell. But he says otherwise
where he is more careful. In those places he makes clear that humans are
originally dominated by nature and their own bodies, therefore other
human beings—because *there is not enough,* not because an undeveloped
society is overpowered by human products become autonomous. Scarcity has one very precise meaning in Sartre's lexicon, the practico-inert
another. This is no small correction, for Sartre first emphasizes the Revolution's formal goal of human control while ignoring its immediate task
of industrializing a backward society. Then he corrects himself. Menacing nature is indeed replaced by a menacing apparatus, but, as he will
point out near the end of volume two, it makes all the difference in the
world that enough food will be produced to make a human life possible
for everyone.

Of course, the fact is that Sartre has not abandoned his original starting
point but has, rather, sought to absorb his original terms into a materialist
analysis, rooted in scarcity. If praxis becomes deviated, it is because, on a
formal level, it takes place in, becomes inscribed in, a material world
which then sets its subsequent limits. But does this imply the a priori
conclusion that all praxis is equally bound to fall victim to the practico-
inert? In fact, Sartre's close analysis points to specific historical reasons.
As Sartre characterizes it, the original Bolshevik project sought precisely

7. Compare this with the first page of his very first published book, *Imagination* (Paris,
1936): "This inert shape, which stands short of all spontaneities of consciousness, which
must be observed and learned about bit by bit, is what we call 'a thing.' Never could my
consciousness be a thing, because its way of being in itself is precisely to be *for* itself; for
consciousness, to exist is to be conscious of its existence. It appears as a pure spontaneity,
confronting a world of things which is sheer inertness. From the start, therefore, we may
posit two types of existence" (trans. Forrest Williams, *Imagination: A Psychologist Critique*
[Ann Arbor, 1962], 1–2).

to liberate the producers to control their own labor: the historical project
of liberation coincides with liberation from the domination by matter.
But under conditions of danger and scarcity the Bolsheviks urgently *had
first to* create a productive apparatus. In order to liberate people they *had
first to* bring them into the modern world, *had to* preserve the conditions
for the Revolution's survival, had to *produce*. We have seen how this
urgency in turn dictated creating the new workers as serial, dictated
massifying, separating, hierarchizing them. However much they might
have wished to do otherwise, the Bolsheviks responded to these urgencies by creating the working class as a practico-inert mass. Practico-inert
in a very precise sense: the inertial structures imposed on the collectivity inevitably became absorbed by the sovereign group managing it,
transforming the Bolsheviks themselves.

Clearly, then, the causes for this are historical rather than ontological.
Not that Sartre's dualism is wholly invalidated: his early vision of the
weight of inert matter, we might say, was a precognition of the role scarcity plays in society, but in a still-reified form. As he pushes his thought
more deeply, the flat and given oppositions with which he began evoke
more genuinely social and historical tensions, especially in emphasizing
scarcity and its consequences.

Peasants into Workers

Sartre now addresses the sovereign group's creation of this vast inertial
mass, the Russian working class. The Bolsheviks inherited a "negative
material given," which offered passive resistance to their goals and may
be symbolized in a single fact: peasant illiteracy. Of course, this negation
of Bolshevik praxis was in itself one dimension of a *positive* reality, namely
the specific way of life of a specific peasantry, in its specific mixture of
powers and inertia. But the peasants' work rhythms, to take a special
example of their (inertially based) powers, stand in the way of their becoming urban factory workers.

Brought to the city and the factory by the Plan—by praxis—they have
extreme difficulty in adjusting to this new world. Their traits generate
resistance: "inert concretions, mechanisms for slowing down or deviation. In short, a practico-inert field" (II, 149). In a particularly trenchant
passage Sartre summarizes the way practico-inertia constitutes the very
being of the atomized, serialized Russian working class of the 1930s and
calls for managers and for an external sovereign who can unify it:

> Mystifying mirage of transcendent unity, reified relations
> with leaders, internal structures of atomization and seriality,

perpetual mixing in contact with the new arrivals: this is the *reality* of the working class in a crisis of growth; this is what renders it a priori inconceivable that it take the levers of command and that it exercise the dictatorship by itself; this is why the managers are constituted *by it* as exercsing this dictatorship *in its place* to the very degree that, by its mode of recruitment, they constitute it as presently incapable of controlling production. (II, 149)

The demographic facts of a vast preponderance of peasants, and their rapid entry into the cities and factories especially after 1928, had a drastic effect on those surviving older workers who made the Revolution. "Invaded," they "will lose their autonomy and their unity" (II, 150). On the one hand, the vast distance between the original workers and these "barbarians" is expressed in the distance between the actual production levels of 1928 and those forecast by the end of the Plan; but in reality the working class is being forced to take in more "foreign elements" than it can absorb. This demographic contradiction will be reflected in production rising faster than productivity, in the temporarily declining political and cultural level of the growing working class. The working class swells with newly urbanized peasants, but in the process becomes ruralized. The new proletariat, the revolutionary class par excellence, becomes shaped as a passive mass, with far-reaching consequences: "this class, penetrated by an ideology simplified and modified by the needs of propaganda, can only find its unity outside itself, by the mediation of the sovereign; and above all this transcendent and superficial unity in fact only represents the unity of sacrifices that are demanded of its members, when the true relations with management remain temporarily reified" (II, 149).

The Necessity of Praxis

Was a gentler, less violent, more humane path possible? As so often in volume two, just as his analysis sounds most necessitarian, Sartre insists that praxis and nothing else has posed the necessities he traces. Starting from *this praxis*, provoked by *these* circumstances, "urbanization *had to be realized* in this and no other way" (II, 150). But this does not at all make the "Soviet way" into a model for other developing countries. In this respect the unsituated and nondialectical point of view of sociology is as distortive as is the transcendental (dogmatic) dialectic: both see *necessity* as imposed from the outside rather than as emerging in and through praxis. The Soviet leaders were not *at the service of* a transcendental reality, rapid industrial growth, but they chose it as their praxis, given their situation.

The "model" is only an "inert objectification of a unity" which is in turn nothing more or less than "the sovereign activity which transcends the present toward the future" (II, 151). To speak of a "model" is also to forget the specific historical situation which produced Stalinist praxis: "industrialization was accomplished practically under foreign cannon" (II, 151); it led to a retreat of workers' movements; it was undertaken amidst a specific evolution of, and conflicts within, revolutionary parties. Even "other models" of socialist industrialization make no sense except as based on *this* one and, therefore, once again refer back to its history and praxis.

For an example of "necessity" revealing praxis as its underside, Sartre takes the inert synthetic relationship set up between two cities when industrial expansion requires that their communications be improved. They now *depend on* each other. A number of risks are built into the new relations, and demands are developed between them; city A might over- or undersupply city B with a vital raw material, leading to a lowering of output or partial unemployment. But it is praxis, based on the Plan, that has created the new objective relations and their risks, by linking the two cities. If there is now a scarcity of transport between A and B, this situation demands new investment of resources. But even this choice will only resolve the problem by posing new ones elsewhere, while retaining the original practico-inert demands engendered by the original praxis. Necessity, then, is "the temporary alienation of this praxis in its own practical field" (II, 153) by creating new relations between elements of the field.

Praxis-Process

The practico-inert field created by praxis imposes further demands on it. And so, at any given moment our action is "overflowed from within" and must resolve the new problems it generates without necessarily even *grasping that it has created them*. Sartre has been describing *praxis-process*.

Volume one describes how "inert perseverance" or "constituted inertia" emerge directly from praxis. "The process develops in accordance with a law from outside which controls it in accordance with earlier conditions; but this necessity is still directed, the future is still prefigured, and the process retains its finality, though it is reversed, passivized and masked by necessity" (I, 643; 543; 551). In other words, it is a kind of passivized praxis. If anything represents the dialectic inscribed in being which Merleau-Ponty found, and rejected, in orthodox Marxism, it is precisely this "permanent obverse of common praxis" (I, 643; 544; 552) engraved in materiality. Sartre cites the state as one example of praxis-process ("not inertia as an inert foundation, as a sclerosis of structures, etc., but inertia as a condition of praxis"; I, 645–46; 546; 554) and then later, at greater length, discusses colonialism and class struggles in France after 1848. Now, in volume two, he describes the process as "the exteriority of praxis insofar as it is revealed in the core of its interiority" (II, 152). "Interiority" refers to the practical field *as practical field:* the conditions and material of sovereign praxis. Sartre's emphasis here is on the dynamic, organizing, controlling character of praxis as sovereign in this field. "Exteriority" suggests that which acts *upon us,* from the outside, and as such has an autonomy that places it beyond our control. We ourselves may, indeed, *must* create exteriority: typically, in praxis, we interiorize that which is exterior to us, and then reexteriorize it as our product. In other words praxis produces a practico-inert field that fulfills its goals but imposes itself on further praxes as an exterior demand.

The process generated by praxis causes *deviation,* imposed on praxis by the practico-inert field it creates. Deviation, let us not forget, involves a change in the group's praxis *and in the group itself.* We have seen the steps with regard to the Bolshevik leadership: the group's stratification stems from the need (resulting from its own praxis) to promote growth, and to do so by measures which result in the workers' impotence and a hierarchy of wage earners. The leadership was "transformed by the entire society and with it, when they stopped being revolutionaries to become dignitaries of the Revolution" (II, 154). They became, we might say, lost within the results of their own praxis, *transformed by the transformations* they themselves imposed. The totalization they would exercise on the masses becomes reciprocal in spite of themselves, as those who are led passively shape their leaders according to their leaders' image of themselves.

Sartre has invoked several key terms—*exis, praxis-process, deviation*—to describe how today's praxis creates new necessities, which set the terms of tomorrow's. He has reached one of the central themes of a Marxism which can negotiate the problems Merleau-Ponty thought insoluble. Sartre's appropriation of Marxism fully respects the weight of the world *and* seeks to give praxis its due. He equally avoids the "objective dialectic" of orthodoxy and the "subjective dialectic" of Lukács as Merleau-Ponty understood him, insisting rather that material reality imposes its pressures to respond in a certain way but without itself moving or acting upon us. Human beings act, Sartre emphasizes, but their praxis leads to its own necessity—ultimately, as we shall see later, because of the urgency of scarcity.

The Political in Charge

In the first stage of industrialization, heavy industry commands the bulk of investment and draws factory workers from the countryside; in the second, productivity itself will rise, demanding relatively fewer new manual workers but more supervisors. These managerial functions are not treated as technical ones, however. First, because of the Bolshevik insistence on retaining the explicitly political character of planning. If overwork and exploitation characterize socialist as well as capitalist accumulation, at least under the Bolsheviks it is a conscious, deliberate praxis, which can be referred to the Plan and, through that, back to the praxis of the whole collectivity. The collectivity, in fact, is shaped to be passive and serial by the sovereign group, as needing first to develop culture and productive, disciplined labor before being *then* granted power. The managers also decide what to do with what in bourgeois societies would be called the *surplus value*, extracted from the workers. They can renounce this political power only at the risk of renouncing the Revolution itself. They extract and apportion it "as the allies of the future community against the masses of the present" (II, 156).

During industrialization, the leaders were isolated "from the masses they had forged," and they in turn reexteriorized this isolation "in suspicion and in coercive measures" (II, 156). In other words, their isolation was not the consequence of terror, but *its source*. Their praxis had produced masses with whom the Bolsheviks had no possible contact, first because of the necessity of exploiting them, and second because the Bolsheviks' own formation, culture, and biographies—as Marxist revolutionaries—radically separated them from these millions of peasants. Many of the millions "had undergone the Revolution without making it, or were too young to take part and . . . were only able to manifest the desperate violence that is born of poverty against the very regime that was making them workers" (II, 156).

How can the Bolsheviks' power be justified in the face of a movement, however constructive, that they so brutally imposed on these masses? Industrialization is actually taking place, following the Plan, and growth is an objective reality. If a hierarchy is needed to inspire workers' voluntarism, then the managing function is justified as its highest level. Moreover, the political must predominate over the economic and the technical as the stable center which produces and oversees the immense changes imposed on the society. Growth becomes the very meaning of the leadership. The dominant social goal, it is the touchstone against which the leadership measures the rest of society. And so the leadership limits and controls the technical, supervisory, and coordinating employees and absorbs them into itself and into the Party. Elevated above him by the necessities of the situation, the technician becomes especially feared and suspected by the political administrator. More than anyone else, the technician has knowledge of what can and cannot be done. He "is a potential saboteur, insofar as he is the one who declares: 'we can do *this* and *no more*'" (II, 158).

The Bureaucracy

The praxis-process described so far is the dynamic basis of the Soviet bureaucracy. Sartre summarizes it in a single sentence:

> A sovereign whose practical field is the totality of national activities, a sovereign which, thrown into a gigantic enterprise, struggles against the scarcity of time as well as against that of tools or consumer goods, which gathers the political and sovereign function together with tertiary functions (administration, coordination, organization), whose very voluntarism— as interiorization of the scarcity of time and as consequence of a void separating the masses from the directors—produces at the same time, at the cost of the most terrible effort, a permanent transformation of Soviet society and a more and more developed stratification of the managerial echelons, which, for this reason, oppose the slowness, the absence of initiative, and the monolithism of their administration to the mobility required of the directed, to their flexible movements, to their adaptation . . . .: do we not recognize the Soviet *bureaucracy* insofar as its functions of management without appropriation has made it thus in the irreversible temporalization of an action which mobilizes the—temporarily—powerless masses to be controlled by it? (II, 158)

In short, the sovereign bureaucratizes itself *for the purpose of action.* But bureaucratization is not its goal, nor is it a *means* of governing. Rather, this stable and inert but directing and motivating apparatus becomes "the being-in-exteriority of praxis." And yet the urgent goal of saving the Revolution led to this group's idealist voluntarism, which in turn leads to its proud claim that the bureaucracy itself is the Revolution. And so it never fails to appeal to the revolutionary praxis in which it arose—for its justification, meaning, and unity.

Masked Conflict

The latent conflict between workers and managers (expressed in sabotage, passive resistance, and the black market) is simply the reactivation of the practico-inert split whose origin we have been tracing. The workers' class-being, like the bureaucratic-being, has been created by the sovereign praxis, and now "the masked conflict, as passive resistance of the ones and authoritarianism of the others, is *assumption* of the congealed opposition that it tries more or less clearly to transform into combat" (II, 159).

How does this conflict differ from the one discussed earlier, between two subgroups? Rather than occurring within a group whose unity it expresses, it reflects the relationship between group and series. The group (leadership) *acts upon* the series (working class) and seeks to keep it *as series* while dissolving those of its practico-inert structures that slow down the overall project. The ruling group may, for example, increase housing construction to avoid potential conflicts that would slow production or, worse, lead the series into becoming a group. Or the ruling group may foster the illusion that there is a working class which functions *as a group* whose members are common individuals. "But, at the same time, they want to maintain the serialities of impotence" in order to be able to *use* the working class "like a hammer in the hands of a carpenter" (II, 160).

However paradoxical it may seem when we think of the history and rhetoric of revolution, the ruling group "*totalizes* the series as series" (II, 160). "Totalization" here does *not* mean the self-totalization of once-serial individuals uniting themselves into a pledged group, which might "change an inert lever into a community forging its own sovereignty" (II, 160). What it does mean is gathering inert matter together like a mathematician totalizing arithmetical recurrences. By mass media techniques appropriate to the goal of sustaining the workers' seriality, the government aims to condition them against their own reality as free and self-determining beings, to be better able to perform certain operations with them. The government's successful totalization of the collective (say to produce ten million tons of pig iron by the end of the Five-year Plan) will keep the workers scattered and separated—*detotalized*. "In this sense the totalization of the series in its product is effected *against it* for it is objectified *as series* and the totality of worked matter reflects back to it its own alienation" (II, 161).

Thus have we seen the original contradiction of the postrevolutionary period, the necessity of building the socialism that was materially impossible to build, becoming interiorized and reexteriorized as "hidden but constantly present oppression." Without justifying it or explicitly calling it necessary, Sartre pungently captures the meaning of the leadership's praxis toward the workers: "to destroy these workers as free practical organisms and as common individuals, in order to be able to create man from their destruction" (II, 162).

Even if it was "required," must we not also register that this was evil? Sartre acknowledges that the leadership has been criticized for such policies. And obviously they went wrong, all the time and everywhere, but this is no less true for any other historical process, any leadership and almost all of the led. In this case particular mistakes may have been involved "in the rigor of the oppression or in the concrete use of organs of coercion" (II, 162), but oppression was already built into any praxis aiming at combining the historical phases of accumulation and industrialization. Lenin's "electrification plus Soviets" could have been thinkable without Stalinist oppression only if the working class had remained more homogeneous and stable during the process, which was on principle impossible.

For Stalin, the original praxis of revolution having engendered the urgent necessity of industrializing *this* country, a working class had to be created, in a massive demographic upheaval, and a surplus squeezed from it—both of which required keeping it as an impotent seriality, often through police-state techniques. Nevertheless, these workers were the end of the praxis and not only its means: with them and in them Stalin sought "to lay the bases of a true socialist community by a considerable effort to raise everyone's cultural level" (II, 163). *This* contradiction, leading to the hidden conflict between workers and bureaucracy, has in turn absorbed the original contradiction of Bolshevik praxis.

The Paradox: Class Demand Becomes Party Project

The contradiction appeared immediately after the moment of victory. Sartre has already indicated that the masses, who made the Revolution by demanding *everything*, will be controlled and guided by leaders who must organize long-term construction to satisfy that demand. Now Sartre returns to the beginning to explore this contradiction.

The insurrection itself depended on the masses' self-transformation into organized groups, carrying the Party with them.[8] The Party guided

8. Sartre indicates that the Party is the would-be "permanent group" which places itself "at the heart of seriality as possible unity of serial individuals by suppression of the series"

this totalization only "by transcending its own limits under revolutionary pressure" (II, 163), adapting itself to the situation and realizing that the socialist revolution was indeed at hand. After recapitulating his description of group formation and the insurrectionary process (under the threat of death, the masses dissolve their practico-inert seriality and, in the heat of the moment, metamorphose into a group), Sartre adds two new themes to the discussion by focusing on the masses' demands and the tension they engendered between the masses and the Party.

When the masses unite to demand something and in so doing attack the regime itself, then they are led to demand *everything*. For the Bolsheviks this means the possibility of taking power and building a new regime. Insofar as they lead the masses and make their goals their own, the Bolsheviks first become the party of popular demands—and then, in power, face the difficulties of fulfilling them.[9] While not demanding everything immediately, neither do the masses, living at a subhuman level, have in mind a long-term project of construction.

On the one hand "*man is born*" by becoming a pledged member of a group, but he will become humanized only by then ending poverty and satisfying his needs. Yet a revolutionary crisis usually occurs only when—through losing a war or during an economic collapse—a country has lost a good part of its resources. Masses become revolutionary when they find themselves threatened by famine or death. *Then* they may attack the social regime itself, demanding everything. The worker frees himself from serial impotence and "affirms himself as a man facing death" in common praxis when allowed to be "a man only in order to die: no regime, no politics, no government at present can give him the means to *live as a man*" (II, 165).

The revolutionary leadership first accepts and presses these demands as its own: "*everything*, as immediate object of the masses, becomes the ultimate objective of an organized action" (II, 165). But in order to then pursue them as long-term goals, a return to order is necessary. Under the aegis of the Revolution itself, the unlivable situation, perhaps further aggravated by the revolutionary conflict, cannot help but continue. A new conflict is inevitable: between revolutionary groups and their own leaders, who thus turn against the masses the very state power that they have together overthrown.[10]

(II, 163). In 1952 he described this at length (although without having yet developed the technical vocabulary) in *The Communists and Peace*.

9. Structurally, the very act of taking power already puts the Party into "contradiction with the movement of liquidation of series" (II, 164).

10. For a remarkable dramatic presentation of this issue see Sartre's virtually unknown

"But this necessity to vegetate in poverty at the very moment of victory" (II, 165) has itself been created by mass praxis (*praxis populaire*), which creates a permanent contradiction between the radicalism of the moment and the long-term radicalism of creating a human order. And it also creates leaders who must oppose the groups from which they emerged.

But, on a deeper level, the workers produce this contradiction *in themselves*. If the upheaval seeks "the satisfaction of *all the needs of everyone*" (II, 166), the workers simultaneously constitute this urgent need and the Revolution's long-term goal—as well as being the mediator between the two. Earlier, when speaking of the origins of the bureaucracy, Sartre indicated that between 1928 and 1932 the conscious worker found that the personal needs—to end overwork and underconsumption—which originally brought him to overthrow the old regime were contradicted by the very requirements of building socialism—intensifying production and limiting consumption!

Such personal needs had stopped being revolutionary watchwords: considered subjective, they were rather reduced and controlled, and their fulfillment became subjected to planning by management. Unsatisfied, the individual's need will lose its physiological urgency but will still drive the process: "in the perspective of socialist construction, undernourishment, which was unbearable, will be borne for some time" (II, 166).

Unity and the Project of Construction

The project became accepted universally. Even vital needs will be framed as those which must be satisfied *in order to keep producing*. Leaders and masses pursuing the same enterprise become united through voluntarism. Even opposition will be framed by shared goals: a self-conscious workers' organization might change the managing personnel responsible for shortages, or perhaps demand a reworking of the Plan, but would not question the project of growth itself. Structural consequences of bureaucracy will be criticized, but only as specific and remediable problems. Critical workers will be unable to see the bureaucracy's basic contradiction of being an inertial center of intense activity. Rather, they too will adopt the "bureaucratic" mode of "attributing faults to men and not to the system which produces them" (II, 167).[11]

---

screenplay, *L'Engrenage* (*In the Mesh*). Its original title, significantly enough, was "Les Mains sales" ("Dirty Hands"). See my discussion of it in *Jean-Paul Sartre*, 189–92.

11. There can be no workers' rebellion against Communism as such, Sartre is implying,

The Alternative

Was there an alternative? If both leadership and workers—the original core of Party members and revolutionary workers—had consciously in-- teriorized the Revolution's original contradiction, it would have been possible, strictly speaking, to avoid oppression. A working class conscious of its own as well as the Revolution's impossible situation may well have moved freely in precisely the direction the leadership wanted. The workers and Party would have created voluntarism in response to the situation, but "one could conceive of a praxis which is centralized, hard, authoritarian but supported (and this time, controlled) by the managed themselves; reciprocally, the managers would have taken more care to find and to suppress abuses if these arrangements had been demanded in the name of a common voluntarism by a working class of which they had been sure" (II, 167–68). Workers' pressure "could, indeed, have tended to suppress bureaucratic excesses and to limit the hierarchy" (II, 168). In fact, struggle within the leading groups and the masses could have become a "factor of unity," leading to the growth of the power of the Soviets even as electrification spread.

Sartre is here, of course, speculating on the alternative to Stalinism projected by many Marxists.[12] But he insists that this is an abstract projection which forgets the reality of industrialization and demographic upheaval, above all the constant remaking of the working class with fresh peasant masses.[13] These essentially "urbanized peasants," lacking all prospect of conceptualizing or actualizing their resistance, serialized by terror, are so radically impotent that their only defiance was the inability/refusal to produce, occasionally expressed in sabotage.

Solidarity in Reverse

We have seen that they live in a world where "everything always comes to them through the mediation of the sovereign . . ." (II, 169). *The bureaucracy* plans the industrial complexes, means of transport, raw materials, housing. *Management* organizes their production, assures their subsis-

---

because the workers' deepest goals are the system's goals. At most they can rebel against those who fail to carry out these goals, who acquire special privileges, or who abuse their mission.

12. Indeed, it is the direction developed by Trotskyists as an alternative, and can rightly claim its intellectual inspiration as Trotsky's *The Platform of the Joint Opposition* (1927) (London, 1973).

13. This has most recently been reemphasized, for example, by Moshe Lewin, *The Making of the Soviet System* (New York, 1985).

tence. A few workers who gain the education and self-consciousness can grasp their own, their factory's, role in the process—but as cogs in a vast practical field planned to the slightest detail by a sovereign praxis. Each worker's own individual work is foreseen within this. "His life, that is, his food, the satisfaction of all his other needs, depend on the way in which he will fulfill the prescribed task (which designated him in advance), and this prescription is a simple specification of the general Plan" (II, 170). In the universal dependency, his or her own ability to execute the order of the sovereign, and fulfill his share of the Plan, depends on other workers' doing likewise and, in turn, on the sovereign's carrying out its functions. This is solidarity *in reverse*. Everyone needs what the management also needs—everyone else's maximum effort—in order to be able to make their own and so to survive.

Retotalization

So far we have been exploring only the workers' totalization *by* the sovereign. Yet the whole of Sartre's thought teaches that the workers are not inert matter, fated to receive determinations from outside and passively reproduce them in their work and lives. The most terrorized worker is engaged in a praxis which must retotalize that of the sovereign if the project is to succeed. The worker "realizes his serial-being" in *his* freedom, even if it is within a totality, developed and coordinated by the sovereign, in which he is expressly designated *as other*.[14] This is what children experience as they discover, in their practical field (which has in fact already been established by their parents), objects which are already seen and named, and whose use is already set. "In this sense, if the propaganda has succeeded, [the worker] grasps the totalization of the sovereign as the depth of his own totalization" (II, 171).

The worker's retotalization is in one sense his impotence and ignorance; in another it is "his possible knowledge and it is his own participation in the praxis of everyone" (II, 171). He retotalizes the totalization of the managing group—exactly insofar as his action is already seen and provided for. The sovereign may even leave certain strategic points open within its overall totalization where seriality will be dissolved by common individuals' "reassuming the decision of the Party or of the Politburo" (II, 172). In such cases, the individual dissolves seriality and deepens the practical field, but his own totalization, ostensibly done for *his*

14. Sartre develops this theme, in a close comparison of the workers' freedom and their enslavement, in "Materialism and Revolution." There the contradiction would lead to revolution; here it results from it.

reasons, is preplanned as a moment of the sovereign's and conforms to *its* objectives. And so it can be said that "the sovereign totalization is nothing other than a praxis whose object is to be realized by the foreseen and effected unity of its retotalizations . . ." (II, 172).

Whatever struggles may now occur, however fierce they may become, they will take place within "the framework of the retotalized totalization." This is the key to understanding the relationship between groups and masses in history. But it is ignored by positivist historians, who see only organized forces acting on the passive masses—as if a physical force is engaged in some "natural" process. Sartre's theme of "retotalization," on the contrary, allows us to grasp the intelligibility of this otherwise puzzling phenomenon: "*the action of action on action.*" The totalizing action of the leaders (the totalization of directed retotalizations) depends on the action of the led (retotalized totalizations) for its success.

Soviet Man

We have already seen that the masses are both the *means* of the revolutionary project and its end. Deeply committed to industrial growth, driven to the maximum exertion, their only freedom lies in the space for advancement offered by Stakhanovism. They are proud of the first great achievements of Soviet industry, which do not, however, increase the level of consumer goods available to them. They are passive toward their supervisors because they are impotent, but also because they deeply believe that it is industrial growth, not changing specific managers, that matters most.

"Soviet man" is indeed "the first to *really* define the present from the vantage point of the future (and on the basis of the past) and his individual future from the vantage point of the socialist future . . ." (II, 174).[15] Bourgeois democracies will never produce this kind of person,[16] who in any case is not easily created and may not fully appear in the Soviet Union until the second generation. He knows that it is one thing to be oppressed as a worker for the sake of profiting one's masters, as under capitalism, and quite another, under conditions of common ownership of resources and the means of production, to be oppressed as a worker

15. This recalls Sartre's discussion, mentioned in chapter one, of why socialism has a privileged status vis-à-vis capitalism (*The Spectre of Stalin*, 4). Here Sartre is reaffirming his acceptance of Merleau-Ponty's original position against Merleau-Ponty's more recent "objectivity."

16. Sartre's claim will appear as simply wrong to anyone familiar with American history. Indeed, the greatest tribute ever written to this aspect of the bourgeois spirit is Marx and Engels's description of capitalist progress in *The Communist Manifesto*.

for the sake of one's children or grandchildren. "Thus, little by little, the newly arrived or their children recover the point of view of the revolutionary workers, except that they have the sense of a constant and constantly reformist evolution at the core of a State that they preserve (with the pious myth that it will wither away of its own accord) because this State comes out of *a revolution that they have not made*" (II, 174–75).

"Soviet man," this "singular mixture of conservatism and progressivism," has thus interiorized a sociohistorical totality, and reexteriorizes it in a praxis seeking "to progress in order to maintain (the essential conquests), and to maintain in order to progress (stratifications born of hierarchization as means of promoting production) . . ." (II, 175). Having *received* this regime but not having created it, he nevertheless *assumes* it and can scarcely place it in question. Interiorized, the Revolution, such as it is, becomes his own future, his own revolution, to the point that even his (hidden) opposition to the sovereign will be framed in the name of the sovereign itself.

The Peasantry under the Bolsheviks

This portrait of the relationship of the working class to the bureaucracy is followed by many qualifications and complexities, all of which will materially affect Sartre's prognosis of the Soviet future. Before further exploring his analysis of the future prospects for the working class, I will reverse Sartre's order and trace his discussion of a far more negative relationship, between the bureaucracy and the great mass of the Soviet population, the peasantry.

So far, we have observed the "real resistance of the temporary result of action on this action itself" (II, 179), but have not yet witnessed a truly autonomous practico-inert, acting, we might say, on its own. Sartre's formal analysis now takes its next step into the comprehension of a society at the same time as he continues his historical analysis of the Revolution's fate. He will sketch how the practico-inert achieved an autonomy which led to a virtual civil war in the countryside. In so doing he will continue to explore the question of the Revolution's deviation-cum-success as it attacked the masses it was dedicated to humanizing.

In a lengthy theoretical and historical discussion, Sartre now tries to clarify how the practico-inert appears where praxis is backward or poorly developed. He explains how scarcity can be seen as a practico-inert force acting on the praxis that would overcome it. He first emphasizes that the practico-inert only becomes a factor within the framework of praxis: the machine itself as inert matter presents no demand unless as "the inert support of a passivized human aim . . ." (II, 179). That aim, rapid industrialization (especially as demanded by Trotsky in the mid-1920s), *requires* that machines be multiplied, which *in turn requires that their servants be multiplied.* In the United States, land of mass immigration, this demand would have a vastly different meaning than in the impoverished and encircled Soviet Union. The simple fact, "there is no foreign immigration" (II, 180), becomes a potential inner negation for each Russian peasant insofar as those who will work the machines must be drawn from the countryside. If we begin with three radically interconnected facts—new machines (even if imagined but not yet constructed), absence of immigration, and huge numbers of illiterate and backward peasants—"the practical synthesis of the *project* establishes immanent links between them" (II, 179). Analytical reason may now calculate these new relations logically and mathematically, but only insofar as the dialectic—praxis—has decided to supply the machines with workers fresh from the countryside.[17]

Trotsky's project of drawing the workers from the peasants implies *unifying* the two social groups. At best, peasants will become workers by a kind of osmosis or "progressive and prudent mixing." Whatever they may have been prior to this new praxis, these elements now become its practico-inert field. The key point is that the practico-inert field constituted by praxis reveals new demands as once-separate elements are linked: to expand industry rapidly demands multiplying both machines and workers; simultaneously, to reduce the number of agricultural producers requires raising their productivity. Yet drafting peasants into heavy industry will mean *reducing* their purchasing power. The dilemma is that the cities, centers of industrialization, will lack the wherewithal to buy foodstuffs.

Collectivization and the "Grain Strike"

The solution to this insoluble problem is advocated by the Left: collectivization. A different praxis may have led elsewhere. By an "absurd and

17. "We thus rediscover the very origins of the practico-inert: the interiorizing integration of relations of pure exteriority. And this origin reveals to us the fundamental contradiction of human history" (II, 180). In this aside, Sartre means that praxis absorbs objects and relationships into its internal field which—before the launching of a practical project—were external both to the practical agent and to each other. The "fundamental contradiction of human history" can only mean that praxis *creates* the practico-inert that obstructs it in seeking precisely to make the world more hospitable. Is this a formal law of any praxis, or is it a result of determinate, historical material conditions? As we shall see in chapter seven, Sartre will give his answer toward the end of volume two.

purely *economic* hypothesis," for example, the leadership may have decided on an investment in consumer goods and transport, perhaps inviting foreign invasion. But the praxis of maximum investment in heavy industry leads to this "fundamental option"—collectivization—on the one side "and nothing on the other" (II, 181).

Why collectivization? As Trotsky sketched it, collectivization combined with mechanization could have led to the smoothest and most humane transformation.[18] On the one hand Soviet Russia desperately needed to rapidly increase productivity. On the other, the lesson of Thermidor, as historian Georges Lefebvre indicates,[19] was that rural Russia must not be left out of Bolshevik praxis, free to follow its own course. Increasing its productivity meant mechanizing agriculture, which in turn made sense only in the framework of large-scale farming through collectivization. The large yields would also encourage the remaining small peasants to join collectives. Collectivization would increase production, discourage the growth of rural capitalists—kulaks—and extend state control to the countryside. In addition it would assimilate now-mechanized agricultural work to urban factory work, creating new similarities of culture and living conditions, and it would extend socialism in the countryside.[20] This vision foresees using the practico-inert—machines, tractors—as the basis and product of a praxis to be constituted "as human relationship of sovereign to citizens" (II, 182). The machine, that inert demand, is used both for fighting famine *and* for "the synthetic enterprise" in which educators try "to convince men by establishing human relations with them" (II, 182).

This was the Left's vision, but Trotsky was defeated—not only politically by Stalin and Bukharin but also socially and economically. Sartre lays the blame on the alleged rapidity with which the peasantry consolidated its smallholdings, leading to rural capitalist concentration, as the New Economic Policy (NEP) largely let the countryside develop "on its own." In this Sartre follows the standard Soviet interpretation, which retrospectively justifies the attack on the countryside as stemming from the growth of the kulaks (the better-off peasants, who employed labor) at the expense of the poor and middle peasants.[21]

By January 1928, this general problem combined with the peasants'

18. See for example Isaac Deutscher, *The Prophet Unarmed: Trotsky 1921–1929* (New York, 1959), 275–77; *The Prophet Outcast: Trotsky 1929–1940* (New York, 1963), 91–98.

19. Sartre is referring to Lefebvre's *The French Revolution*, vol. 2: *From 1793 to 1799* (New York, 1964).

20. This is developed in *The Platform of the Joint Opposition*.

21. The problems of the late 1920s can far more convincingly be explained as resulting from the Revolution itself and the remarkable spread of unproductive and primitive small-

understandable refusal to sell grain at low prices and their decision to produce higher-paying crops. Although weather conditions were favorable, grain procurements dropped from the previous year by nearly one-quarter. Sartre does not discuss the details, but indicates that the "grain strike" signaled the new situation whose root problem was a "*real indetermination* of the relations between the sovereign and the agricultural masses" (II, 182). In other words, it was the Bolsheviks' relative impotence that had allowed the peasantry to remain "*relatively autonomous.*"

Certainly in 1917 and during the civil war, the countryside has been a vital revolutionary battleground. "But the existence of a unified practical field should never be confused with the total exploitation and the total control of this field" (II, 183). To be sure, praxis—such as NEP—remains praxis even where its own field of action incorporates ignorance or indetermination due to its inadequate development or lack of means. Even if praxis retains its formal unity in such a situation, its poor development may doom it to failure. In other words, the countryside remained a dangerously independent and undeveloped realm within the Bolshevik practical field.

The "grain strike" in fact incarnates the principal features of the Bolsheviks' rural praxis to 1928. First, they had decided to base the Revolution on the working class and in the cities. As a result, as well as by formation and orientation, they continued to lack knowledge and understanding of the peasantry. But rapid industrialization meant that the cities needed greater quantities of foodstuffs while lacking the means to pay for them as well as transport. The situation highlighted the vast size of the peasantry vis-à-vis the working class, and the absence of rural Party members.

These features add up to a "practico-inert zone of separation" which cannot help but act negatively on any Bolshevik effort. One way this is expressed is in the capitalist redivision of land, a *serial* process indicating the "impotent isolation of the poor peasants," which generates the kulaks. The creation of a rural autocracy was itself internal negation of the sovereign, taking place "in the unity of praxis and the practical field as nonreciprocal reconditioning of praxis by the content of its field" (II, 184). This is the very reverse of what Sartre described in his earlier aside on unity and retotalization. Rural serialization, meaning, in Sartre's interpretation, the growth of the kulaks, happens "on its own" to the degree that Bolshevik praxis cannot gain control of the countryside. Rural

holdings, which were incapable of producing adequate surpluses. See Moshe Lewin, *Russian Peasants and Soviet Power* (London, 1968).

Russia undermines Bolshevik praxis due to its independence, based in turn on its backwardness. This serialization is radically different than that deliberately imposed on the working class (the Stakhanovite hierarchies, for example) by the sovereign praxis: that was within the practical field, this "mediation of man by the earth" lies outside of it; that was done *in order to* realize the Revolution's urgent goals, this mortally threatens them.

Facing the Bolsheviks, then, is a practico-inert "object being posed for itself"—rural Russia—which casts the entire practical field "as the inert demand that this foreign concretion be dissolved" (II, 184). It is experienced as a problem of feeding the cities and therefore as endangering the project of industrialization itself. Of course, as we have seen Sartre say, it is revolutionary praxis itself that has made this particular practico-inert appear, as its own counterfinality. After all, under a different, a bourgeois revolution, serial processes would have led to an industrialization which would have followed, we may say, "its own" pace free from the Soviet urgency, breadth, and unity.

Within the Soviet conditions of the late 1920s, however, Sartre seeks to highlight the Bolsheviks' *deficiency of power*, rooted in turn in Russia's lack of transport and the vast size and backwardness of the peasantry compared with the working class. The paradox is that in acting to transform Russia, the sovereign only *increases* its deficiency by intensifying its terms. Suffered, lived, this deficiency that has become conscious and re-exteriorized in solutions such as collectivization "becomes, *in its practico-inert consequence, the internal vice* of action and *its own risk* of failing radically . . ." (II, 185). The peasantry becomes integrated into the sweep of the sovereign's unifying praxis, yes, but only as "the fleeing disunity which puts unity in peril" (II, 185).

Sartre focuses on the threat of famine. To call it the "grain strike," implying consciousness, organization, intention, reflects the leadership's incorrect grasp of the nature of this danger. In fact, it also reflects the complex historical reality of Bolshevik rural policy, which may be summarized as "the decay of a sovereign action which was neglected because the means of pursuing it were lacking" (II, 186). By this Sartre is referring to NEP, although his highly suggestive formulations do not even outline Soviet agricultural policy before 1928. The point is that to call the result a "strike" was to see it through the eyes of the Bolsheviks' praxis.[22] And

22. Writing separately almost a decade after Sartre, an American and a Soviet scholar confirmed that "the extent of the shortfall was deliberately exaggerated by Stalin. In 1927 the proportion of grain marketed was only half of what it had been in 1913." These scholars pointed out that marketed grain fell somewhat between 1909–13 and 1926–28 (from 16.7 to

they were not wrong to see it this way. It was a "strike" from the point of view of the sovereign or the city, engaged in their particular struggles, because "in the milieu of action, everything is always action (positive or negative)" (II, 186). After all, the more urgent the praxis, the more the resistance of things appears as *sabotage*.

Conversely, voluntarism is necessarily terror, especially when at its most optimistic. If it seems that everything can be done, it also seems that those who "cannot" do it *will* not: they must not be trying hard enough, or must be saboteurs. Voluntarism—a response, we must not forget, to the Revolution's fundamental contradiction—*must* "underestimate the coefficient of adversity of things; therefore, in the name of its confidence in the power of man, it ignores the resistances of inertia, counterfinality, the slowness of osmoses and penetrations (insofar as they increase the scarcity of time). It knows only treason" (II, 186).[23]

Forced Collectivization

In the Manichean worldview accompanying Bolshevik praxis, any resistance is perforce seen as praxis, and, to the degree that it threatens socialism, as produced by counterrevolutionary groups. So, threatened by the "grain strike," sovereign praxis pretends to recreate the sense of the group-in-fusion—whose original purpose, we may recall from volume one, was to combat a mortal threat. Now the sovereign seeks to unify the peasantry to meet the threat, but from the outside, by coercion and, we might add, against itself.

The result is collectivization, doubling the state's ability to requisition crops, suppressing the kulaks, and beginning the socialist transformation of the countryside. But under the urgent conditions of 1928 the scarcity of time led to *forced* collectivization without the anticipated prerequisite number of tractors or years of education and modernization. This brutal policy created, on the one hand, huge collective farms dominated by the authorities and, on the other, groups of peasants united in resistance to the dominant praxis, sometimes even led by genuine counterrevolutionaries.

Sartre applies his earlier analysis of contradiction here. "The scarcity

---

16 million tons, from 25 to 21 percent of total output) but nowhere near the amounts and proportions claimed by Stalin. See Alec Nove, *An Economic History of the Soviet Union* (Harmondsworth, 1972), 110–11.

23. Under Rakosi, Sartre notes, the engineers decided, after months of work, that the subsoil under Budapest would not support the subway. In jailing them, "it was this subsoil that he imprisoned" (II, 186).

of time, joined to the scarcity of resources, transforms the contradiction into conflict. But the conflict itself, as contradiction assumed by adversaries, although it is yet more dangerous for the total praxis, represents a degree of higher integration" (II, 187). First, the urban masses *unite* against the countryside—after all, *every* peasant was seen as a possible kulak, hoarding grain for private profit while workers were starving, and every opponent was treated as a kulak. Second, the old rural serial collectivity was broken. The results included the mass destruction of grain and livestock, which were accompanied by the famine of 1932–33.

Why did the regime survive the adventure? Because the workers had become aware that continuing the alliance with the peasants, source of the Revolution (and of victory in the civil war), was impossible in the conditions of 1928. In general the resisting peasants rejected the socialization which the workers had accepted; in particular they rejected the overwork needed to build the national community which the workers had accepted. And this overwork was essential for supplying the workers with *their* very means of survival. Imposing it on the peasants, the workers incarnated the ruling praxis of voluntarism and coercion, seeing it as *their own* demand.

The regime also survived the induced upheaval because of the peasantry's *underdevelopment:* "impossibility of uniting themselves in a large organization, of clearly becoming conscious of a common objective, lack of culture, illiteracy, technical weakness, lack of arms . . ." (II, 188). But this complex set of sociohistorical facts, reflected in rural dispersion and the fact that the original Revolution had been *urban*—and leading to the peasantry's self-destructive and passive tactics—had been, after all, a source of the October Revolution itself. Condition of Bolshevik power in the first place, the nature and balance of forces in Russia both defined the revolutionary project (to overcome underdevelopment) and assured victory in 1929–31 no less than in 1917–21. Collectivizing the peasantry meant "breaking the resistance of the men who are the very incarnation of this underdevelopment" (II, 188).

A few pages later Sartre will return to this question, to emphasize that the peasantry's technical and cultural underdevelopment kept them from even unifying around a program. Knowing only that they did not want forced collectivization, they had no clear sense of what they did want—not only because of their class orientation, but above all because their resistance was *regressive* and sovereign praxis *progressive.*

Once again, Sartre claims not to be speaking in value-charged terms, and certainly does his best to evacuate any specific sociohistorical content and make this a formal judgment. *Progressive* means helping to allow praxis "to realize the projected totalization" (II, 185); *regressive* (*retardataire*) means *retarding* its realization. Sartre's explicit point is that the peasantry was doomed in advance. Does this mean that the Party leadership knew it? In a sense, yes, but the very character of praxis, with its built-in blind spots, kept the leadership in the dark.[24]

Terror and Unity

The ferocity with which the peasants were suppressed incarnates the "scarcity of time," which in turn reflects the urgency of the foreign and internal threats, as conditioned by underdevelopment. The foreign threat demands rapid industrialization, but *there is not enough time* to develop consumer goods industries; the lack of tractors demands forced collectivization and *there is not enough time* to educate the peasantry. "It is *through* the struggle against the peasants that the dictatorship will radicalize itself everywhere and in every sector as Terror; it is starting with this Terror—which requires a consolidated power—that the improvised hierarchy little by little becomes sclerosed" (II, 189).

Terror will turn inward on the "sovereign organs" themselves. As such, it is a mode of "radical unification of practico-inert diversities." Since terror is the integrator par excellence, may we not conclude that it is a source of progress in dialectical terms? Its intelligibility lies in the need of the sovereign—seen here as the bureaucracy, not yet as Stalin alone—to drive out its *own* passivity, to make itself the rigorous and inflexible unity of its practical field by first making itself "pure unifying power." But since passivity is always present, as we have seen, the sovereign must continue attacking it. The leaders "must be as one" *in order to* apply the Draconian measures required by rapid industrialization, but, in doing so, they may discover that they are indeed *several*. Thus the logic of terror is rooted in the dialectic of praxis itself.[25]

By substituting class struggle for the "inert impossibility of exchange" the assault marks a *progress* toward unity (similar to the progress served by the conflict between subgroups explored earlier). Or, rather, given the seriality of the working class and the scattering of the peasantry, it is the sovereign group that declares and mediates the conflict. *It* decides that resolving the question of feeding the cities is urgent; and rather than seeing the peasants remake the workers and itself, uses *its* apparatus of

24. This repeats the point made above, in the discussion of military schools. See chapter two above.

25. Compare this discussion of terror with I, 527–42; 447–59; 430–44.

coercion in the workers' name to reshape the peasants. However bloody, Sartre argues that the conflict's goal was not to liquidate the peasants, but to gain control over and increase agricultural production—"*under no circumstances* to suppress the peasant class in the way the bourgeoisie was suppressed as a class" (II, 190).

Collective Farmer and Worker Today

The project of unity is still being pursued as Sartre writes. Mechanization, still incomplete in 1958, seeks to create a rapprochement between peasant and worker—but by erasing their differences, not by bringing them into reciprocal relations, and, to be sure, under the constraint of bureaucratic domination. Sovereign praxis has thus slowly given means of production to the peasants that both increase their productivity and produce "the man of this growth, kolkhozian man." Raised into collectivized agriculture, he will be at home with machines. Perhaps then the difference between city and country will tend to disappear?

In fact the growth of Soviet agricultural production has lagged: in 1958, 6,900,000 farmers fed 165 million Americans while 50 million were needed to feed over 200 million Russians. Soviet agricultural growth has not even kept pace with the increased mechanization of Soviet agriculture. The explanation throws light on how its own counterfinalities have distorted Soviet praxis: coercion has kept Soviet peasants "in a state of permanent resistance." Held in a state of serial impotence, they have re-exteriorized this as passive resistance: "nothing is *done* against the regime; something *is not done*" (II, 191). Tasks are not accomplished, tractors do not help to reorganize farming, machines are seen as a new method of control even as they increase productivity. If sovereign praxis sought to forcibly collectivize peasants, and *then* to give them the means of accepting it, these two strands remain opposed.

Produced by mechanization and Marxist education, the new generation "still carries the mark that impotent rage and the miseries of the preceding generation have left on it" (II, 192). Under Khrushchev, it still manifests "a separation within the nation, at least a sort of particularism" which points toward its own *class-consciousness*. If the farmers of this generation have been produced as "Soviet men," they have also been formed by terror and still reject the workers' leadership. This disposition, which Sartre describes as "*exteriority from within*," "in itself summarizes thirty years of sovereign praxis and simultaneously passes sentence on it" (II, 192).

Where will it end? Perhaps with genuine unity between city and country? Sartre does not explain what this "unity" might mean, and in any case this section is specifically focused on the collective farmers. Can they follow their proletarian cousins? If they can, the leadership praxis between 1928 and 1950 will retroactively and passively receive new meanings. So far we have a temporary conclusion of praxis, capturing today's relationships and conveying the positive achievements and negative limits of Stalinist terror. At the moment Sartre writes in 1958, it indicates both "the ambiguity of Soviet society as a whole and the possibility, under certain conditions, of accomplishing progress again" (II, 193). For now, the oppression of the peasants, undertaken to carry out industrialization, makes impossible both their integration into the "classless society" and any significant increase of productivity.

The Prognosis for Soviet Socialism

Sartre concludes his discussion of the collective farmer in a rather formalistic and ahistorical tenor: the situation remains open to change, as the people produced by it transcend it in *their* action. And then he moves, characteristically, to wonder about the political issue in formal terms. He suggests that, having rendered a specific class conflict intelligible—that between the workers and peasants, taking place within a sovereign praxis which mediates it—the current situation can be grasped as its product. He shifts from the plane of political assessment, returning to the theoretical goal of showing that the complex analysis of a society (incorporating the series, the process of praxis, the sovereign as dictator, and classes in conflict) reflects the same logic as his earlier discussion of contradiction. Practico-inert conflicts do not *destroy* unity but "are both the consequences of this unification and the means it chooses for tightening it even more" (II, 196). The historian should be able to grasp the logic of Russia's enormous upheaval between 1917 and 1958: a sovereign praxis, continually overflowed by its process, endlessly reintegrated into itself. Certainly, Sartre insists, the attack on the peasantry was "atrocious," but he insists that the analysis has not reached the point of being able to argue that another course was or was not impossible. It has established only that sovereign praxis appears as *totalization*, and that as *praxis-process* it is intelligible as *constituted dialectic*: "this is our only optimism."

Sartre leaves us, however, with a pressing problem. As his analysis ends, the bureaucracy has a stake in the hierarchical system, the working class is partially transformed into "socialist man," partially Stakhanovized, serialized, and dominated—and the kolkhozian remains in a condition of permanent passive fury. What conclusions does this suggest

about the Revolution's itinerary—its deviation and its prospects of re-
gaining its original direction? How has Sartre absorbed and gone beyond Merleau-Ponty's discussion of deviation and his renunciation of the
Soviet experiment? What conclusions can one draw, in 1958, about the
success and/or failure of the Bolshevik Revolution? Can one expect
the suffering it brought about to be offset by its achievements, or at least
by a reasonable prospect of its return to its original socialist goals? Or
will it take a revolution, in the Soviet Union no less than the West, to
institute a socialism worthy of the name?

If such questions emerge naturally in reading Sartre, his detailed
analysis takes us much further than his own conclusions, providing
many of the keys needed for the answers. He is aware, from the beginning, of the differences between the early Soviet working class and the
one of 1958. When he spoke of the project of building of a *future* community against the one of 1928, Sartre noted that, thirty years later, the future community now exists. It is the educated, skilled, productive—
even if also serialized and alienated—young Russians of 1958 who "make
Terror useless; soon, perhaps, they will make it impossible" (II, 156). Later
he noted that only since Stalin's death has its radical transformation and
high cultural level become apparent. When discussing Stakhanovism as
a way of encouraging productivity, he remarked that by the late 1950s the
level of technique and culture have become so high that the masses can
be "interested" in production only by self-management.

Certainly, if we adhere to his main line of thought, we cannot be very
sanguine. The discussion of deviation suggests that not only has a very
different Soviet Union been built than the one originally intended, but
that, above all, those who have built it and their children think of themselves and their project very differently than did the first Bolsheviks.
With their stake in the bureaucratic domination of Soviet life and the hierarchical organization of the working class, contemporary Soviet citizens can scarcely be expected to return to more democratic and egalitarian visions of socialism.

Yet at a decisive point in the analysis, after describing the creation
of "socialist man," Sartre reflects at greater length on the situation in
1958 and anticipates a reversal of the Revolution's deviation. An increasingly conscious working class reflects that Stalinist praxis is accumulat-
ing "transformations which deny it; and this negation is returned to it
through new generations of workers" (II, 176). This very project of negation "is explicitly contained in sovereign praxis as one of its long-term
objectives" (II, 176) in its own theory of the withering away of the state,
and in its emphasis on the *temporary* character of the hardships of the
period of construction.

The reason why the future bureaucracy will need "to disappear or to adapt the forms of government to circumstances" (II, 176) is that (although Sartre does not say so explicitly) Bolshevism has survived its own deviation. Once they are made explicit, "the demands of the masses would be a first control exercised on the sovereign *in the name of its own projects and of the praxis which realizes them*" (II, 175)." Stalinist *dirigisme* builds *into itself* its own abolition as its goals are attained: this contradiction is only another, if inverted, expression of the original contradiction of the Revolution.

Sartre knows that this optimistic projection cannot deny the powerful fact whose origin we have already witnessed: the workers themselves in fact absorbed the same contradiction by becoming structured as a hierarchy in which the hardest, fastest workers would be the best paid and most honored. Similarly the bureaucracy developed both *"for itself and against the masses,"* and *"for the greatest efficacy of the common praxis*, such as this efficacy can appear to bureaucratized agents" (II, 176). Why is this last qualification not fatal? Because the sense of their *temporary* character was built into the bureaucrats' very consciousness at their formation: they existed only for the "interim." "They can build the USSR but not construct a class: their action itself forbids them doing this in spite of the privileges it confers on them" (II, 177). But if the bureaucracy has prepared this emancipation of Soviet workers, will it not be swept away by it?

Sartre leaves unclear what kinds of changes are required, except that he sees them stemming quite naturally from the existing structure and ideology. Will the bureaucracy itself refuse them and thus either restore terror or be overthrown? Even if emancipation has already been enshrined in principle, it may not happen calmly. Only circumstances will decide how rapidly or violently this reform is carried out. And above all Sartre notes that it will be "in the framework of a *reformist* praxis" (II, 177n). Not necessarily a nonviolent one, to be sure, but one which accepts the basic achievements of the Bolshevik Revolution as its starting point.

Limits to Change?

Sartre now seems to veer in a puzzling direction, returning to consider the peculiar nonreciprocal unity of managers and managed. It is as if his most optimistic thoughts must be immediately followed by a close look at the negative factors which inhibit their realization. In this case it is the kind of unity that is imposed on the actors by the material they unify— not the kind that dissolves collectives or one that draws a multiplicity into a group. If one can speak of the practical field *transforming* the actors and their praxes, this is not in a reciprocal relationship with another, who modifies as he is modified, but rather as the repercussion of praxis upon itself. Praxis having brought disparate elements into relationship in the practical field, *it* will now find itself limited by these new relationships.

This nonreciprocity is the key to understanding relationships between managers and the workers they treat as "inert and maneuvered serialities." The workers, treated as passive material, in turn affect those who shape them, but they never question the fundamentally hierarchical character of this nonreciprocity. For all the workers' ontological freedom in transcending the situation which has produced them, they cannot create a reciprocal relationship with the sovereign. Rather, they are always "seen, foreseen, produced, provided with a destiny by the sovereign . . ." (II, 178). In a "circular and nonreciprocal unity," they are organized by the sovereign as part of the practico-inert totality.

I have suggested that Sartre's insistence on *reform* contains his hope that the Revolution will have been successful, deviations and all. This success will depend on it having created a *socialist* structural framework, system of values, and social force—all capable of being modulated back to their original intent and destination. But who will lead the working class from bureaucratized seriality, one aspect of its situation and heritage, toward the other, socialism? Obviously not the bureaucracy, which Sartre has shown as *believing* in and having a structural *stake in* both its privileged position and workers' seriality. Equally obviously, if it is to be possible, only loyal socialist workers can accomplish such a reformist correction of the Bolshevik Revolution's actual evolution. But, as Sartre now shows us in this aside on nonreciprocity, the proletariat is encased in profound structural chains, hardly admitting any easy reformist dissolution.

The comment contains his doubt. Two years earlier, in writing about Hungary, Sartre accepted the Soviet Union as socialist and hoped that a decisive number among the leadership could accept democratization now that the objective basis for authoritarianism had been overcome.[26] In ten more years, Sartre will carry the *Critique*'s doubting side to its conclusion, insisting (after the invasion of Czechoslovakia) that "the machine cannot be repaired; the peoples of Eastern Europe must seize hold of it and destroy it."[27] For now he is still wrestling with the problem, leaving us with a question mark.

---

26. See *The Spectre of Stalin*, 77–91.
27. "Le Socialisme que venait du froid," *Situations* IX; trans. John Matthews, "Czechoslovakia: The Socialism that Came in from the Cold," *Between Marxism and Existentialism*, 117.

6 Why Stalin?

When Sartre discusses the pressure on the Revolution to abandon its principles, we have seen him insist that the Revolution had to choose between collapse and deviation. "Deviation," we have seen him say, "is also detour." And then he adds: "Stalin is the man of this detour" (II, 140).

So far, Sartre has mentioned Stalin very little, Stalinism scarcely at all. He has not yet arrived at the period of "the cult of personality." He has focused, if selectively, on trends and events between the death of Lenin (1924) and the end of the first Five-year Plan (1932): the Trotsky-Stalin conflict, collectivization, and the beginnings of forced industrialization. The cult of Stalin does not dominate Soviet life until after the "Congress of the Victors" in 1934, which proclaimed the success of the gigantic transformation. If Sartre's is to be taken as a historical reflection, it certainly calls for discussion of Stalinism.

However, in keeping with his plan, he seems poised to leave the Soviet Union without such a discussion in order to move on to bourgeois society and the promised "totalization without a totalizer."[1] But before doing so, he says, he wants to "return to our example" of the Soviet Union to understand it as a totalization of envelopment[2]—as a single, overarching praxis-process which absorbs and shapes every individual praxis. By clearly grasping this here, "in the obviously less complex structures which define it at the level of dictatorial societies" (II, 198), we will be better able to understand societies dominated by no single total-

1. Elkaïm-Sartre indicates that Sartre's own notes, gathered in the appendix (II, 451–52), make it seem "that the interrogation of the synchronic totalization (intelligibility of struggles) would have fitted very well here" (II, 197n).

2. Sartre most often uses "*totalisation d'enveloppement*" but also employs "*totalité d'enveloppement*" and "*totalisation enveloppante.*" The first usage seems to emphasize the objective reality of the phenomenon, the last its actively integrating character. Below I follow his usage.

izing party or individual. This brief return, and his general ontological conclusions, will occupy the remainder of volume two. Sartre will never recover his original thread, except to briefly reflect on "disunited societies" in the notes he made in 1961–62.

Singularity

Drawing every individual praxis into the dominant social praxis-process, the Soviet Union in the 1930s is a particularly clear example of an enveloping totalization. In posing this, Sartre is now himself asking the very question I suggested (in chapter three above) he begged when talking about incarnating the world of boxing: "What kind of objective reality does this synthesis possess" (II, 199)? His answer returns directly to his treatment of the theme of incarnation. If every local praxis and singular destiny "gathers in itself all the traits of the praxis-process taken in its totality" (II, 199), it does so not as specification of the abstract, but as a singular activity or system. If there is an enveloping totalization, it will not be a simple general rule or abstract synthetic schema but, rather, will only be realized "as singular incarnation in such a moment and in such a fact (or in such an action) as if it is itself in itself singularity and incarnation" (II, 199). This specificity is its *historicity* which, for example, makes the Bolshevik Revolution a unique adventure and Stalinism a specific phase of its development.

All incarnation is linked to the specific historical totality in two ways: it singularizes it—"condensation"—and it opens to it, is enveloped by it. It "expresses" it, we might say, after having "absorbed" and been "absorbed" by it. A French boxing match at the time of Hitler's occupation of Austria, for example, may be poorly attended as "the incarnation *here* and *at this moment* of the French fears" (II, 199). Its promoters lament their reduced receipts, each member of the small crowd experiences the vaguely sinister feeling given off by a near-empty hall—these are incarnations of the fear, as are the empty movie theaters on the same day. In the Soviet Union under Stalin, *every* event "is defined in relation to the sovereign praxis and as singular determination of the unified practical field" (II, 200). Whether by working in conformity to the Plan or by resisting it, everyone incarnates the sovereign praxis.

Universality: An Economy of Means

In keeping with his attack in *Search for a Method* on "today's Marxists" for seeing individuals and events only as expressions of more general forces and structures (*QM* 19–71; 24–59; *SM* 21–84), Sartre now insists further on *specificity*. In so doing he brings to a climax volume two's attack on universality and generality. If we have had any doubts before, it now becomes quite clear that Sartre's animus is directed against universality as such. *All reality*, he will now say, is specific. But what then is the meaning of the general orders and commands through which organizations seem to function? *Specific* individuals are always in play: a specific regiment, possessing *specific* characteristics, even if these are not known to those who issue orders. They may speak hypothetically and normatively ("every *X* should be *Y*") but this universalism draws its abstract generality from their "indetermination of knowledge."

In explaining this rather startling idea—which asserts a radical particularism and denies the existence, in any meaningful form, of generality as such—Sartre's example cannot support his argument. After all, he soon shows that in its general knowledge the General Staff knows all it needs to know to be able to give its orders, and in fact *ignores* its particular soldiers "except as units." But, he argues, to treat specific individuals as universals is to see them in exteriority and in fundamental ignorance. Sartre's discussion verges on confusion because at every turn he must use general meanings and intentions which are *not* simply a matter of bureaucratic shorthand or ignorance, as he originally asserts, but are rooted in the very way we experience and conceptualize reality. Without theorizing them he does yet remain true to these facts. Accordingly, Sartre seems to go beyond his hypotheses of ignorance and indetermination by concluding: "Thus these rigorously individual soldiers are aimed at as universals, insofar as their *given* individuality is both useless here and ignored *and* insofar as their conduct as common individuals should be everywhere the *same* as practical transcendence of this given" (II, 202).

He presses this point by arguing that a sovereign's decision seems to have the aspect of *universality* (for example, a law limiting *all* civil servants' right to strike). "But this universality is in fact a historical and singular determination . . ." (II, 203). Nobody has in mind strikes *in general*, state employees *in general:* specific events and the sovereign's specific political relationships have provoked *this* response at *this* historical conjuncture.[3]

3. Again, his notion of "determined indetermination," and his reference to the problem of the *concrete universal*, can only have in mind a reciprocal relation between universal and individual, rather than taking the one as standing for the other. In any case, he indicates he will study the problem later, which he does in two places: in his biography of Flaubert, *The Family Idiot*, especially the last volume, and in an essay on Kierkegaard, "L'Universal singulier," *Situations* IX; "Kierkegaard: The Singular Universal," *Between Existentialism and Marxism*.

To universalize is to treat people as means necessary to certain specific practical results (as the number of tons of pig iron required to be produced). Or it is to treat them as agents determined in a single important respect but otherwise totally undetermined (as the civilian population which must be evacuated before an enemy bombardment). In either case, "the agent is only an inertly defined instrument: the true concrete is these women, these children, in these burning houses; the relative indetermination of the agent comes from the full and concrete determination of the situation and of civilians who risk death, and each one of whom defines the death he risks because of his age, his sex, his state of health, his situation in the spatializing field of forces which enclose him" (II, 205).

And, inversely, *these* soldiers who save them are not *any soldiers whatever* but in each case a specific, free, practical organism with a specific history, using specific means to save this old person. Their actions are the real point of the abstract order which, out of urgency and the need to save time, commands that "the population" be evacuated. "Universality—through the necessary ignorance of the leaders—is only an economy of means: but it does not refer to any species, to any genre; this *abstract* determination is swallowed up and dissolved by the true practical temporalization of the agents" (II, 205).[4]

Stalin

It would seem that Sartre, having briefly made his point about the specificity of any given enveloping totalization, might now rejoin the main line of his study and tackle bourgeois society and its specific enveloping totalizations, which unfold without being presided over by a totalizing party or individual. But he never returns to his main question. In an unannounced and undramatic manner, Sartre begins an eighty-page exploration of the totalization of envelopment under Stalin and its singularization in this particular individual. At the same time, Sartre fully returns to his political-historical analysis. As an "example" of the specific nature of the enveloping totalization he pursues what every reader must expect as the next step of his analysis of the Soviet Union, asking its climactic question: why Stalin?

4. Generality, in Sartre's analysis, turns out to be a device and no more. Thus does Sartre echo the argument of philosophers such as Locke and Hume, with whose analytical and positivistic spirit he is otherwise totally out of sympathy, while he emphasizes the weakness of Marxists like Trotsky for being overly given to abstractions. How then would he have characterized Marx's effort to grasp and portray the general laws and dynamic of capitalism? Obviously, Sartre's rhetoric here goes much further than his practice, otherwise there is utterly no point to pursuing *the* dialectic.

In exploring the phenomenon of Stalinism, Sartre presents some of the *Critique's* most brilliant historical and political analyses. In so doing he will begin by casting the individualization of the society's leadership in Stalin as a praxis-process sufficiently abnormal to require explanation. Individualization, we may say, remains his theme, but now as historical aberration rather than ontological phenomenon. Then, in another major shift, he will return to the more abstract line he has now begun, questioning the "real-being" of the totalization of envelopment.

1928: Adapting to the Situation

In the summer of 1928, "a *historical* resistance of the rural class brings the cities to the edge of famine and socialism to the edge of ruin *in the lived present*" (II, 206). The decision to plunge the country into forced collectivization and industrialization is doubly singular—first, seen by the sovereign as the "only *possible* response" to the danger, second, initiating the historical phase which will become Stalinism.

Having earlier defeated and exiled Trotsky—in a triumph for specificity over abstract radicalism—Stalin now breaks with the Right in taking the leftward course, winding up in power alone. For Stalin, we may recall, "the only decisions which inspire his confidence are those which are *required* by the circumstances" (II, 207). Trotsky could *never* be right in his eyes, for his solutions, even collectivization, were never chosen for the right reason but rather from a kind of intellectual's apriorism. The Right, too, in pursuing "socialism at a snail's pace" for abstract theoretical reasons about the nature of undeveloped countries, and out of a prudence which froze it in "theoretical inertia," was unable to adapt to the danger of 1928.

Stalin triumphs. Not because the situation required and used him— Marxists too often think this—but because "Stalin makes himself the man of the situation by the response he gives to the requirements of the moment" (II, 208).[5] The adaptation of the first Five-year Plan initiates a "definite and individualized praxis" in place of the hesitation and oscillations that had been followed since before Lenin's death. It requires and is expressed through a remaking of the leading group, replacing collective leadership with individual sovereignty.

5. As I indicated in chapter four, Sartre later lauds Castro for the very same specificity. In addition to the discussion referred to there, I have commented on the anti-intellectualism and anti-Marxism of Sartre's approach in "Sartre and the Radical Intellectual's Role," *Science and Society*, Winter 1975–76.

The Need for a Sovereign Individual

In volume one, Sartre traced the devolution of authority to an institution and then to a sovereign individual, who "gathers up the multiplicity of institutional relations and gives them the synthetic unity of a real praxis" (I, 694; 587; 609). This common individual raised above all others reflects the vicissitudes of the group: having more and more fallen into serial impotence in order to sustain itself, the group/institution still seeks to realize itself in common action. It incarnates itself, we have seen, in the individual who "reveals common unity to the half-dead group . . ." (I, 707; 598; 623).

Sartre claims, wrongly, we shall see, that his goal is *not* to explore the individual dictatorship or the meaning of the cult of personality. "What matters, here, is something completely different . . . If, in the organisms of leadership the sovereign is *an individual* (a *common* individual), it is because the type of integration demanded by their praxis and by their objectives can only be realized and guaranteed by abandoning, to the advantage of one alone, the powers proper to each one" (II, 208–9). They do this because of insoluble conflicts within the group and its crippling infiltration by the practico-inert. His power and effectiveness are drawn from the fact that the leading groups, frozen into impotence by inertia, turn to him as "*the only one through whom this serialization can be dissolved and the groups reconstituted*" (II, 209).

The secret of Stalin is that he constantly dissolves this seriality, which would return the moment he stopped, by a totalizing praxis that keeps his collaborators impotent. If he is not simply *a* person but a sovereign and a *common individual*, then "he is a human pyramid who draws his practical sovereignty from all the inert structures and from the entire adherence of each leading subgroup (and from each individual); thus he is everywhere, at every level and at all the points of the pyramid, since his totalizing praxis is transcendence and conservation of all structures or, if one prefers, since his praxis is the synthetic temporalization of this entire inert structuring" (II, 209).

As *sovereign* he interiorizes, "in the synthetic unity of an individual, the strata, the hierarchy, the zones of cleavage, the serial configurations, etc., which are precisely the passive means of his action and the inert directions of the regroupings he carries out" (II, 209). *He* is incarnated in the pyramid of authority, and it is incarnated *in him*.

This sovereign common individual is not an abstraction but a unique individual with his own original *exis* (described here "as simple interiorization of the conditioning that he has transcended" [II, 210])—shaped through his struggles, in relation to his background, childhood, and sur-roundings. He is, as a specific individual, "the *facticity* of this sovereign praxis and of this pyramid" (II, 210). Sartre emphasizes the paradox that *this particular* man, Stalin, is *everywhere*. He appears not only on the walls, as image of the Soviet project, but also "as structure of inertia inte-riorized in each one . . ." (II, 210). This man incarnates *their* wills but as *other* because he is, after all, *his own* body, *his own* past, *his own* face.[6]

The first conclusion of this analysis is that Stalin's individual *facticity* (as private person) cannot be separated from the public Stalin. In the case of a king we see a separation between the individual and the office, but Stalin was *himself* sacred, was in his own person the "synthetic con-crete unity of the social transformation" (II, 211) that he brought about. In this sense it is virtually impossible to separate out Stalin's individual contribution from the policies "called for" by a given situation. In real-ity, every administrator acts in obedience to, and as emanation of, Stalin: "Stalin is incarnated in the local leader *as Other*" (II, 212).

This Sovereign Individual

The irony is that this *socialist* society, understanding people through the social environment which produces them, and trying to reduce the his-torical importance of individuals to a minimum, should be driven to rely decisively on the mediation of a single individual. Stalin's mediation was needed so that "the unity of the practical organism be conferred on the activity of organized groups" (II, 213). But his own individual pecu-liarities were then thrown in to the bargain, giving the praxis *his* stamp "in spite of itself." At the same time, his own individual mortality meant that *Stalinism* could only last until his death. His very presence, aging, will contain the contradictions of a sclerosed Soviet society until after he dies.

All of this testifies to the fundamental contingency which has perme-ated Soviet society from the beginning. Sartre only means, in spite of diverting and confusing references to the formal definition of contin-gency in *Being and Nothingness*,[7] that as sovereign Stalin had to resolve problems bequeathed by the past by using *his own* limited tools, thus considerably adding to the ignorance and blindness characteristic of any

6. The incarnation, we might say, is thus an alienation because it creates a non-reciprocal relationship in which Stalin gives back the power surrendered to him only at his pleasure, as *gift*.

7. Every individual dwells in "*the necessity of his contingency*" insofar as he "*is not in the situation of founding his own existence*" (II, 214).

undertaking. This particularistic reinforcement of the social undertaking by its sovereign's individual peculiarities can have positive results as well: "it is the good luck of the Russian Revolution that its voluntarism is incarnated in the will of 'the *man of steel'*" (II, 215). Its negative traits can be exaggerated *for the same reason:* Stalin's personal lack of culture will intensify the general lack of culture in his officials into a "universal incompetence."

Certainly cultural progress, in a society of mass illiteracy, meant Marxism's vulgarization, but Stalin added his *own* "dogmatic heaviness" to the process. "Stalinist also, the perpetual invention of new principles which are added to the others without contradicting them . . . and whose only purpose is to furnish a theoretical justification of an opportunist decision: this mixture of empiricism and pedantry is certainly not *rejected* by the circumstances, but its own origin is Stalin himself" (II, 216).

What Was Required?

If we could speculate, however abstractly, about exactly what program was required by the circumstances, then its distance from the actual program could be explained by the *contingency* of *this* man. Many non-Stalinist Marxists do this, arguing that the "unbelievable tensions" generated by industrialization and rapid collectivization—seen as the only possible policies—made force necessary. "They simply wonder *if it was not possible* to avoid the propaganda lies, the purges, the police oppression in the workers' centers, and the terrible repression of the peasant revolts" (II, 216). Sartre's reply is that, since sovereignty was in fact *singularized*, Stalin's deformation of the "required" praxis was *inseparable* from his effort to carry it out.

A positivist analysis might hypothesize an alternative: "with greater flexibility, more foresight, greater respect for human lives, *one* might have been able to obtain the same result (e.g. collectivization) without spilling a drop of blood; but Stalin, the more inflexible the more narrow-minded he is, less imaginative, carries to an extreme the tendency of Russian constructivism, which is to subordinate man to the construction of machines . . ." (II, 217). Sartre rejects such reasoning because, by proposing two quite independent sets of factors, the personal and the political, it makes history a matter of sheer chance.

It has already become obvious that the demands of industrialization did not require Stalin's methods, and that its results were different from the results praxis demanded. Even if, on hypothesis, the amounts pro-

duced could be quantitatively the same, "ten million tons of pig iron obtained by threat and by measures of bloody coercion (executions, concentration camps, etc.), are not *in any case* comparable to ten million tons
of pig iron obtained in the same perspective and by an authoritarian government but without coercive measures" (II, 217). For one thing, praxis
will be deviated by the consequences of Stalinist violence. This will not
be in the sense already studied of its internal reaction to the counter-
finalities it produces, but "the deviation which results from it should be
attributed to personal factors and, because of this, [may be regarded as]
foreign to the revolutionary totalization" (II, 218).

Yet, looking at this more closely, what does *praxis itself* demand, if not
that the only way the organs of sovereignty can survive and act is to surrender their power to a single individual? And isn't this after all an "internal and fundamental" determination of *this* praxis, even if in contradiction to cherished Bolshevik doctrine about the centrality of the Party?
The point is, from the very moment of its recourse to a single individual,
praxis must be stamped by his individuality. To be sure, even where
a group of common individuals collectively decides and applies policy
after sifting out all personal factors, there cannot help but be "a certain
inequality" between demand and response: they are inevitably *these* men
of *this* situation using *their* instruments of thought. But they can go quite
far toward achieving "a strictly objective response to the objective demands of the praxis and of its field" (II, 218). While their effort of "pure
and anonymous action" will be based on the *negation* of each person as
specific individual, the precise opposite takes place when the sovereign
is *a* person.

The regime turns to him in the name of "*maximum integration* and in
order that he be, at the summit of the pyramid, the living suppression of
every multiplicity . . ." (II, 219). Because the enormous effort of construction demands that the Soviet Union "find its unity in the biological
indissolubility of one individual," it cannot then eliminate the particular
idiosyncrasies of *this* individual and instead achieve an abstract objectivity of praxis.

It has been argued that someone else would have had more scope, a
broader perspective, a fuller consciousness, but the correct comparison
(as many Stalinists know) would not be between pure objectivity and
idiosyncrasy but between two singularities. Trotsky's praxis as sovereign
would have been marked by his greater intelligence and cultivation
and his organizational skill, but also by the abstract radicalism stemming
from *his* idiosyncrasies. Whoever became sovereign, the Revolution
would inevitably, in its faults, in its excesses, have become "this indi-

vidual in person." This is an example of overdetermination in history: the individual called for gives more or less than the situation calls for; the Revolution turns to a single individual to unify it but becomes individualized according to his idiosyncrasies.

We can imagine—but *only* imagine—a sovereign individual who would have done precisely what was needed, neither more nor less. In reality the Soviet Union, by turning to an individual, made essential his "accidental" individual traits. In a marvelous passage which "reduces the role of accident without eliminating it," Sartre caps this discussion:

> And undoubtedly, if the process of planned growth could be directed by an angel, praxis would have the maximum unity joined to the maximum objectivity. The angel would never be blind, or spiteful, or brutal. It would do in each case whatever has to be done. But, precisely for this reason, angels are not individuals; they are abstract models of virtue and wisdom. In a situation the real individual, ignorant, worried, fallible, flustered by the brusque urgency of perils, will react (according to his history) at first too softly, then, at the point of being overwhelmed, too brutally. Those jerks, those accelerations, those brakings, those hairpin turns, those violences that characterize Stalinism were not all required by the objectives and the demands of socialization. However, they were inevitable insofar as this socialization demanded, in its first phase, to be directed by one individual. (II, 220)

Why Stalin?

Why did circumstances tilt the balance in Stalin's favor rather than Trotsky's? Sartre returns to this question by noting that each common individual of the revolutionary party lived the same past as the working masses and that certain among them had lived it "in a certain particular way which makes them better understand the situation and demands of those being directed" (II, 222). But because the proletarian revolution occurred only in Russia, it was followed by a weakening of the position of the internationalist émigrés such as Trotsky. In a situation when Russia's own particularities were bound to come to the fore, it is hardly surprising that the Party leaders would turn to the man who shared their past as militant in Russia. It was as representative of Russian particularism,

> believing in *dogmas* and mistrusting *theories*, penetrated with the particularity of the problem of socialization in Russia (that is, the fundamental singularity of the Russian fact), convinced

that no Western conception could find a field of application in
this complex country, assured *both* of the technical and cultural inferiority of the Russians in relation to other Europeans
and of their *human* superiority (energy, courage, endurance,
etc.), it is indeed as patient militant, slow of mind, tenacious,
wanting to progressively discover the Russian truth, that he
found the necessary alliances in the Party and even in the factories to get rid of the theoreticians of the Right and Left
who opposed each other in the name of the same universality.
(II, 223)

Sartre goes so far as to say (speaking rhetorically, no doubt) that the revolutionary incarnation chose "the singular against the universal and the
national against the international" (II, 223).

Two movements led to Stalin, then, precisely as they led to *suspicion's*
becoming one of the Revolution's major attitudes. First was the fact of
encirclement, leading to urgency, then to terror; second was the fact
of national singularization ("as distrust of the foreigner and of intellectuals" [II, 223]). Based on objective reality inasmuch as its military-
industrial weakness placed the Revolution in danger, suspicion became
vigilance against traitors who might hurt the effort to catch up and meet
the threat. "But this mistrust, as interior consequence of singularization,
is exactly one of the habitual conducts of Stalin, that is, a residue of his
history" (II, 224).

If under siege the Revolution has turned to the accidental and from
group to individual praxis, it still circumscribes and determines the role
played by either. It can only be incarnated in a particular kind of person.
First of all, he will not be Trotsky. Trotsky is rejected because, very
simply, he incarnates the international revolution. But why will it be
Stalin? Insofar as the Revolution, incarnated only here, must abandon its
principles, it both leans more heavily on its dogmas and keeps them distant. It must then seek to place itself in the hands of a "dogmatic opportunist." To integrate the Party it also demands a "militant known by militants," someone who, to impose enormous demands on workers and
peasants, must be "inflexible, without nerves and without imagination."
"Finally, by the very fact that the experience is *singular*, he has to adapt
action *to singular circumstances* without any but a formal reference to
principles, and this distrust engendered by isolation—result and source
of national singularization—is lived practically by him as his own singularization" (II, 226). The demands must become, "under the compres-
sion of biological unity," the sovereign's personal qualities—not by some
"happy chance" but as "a certain manner of having transcended and
preserved the common past" (II, 226) by his present praxis.

Does this mean that Stalin was required in his most singular traits, right down to "the determinations which came to him from his environment, his childhood, the *private* features of his adventure (for example going to the seminary, etc.)? Was *this former Georgian seminarian* really necessary" (II, 226)? *Search for a Method,* Sartre now says, would at first glance suggest *yes.* Through his family situation the child singularizes the various generalities: Stalin's childhood "interiorizes, in toughness, a factor of his future adaptation to revolutionary praxis" (II, 227).

Stalin's hardness, his inflexibility, can indeed be traced to social contradictions which "are certainly among the fundamental factors of the Russian Revolution; more exactly, the child by his rough childhood and by the violence of his revolt, incarnates and singularizes the practical totalization which constitutes this moment of Russian history" (II, 227). The crisis of 1928 demanded inflexibility on the sovereign's part, but "this demand leaves undetermined the question of the individual origins of this inflexibility" (II, 228). An infinity of childhoods might have produced the quality required—but this implies that it could never be "*precisely the required inflexibility.*" Had it been created *directly* by the situation, it may have been the precise quality and quantity needed. But because it came from elsewhere, "its practical goal cannot originally be the difficult construction of a new society, and the very situation that requires it implies that it is not *adapted to its task* but only more or less disadapted" (II, 228).

The Individual Deviates the Required Praxis

No, this particular individual was not required, but certain qualities were, which *he* approximated better than anyone else. In the end, the sovereign individual will have to adapt himself to the praxis required insofar as that praxis is adapted to his "prefabricated idiosyncrasy." The result is a slow movement toward an equilibrium achieved only "by a transformation of the man and a deviation of the enterprise" (II, 228).

Plekhanov would have removed this individual dimension from history entirely, arguing that history will create the man to fit the situation.[8] To his universalism Sartre opposes the "concrete and incarnated totalization" he has been describing. A dead Napoleon, for example, could in Plekhanov's eyes have been replaced by Augereau or Moreau, who would have adapted themselves to fill his office without being overthrown by other generals, without losing wars he wouldn't have lost or provoking fatal mistrust in the army. Plekhanov fails to understand that once so-

8. Sartre is referring to George V. Plekhanov, "The Role of the Individual in History," *Fundamental Problems of Materialism* (New York, 1969); see especially 165–68.

ciety turns to a sovereign individual, *it* becomes individualized in *him* and his personal peculiarities are decisive. For Plekhanov, history moves as a general and abstract force, producing men to fit its functions, neither incarnating nor individualizing itself. Any idiosyncratic moments are deviations to be corrected by the universal process.

Granted that the function to be filled in the circumstances does indeed give individual action its scope and opportunity, the individual must nevertheless adapt himself to it, and, in so doing, he transforms the function. Scarcity is an "iron law" here as elsewhere; the exact inflexibility is not only not readily available, it may not be available at all. There may indeed be too many candidates for the position, without any of them meeting the requirements.[9] The men history makes are never those needed to make it. The situation in France *needed* a man of peace after Thermidor, for example, but he was missing (perhaps killed in the Terror); Napoleon was available, however.

In the case of Stalin the situation required Russia to turn in on itself but not its "absurd cultural isolation"; the great difference between Western and Soviet standards of living "*proposed* the 'Iron Curtain'; but it did not *demand* endless lies about the condition of the European worker" (II, 233). After the first sustained contact with the West in 1945, the curtain could have slowly been lifted, but was kept by Stalin, who instead intensified Soviet distrust. In a new situation Stalin only repeated, and extended, his original rejection of universalism between 1924 and 1928, even if he also eagerly imported foreign technology.

This new situation, and most notably the Soviet Union's extraordinary industrial growth, now *required* going outward: Stalin kept it turned in on itself, and even led it into political antisemitism[10] in an attack on "foreign" influences at home. The attitude of mistrust, having been generated and in a sense needed at the time of encirclement and industrialization, now perpetuated itself. "Thus the movement—it has been said a hundred times—toward the future is realized as evolution or revolutionary overthrow when it is *hot* [*à chaud*]; but it remains, as past signification, aging, but its inert materiality still weighs as one of the most effective brakes on future action" (II, 234n). Outdated significations are thus

9. "We have seen scarcity, a dialectical fact, an interiorization of a practical relationship of man to the [practical] field, reach every sector, all levels, every reality according to the requirement of the circumstances. And *each time* it signifies that *the world is not made for man*" (II, 231). A few lines later, he adds: "If it is true that there are not enough men or not the right men for a definite enterprise, we feel through this scarcity the incarnation of this historical truth: man, insofar as product of the world, is not made for men" (II, 231–32).

10. Following Yehuda Bauer, I use here *antisemitism* rather than *anti-Semitism*. See *The Holocaust in Historical Perspective* (Seattle, 1978), 8.

a major historical force: even after Khrushchev's "Secret Speech," Stalin remains interiorized and reexteriorized by most Soviet groups and individuals, blocking their adaptation to the problems at hand.

Deviation and Poverty

This emphasis on the individual does not at all mean that his individual biographical details, such as Stalin's sexuality, *explain* his social praxis: they are, on the contrary "practically without influence on the practical totalization or have only, from the point of view of the social task, anecdotal importance . . ." (II, 235). It was not Robespierre's inferiority complex, but the necessities of praxis, that caused the Terror. Thrown back on his personal particularities in the course of his action, Robespierre would have stopped being a common individual engaged in group action. Sartre thus rejects "subjective idealism," which would emphasize the effects of Stalin's "private" character, no less than Plekhanov's "objective idealism" (which, by arguing that praxis is always what it needs to be, makes social struggles into a practico-inert process).

Yet Sartre's point has been precisely that the sovereign individual's peculiar effect on history appears in the *differential* between what is needed and what he supplies, due to *his own* origins. Stalin, we might say in explicating Sartre's point, certainly gave the stamp of his personal idiosyncrasies to his praxis, but did so in a way that was both objective and subjective. History called for *him*, and so he was able to impose on it his and no one else's hardness, suspicions, dogmatism, and opportunism. If these traits roughly approximated the situation's needs, they were also rooted in Russian history. Of course, strictly speaking, every individual trait is social and historical and, as *Search for a Method* has argued, develops through the mediation of the family. But no matter how much an individual biography might make of such traits, the study of history is concerned with the demands imposed by praxis, the interiorization of these demands, and the exteriorization of practical responses to them.

Does Sartre imply that the *deviation* lies in this historical-personal dimension being inevitably *added to* (or *subtracting from*) the practical requirements, making deviation inseparable from individual sovereignty as its individual side?[11] He will now answer this in a step-by-step conclusion of his study of individual sovereignty. His main claim is to have grasped the dialectical intelligibility of the *differential* between objective

11. Sartre adds an important aside, never pursued, that "we will see later" that this deviation is also present when the sovereign is not an individual.

demands and their realizations by *this* individual. First, we have seen
how power was individualized, demanded by a praxis which was conditioned by a specific past and which drove the Revolution back on itself
and into oppression. Terror was the consequence of this specific situation, as was Stalin—*especially* of this specific situation, as was Stalin—
particularly given the scarcity of available leaders.

Sartre's next insight, which has been implicit in his characterization of
Stalinism, dramatically deepens the capacity of historical materialism to
understand our history: all praxis, insofar as it is a struggle against poverty, absorbs this poverty as its own dialectic. At worst its result is fatal,
but even at best it is a deviation. It matters little whether praxis itself is
partially responsible. Every praxis interiorizes its poverty and thus becomes responsible for it. Stalinism, as the Revolution's "reincarnation
into individual contingency," thus reflects the fact that "praxis, as poverty, incarnates the dialectical intelligibility of all the internal poverties of
the practical field, from shortage of machines to the peasants' lack of culture" (II, 237). Stalinism, in short, is the incarnation of the society's
poverty.

Stalin adds to the insufficiencies as he adds *his own* deviations to the
Revolution's course. In its very submission to contingency the Revolution
follows a logic, not the a priori logic of some transcendental dialectic imposing itself on human action from the outside, but the logic of praxis
with all its complexities, detours, corrections, regressions, and rup-
tures. The logic of scarcity drives praxis toward its incarnation in contingent sovereign individuals. And so history is not rigorous,

> because it always proceeds by faults and corrections, because
> it is *in no way* a universal schematism but a unique adven-
> ture that takes place starting from prehistoric circumstances,
> which constitute in themselves and by relation to every objec-
> tive and to every practice a heavy and little known legacy of
> fundamental deviations. In a word, Stalinism saved socializa-
> tion in deviating socialism; it remains for his successors, who
> have received the means from him, to correct the deviation.
> (II, 238)

Totalization of Envelopment, Cult of Personality

With this powerful conclusion, are we now ready to move to the *Critique*'s planned next stage? Although Sartre has seemed to stray from his
formal purpose to reach this point, not only have we seen him deal brilliantly with Stalin and his role, but he has also taken the further vital

formal steps of analyzing the nature of individual sovereignty and the process of deviation specific to it. We may recall that the context was a discussion "specifying several points" about the totalization of envelopment and, within that, of the nature of singularization. Stalin, the great singularizer, himself became the Revolution's singularization. Does this mean that he himself became the totalization of envelopment? In posing this question now, Sartre rejoins the thread leading back to his original path. The example of Stalinism reveals totalization as singularizing incarnation. But if the totalization of envelopment is neither a being nor an existent nor a rule, we return to the original question of what it is.

Constituent praxis, we may recall from volume one, referred to (in abstraction from the social conditions of its accomplishment) the concrete reality, "*a-man-informing-matter-by-his-labor*" (II, 239).[12] Its emphasis is on the individual practical agent himself, insofar as he totalizes by transcending continually. "It is one and the same, for each one of us, to exist, to be transcended toward his ends, to be totalized by this very transcendence, and to produce the demoniacal and inverted reflex of totalization, the basis of history: inert syntheses, worked matter" (II, 239).

But as a member of a group or collectivity in a society—which is the terrain of the totalization of envelopment—this individual's praxis becomes posed for itself. For the group as well as the series, we have seen a given individual's praxis become an object to be controlled, rearranged, coordinated from the outside according to the common purpose or goals others have set for it. The subgroup to which the individual may belong becomes itself treated as *inertia* to be manipulated for the group's purposes, as its organ. It *incarnates* common praxis as a predictable structure, becoming a cog in a complex machine, now passive element conditioned by others, now active demand upon others. Thus constituted praxis emerges. The thousand and one possible ways it may be disrupted show it "as material and inert reality to be supported and ceaselessly corrected by the labor of man" (II, 240).

Yet the practico-inert exteriority of constituted praxis always refers back to the "*living* unity of common activity" (II, 241). The contradiction is that this "totality of passive syntheses forms a group in action only if it represents, in some way, *the body* of praxis, this very inertia by which the solitary organism as well as the community act on the inertia of the field" (II, 241).

If there can be such a thing as an enveloping totalization, it must explain this *body of praxis:* how common praxis, becoming compressed and

---

12. See also his original discussion of praxis in I, 193–207; 165–77; 79–94.

incarnated in each subgroup, in that very process becomes decompressed into this exteriority. This highly structured skeleton of inert relations, governing all possible incarnation, is produced by praxis which governs and transforms it endlessly *from the outside*. The totalization of envelopment is praxis, then, but praxis which generates its sustaining corporeality, is deviated by it, and continually seeks to dissolve this exteriority even as it continues to animate it.

These ontological thoughts, to which we will return in the next chapter, seem remote from Sartre's discussion of the Soviet Union. For now, however, they have a specific relevance. Sartre has Stalin in mind. Stalin is the *being* who is everywhere—as leader, as observer watching everyone at work, as Soviet society "in a single person." *He* is the indissoluble unity of the vast multiplicity which is the Soviet Union. "His millions of portraits are only *one* portrait; in each dwelling, in each office, in each workplace, he realizes the presence of all the others, under form of synthetic environment and of inflexible surveillance" (II, 243). Although Sartre suggests that the unity thereby achieved is the deceptive one of serial recurrence, he also emphasizes that the "cult of personality" is *more* than deception: we might say that it achieves *the only possible* unity under the conditions of seriality described earlier. Indeed, this "identity of the exterior and the interior" permits the interiorization in everyone of the great fact of Russia's socialization.

During this moment of Soviet history, then, Stalin is indeed the enveloping totalization. But we have seen what this means: *he* is created and maintained by everyone's praxis. As sovereign individual, he unifies all individuals and structures *and* pursues the "illusory mandate" of dissolving the petrified structures of constituted praxis in the dialectic of one man's free praxis. Because his "untranscendable model of unity" is retotalized in everyone's praxis, the society determines Stalin as he determines its tasks. Because it becomes internalized in him by surrendering all sovereignty to him, the society constitutes Stalin's depth. Then, adding his own personal idiosyncrasies and so deviating it, Stalin re-exteriorizes this interiorized depth: "at this moment of praxis, he sovereignly grasps the national field and by it he integrates the practico-inert totality into the unity of one praxis . . ." (II, 244).

And so we have grasped a particular version of the enveloping totalization: the cult of personality unites the serialized and separate incarnations of common praxis into one man's *organic interiority*. Soviet society, by assimilating Stalin, makes his singularity the unity of what is in truth a dispersed, split society. In a circular movement he retotalizes the Soviet Union and it retotalizes him.

The political goal of this process is the *auto-domestication* of every individual: a Stalinist withering away of the state, in which serialized "common individuals" would be created who have so interiorized the constraints imposed on them that they have become "second nature." The Other is to be internalized as superego or censor, for example in the benevolent and sympathetic portraits of Stalin, so that the "obligations of each worker are singularized by the face and the voice of he who imposes them" (II, 245). Stalin, "indissoluble organic incarnation of the socialist fatherland (II, 245)," penetrates everyone. And serialized mass man, conditioned from outside, takes on the semblance of the common individual of groups, united by oath and common praxis.

Stalin Outlives the Need for Stalinism

Five years before Stalin's death, his "praxis becomes a monstrous caricature of itself" (II, 246). The Soviet Union is no longer isolated, but "the man of withdrawal and solitude" cannot adapt to the new situation. Witness the break with Tito, the horrible trials in Eastern Europe, the revival of terror, purges and antisemitism in the Soviet Union, the failure to understand or appreciate the Chinese Revolution. Aging, Stalin was no more than the "pure product of his prior praxis," and responded to the new situation through the inertia of old formulas even as the society they had created demanded radically new policies. Stalin had earlier supplied/been the praxis-process demanded by the urgent situation. He did/was so only approximately, and given all the qualifications of Sartre's analysis. But now Stalin becomes a form of sclerosis. "He becomes for every Soviet man the *negative* element which separates him from others, from the practical field, and from his own reality; he is the source of ignorance [*non-savoir*] and unconsciousness" (II, 246).

Does this mean that Stalin's death, freeing the Soviet Union from the man who outlived the need for him, will catalyze a new politics? Politically this is the most important question for the *Critique*. So far we have seen Sartre suggest both that the Revolution may be fatally deviated and that the newly created Soviet workers, farmers, and leaders have the capacity to now fulfill the Revolution's promise. In fact, Sartre already carried this line of thought beyond Stalin in his critique of the Soviet invasion of Hungary. There he argues that a new situation, of Soviet power and economic development, necessitates a new foreign and domestic policy based on revolutionary self-confidence. Thus the invasion of Hungary is objectively *unnecessary*.

Now, however, in talking about the totalization of envelopment, Sartre returns to his emphasis that the Soviet people and their leadership have been deviated, consciousness and all, from the goals of the Revolution. The totalization of envelopment in a highly integrated society under a sovereign individual must be understood as a form of incomplete circularity—in fact, a spiral. It is a praxis which escapes its makers, changes them without them knowing it, and deviates itself as it interacts with its accompanying counterfinalities. The totality slowly becomes deviated. In time "these men have become other men occupied in attaining other objectives by other means: and they do not even know it" (II, 248). In general, the "spiral of envelopment," although it may be reversed if too sudden or visible, reveals a series of small, slow, unconscious alterations of practice.

Sartre's earlier thinking on this question appears in the screenplay *In the Mesh*. There the Communist leader Jean Aguerra acted brutally to save the Revolution but *also* retained intact his lucidity and his original commitments. Thus he went to his death aware of and lamenting the evil he had to commit to preserve the Revolution. Now Sartre seems to be refuting both this early hope and—with considerable theoretical and historical basis—his optimistic remark about Stalin's successors "correcting the deviation" and returning Bolshevik praxis to its original commitments. For, as he says a few pages further on, the totalization of envelopment "practically realizes the agents' (leaders and others) objectives and in another fashion it transforms them into other men discovering other results but believing that they have attained their objectives since these are transformed at the same time as [the objectives]" (II, 255). Without renouncing historical materialism, then—indeed, while using it to explain the Soviet itinerary—Sartre might here seem to be laying a sophisticated basis for Merleau-Ponty's renunciation of the entire deviated project.

Illusions of Pure Necessity and Pure Action

The totalization of envelopment "represents the moment of temporalization in which the agent—*in spite* of his success, if he succeeds, or perhaps *because* of it—is lost in the act which produces him, which disorients [*déroute*] him and which deviates *itself* through him" (II, 249). Sartre further concretizes this in one of the great discussions of volume two, a masterly reflection on the illusions surrounding action in history.

While foreign Communists see every one of Stalin's acts as required by the objective circumstances, anti-Communists have indulged themselves in the opposite illusion—of absolute activity. According to them *nothing* was required. With alleged absolute freedom the Bolsheviks ineffectively intervened in an economy which would have developed quite well "on its own" *and* effectively built the machinery to oppress and murder. Their action was no longer "dominated by its own objectification, by the inert synthesis it creates" (II, 250) but, rather, developed gratuitously as absolute action, according to Communist theories or urges for power. If they modified their action, it was not because they had to, but in the "highest degree of praxis," out of total lucidity.

The anti-Communist illusion is in turn based on the Stalinist one—of pure praxis without passivity. In the Soviet Union the totalization of envelopment *seems* to be a unified praxis, while in fact its exteriority "is hidden in its very transparency" (II, 251). For most observers, for example, "stratification and the appearance of interests as backlash [*contrecoup*] of praxis have remained invisible" (II, 251). Communists have simply seen the privileges as deserved rewards, anti-Communists as the rulers imposing their *interests* by carrying off the lion's share.

The latter posit *interest* as a given of human nature which predates, then acts itself out in, any situation, deviating its original praxis for the advantage of the few in power. Against this theory, which hypothesizes an unchanging human nature, Sartre insists that "interest" is a practico-inert *product* of praxis which has in turn deviated that praxis and changed its agents. Correctly understanding the totalization of envelopment can free us from these errors, as well as from the inability of sociologists to see how the social unities they study are unified: the totalization of envelopment is overarching praxis, which continues as praxis even as it has been deviated by its own byproducts. "In this sense the totalization of envelopment is revealed as dialectical connection of the result aimed at (with its foreseen consequences) and the unforeseen consequences of this result insofar as its incarnation in the totalization of the practical field must condition at a distance all the elements of this field including the agents themselves" (II, 252).

Society Explained

We may recall that the detailed study of the Soviet Union was begun for the formal purpose of examining deviation in a society. Sartre has now described a society, as a unitary praxis emanating from its leading group which *acts on* other social collectivities to accomplish the praxis and finds itself, and the society, deviated in its accomplishment. In this sense the totalization of envelopment is nothing other than the Soviet Union as a whole, understood both structurally and as developing historically. Under Stalin the common undertaking becomes an "enormous *society-*

object" that is *both* a specific social totality and an "inert movement of industrial growth." Sartre insists that "it is the undertaking itself—in its
calculated responses to vital questions that the practical field poses—
that produces *itself* and instrumentalizes *itself* as *this* society-object . . ."
(II, 252–53).

Sartre indicates rather trenchantly that he has presented a decisive
corrective to all disciplines of analytical reason. A sociologist watching a
game of bridge from the outside would give an account of what is happening by concentrating on "the movement of cards, their successive
positions, the redistribution of packs [*paquets*], their sudden reunion
then their new separation, without ever mentioning either the presence
of the players (and of their eyes which see, and of their hands which
play) or the rules of the game . . ." (II, 253). And he also indicates that he
has presented a decisive critique of the Marxist illusion which, in its
boundless optimism, would see men as making history without being
made *by* it. And, on the theoretical plane, we may add, he has answered
the core of Merleau-Ponty's critiques of Marxism and of himself. Sartre
has done this by correcting the Stalinized historical materialism that be-
lieves "the builders escape from the consequences of the construction,
the construction is in conformity with the objectives of the builders" (II,
254). Stalin, he is saying to the illusionary outlooks, was within and deviated by the totalization of envelopment *and* was its unifying force. The
only adequate way of understanding the totalization of envelopment,
then, is one which passes from the being created by praxis to the act
which creates it, falls victim to it, and transcends it, while ascending "to
the summit of sovereignty to redescend to the base . . ." (II, 254).

The Totalization of Envelopment as All-Encompassing Unity

Under Stalinism, the society-object, produced by everyone, draws every
element of the practical field into it: "men, things, praxis, practico-inert,
series, groups, individuals." The totalization of envelopment is not just a
formal or abstract signification, but a *reality*, "with its opponents, its partisans, its neutrals, with its hierarchy, its astonishing *élan* and its inertia,
with its relationships of production, its relations of leaders to led, its
'infrastructure' and its 'superstructures'" (II, 256). As such it has "a
practical efficacy, an idiosyncrasy, a concrete richness, and a future" (II,
256). This does not suggest it is a "hyperorganism." The society-object
never can become a superhuman synthesis moving on its own because it
remains rooted in the transcending praxes of millions of free practical
organisms who produce it.

What creates its unity? First of all, the often foul, coercive labor of integration performed by the sovereign, establishing unity through the Party and police apparatuses. This real, material labor includes all the measures by men upon other men to reduce opposition and generate submission: "tracking down, arresting, throwing into prison, beating or simply surveilling, following, searching . . ." (II, 256).

Second, this coercive unification transforms the environment in which everyone lives into the *sovereign's*. Sartre emphasizes the objective internal interconnectedness of every human fact: a modification *here* modifies *every* human fact everywhere. If all humans are generally linked to all others by a formal but indeterminate reciprocity, under a sovereign's unifying action this becomes more rigorously determined and objective. In this relational world a modification of the paths linking certain people and things will effect everyone and everything.

Specifically, in the case of the Soviet Union, each person's standard of living conditions everyone's productivity. "Thus each is determined by everyone in the very perspective of the praxis of socialization . . ." (II, 258), giving the statistical notion of the average standard of living a meaning and truth it might not have elsewhere under conditions of dispersion and detotalization.

Differential salaries, varying not only from occupation to occupation but from region to region, establish a complex relationship between each and everyone else—including solidarity or hostility—to the point that another's salary enters *into one's own salary*. The poverty of the inhabitants of a given province, contained in their low purchasing power, threatens the higher standards of living prevailing elsewhere. Their hypothetical demand, even if implicit, that the others' privileges be reduced to a minimum, would join a second, that their own suppliers receive enough to eat, and in turn a third, that their own standard of living be raised. They would aim at an ideal salary, slightly reducing that of the privileged in order to raise the others' and their own.

This synthetic interconditioning of each by all is seen diachronically when changed circumstances transform the meaning of specific intellectual works. An earlier work celebrating the spirit of the masses (published, say, in 1930) will be revised during the war to emphasize the leadership role played by the Party and to remove the *subversive* emphasis on popular spontaneity. New circumstances *objectively* change a work's meaning:[13] "its relationship to actuality is modified through the

13. See Sartre's discussion of how the objective circumstances of the Cold War "changed the meaning" of *Dirty Hands* from his original intention, and my critical comment, in *Jean-Paul Sartre*, 162–64, 192–97.

modifications of that actuality itself . . ." (II, 262). Because the work has *not* changed, an author may be asked to submit to self-criticism to undermine its ability to promote self-consciousness about the deviation that praxis has undergone. Soviet Party histories and encyclopedias are constantly being rewritten in order to adapt them to the changing situation. To preserve the original meanings when the environment has deviated would subvert the environment. Instead, the work is condemned by readers who perceive the deviation to be the book's, not theirs. We have seen how, as it deviates, action "loses all possibility of knowing its deviation": the later Soviet society thus further renders itself unable to measure its divergence from the earlier.

All current condemnations in this sense become retrospective, as the dissident's past actions are examined to find a basis for guilt in the present, even if they were performed in totally different circumstances—such as the American official who had cried "Long live Russia!" at the victory of America's Soviet ally at Stalingrad but was hounded about it ten years later. This denunciation of the past by the present was probably more extreme under Soviet conditions of building socialism. One-time oppositionists, mildly punished for having erred slightly ten years earlier, now under the Terror are killed for having *always* been traitors. They are seen as having an "immutable-being" by a sovereign bureaucracy peering through the lenses of its own sclerosis. Their past is examined carefully for old errors, all the more so given that in the present they might be deceiving the security apparatus and pretending to be loyal. This mode of judgment, of self-judgment, makes deviated Stalinist man into a suspect living an extraordinary contradiction: bridge toward the socialist future, haunted by his past as his unalterable law.

Incarnating the Totalization of Envelopment

Sartre now moves on to discuss the "retotalization by each event, each praxis, and each particular *exis*, of the totalization of envelopment" (II, 266). Having already spoken about this, Sartre now wishes only to mention the specific way in which individual conduct freely reproduces the totalization of envelopment, so as to become enveloped by it.

After some preliminary observations on how sexual behavior can incarnate other violations undergone by a person, Sartre describes how, in the Soviet Union, the traumas of accelerated urbanization must also have been incarnated in sexual behavior. The traumas are incarnated simultaneously as sexual indifference on the one hand and *activism* ("a practice entirely devoted to labor and social action" [II, 269]) on the other, the first enveloped in the second. As in every form of behavior, the activist-celibate conserves what he transcends, because his own flesh remains with him as permanent provocation: "will he be chaste or will he limit himself to brief encounters, in conformity with his desires" (II, 269–70)? A number of factors—including his past, his position, his ambition—will enter into his actual sexual behavior in the fundamental "relationship of reciprocal immanence" with every woman.[14]

His attitude is the totalization of a free, constituent praxis, but it is that of an enveloped totality as well. Sartre now embarks on a discussion, for which there is no preparation or context in the *Critique*, of the general way in which a given sexual behavior incarnates the person's total conduct. Reference to the totalization of envelopment is either assumed or let slide here, while Sartre pursues an exceptionally arduous line of reasoning remote from questions of the source of unity under a sovereign individual. Sartre does move toward his goal, however, by describing the activist under study as living his body as "an instrument to manage other instruments," under conditions of sexual socialization. His sexual behavior runs the danger of becoming more instrumental than erotic even as he tries to split himself "here, in this instant, in and by these acts, which keep a sort of *private singularity* and, because of this, fall outside the grand historical enterprise in which he wants to play his role" (II, 272). *His* praxis is, after all, the incarnation of his objective relations "with his work and his bosses, his possibilities of 'advancing,' of tearing himself from the masses, and as a function of this, his opportunism . . . or, on the contrary, his sectarianism, etc." (II, 273).

Sartre's conclusion is that every totalizing singularity incarnates the enveloping totalization, and, in the process, each singularity becomes an enveloped totalization. Sartre is trying, once again, to convey the circular and reciprocal relationships creating both society and individual while avoiding various pitfalls, above all, hyperorganicism. "The enveloped totalizations incarnate the totalization of envelopment for the sole reason that individuals as practical organisms are totalizing projects and that there is nothing else to totalize, in a society integrated by an individual sovereign, than the totalization of envelopment itself" (II, 274). The language is unwieldy but decisive: the activist incarnates the specific

14. Sartre parenthetically adds a remarkable characterization of (hetero-)sexual relations, worth citing in full: "On the plane of total praxis that characterizes the individual and always mobilizes him completely in whatever he does . . . at the very level of social, ethical options and relations with institutions, sex is present as synthetic determination in interiority, and as the relationship of reciprocal immanence of this man with every woman, insofar as each women—absent or present and in one way or another—*also* determines his praxis-body as carnal body" (II, 270).

traumas of his existence as a specific pattern of sexual behavior but is in turn enveloped by—contained within the terms of, surrounded by—the surrounding society.

The individuals totalize it, yes; but, as we know, the society also totalizes *them:* "insofar as it produces them, they retotalize it insofar as they themselves are made its products by the practical transcendence of interiorized factors" (II, 274). Thus *within* each individual totalization, as its meaning, we find none other than the totalization of envelopment. And so in this discussion of a totalitarian society, Sartre presents his answer to the riddle of the Sphinx, the question of individual and society. At the heart of the individual (who reexteriorizes the society in making himself, and whose individual praxis sustains the society) we find the society—just as at the heart of the society we found the individual. We can only wonder if the same would be true *without* a sovereign individual as totalizer.

Idiosyncrasy and Antisemitism

Sartre begins his last concrete discussion of the Soviet Union by reminding us of the objective gap between what was called for and what was done. Stalin's "brutality" reflects this distance. Best understood as "a gap between the demands of the objective and real situation and the tasks . . . sovereignly demanded by *real* praxis" (II, 276), it can be observed in his campaign of antisemitism.

Stalin, and Marxism as well, would deny and denounce seeing Jews as a race who, as such, are driven to evil, to antisocial or anti-Soviet behavior. Stalin's antisemitic actions are, rather, based, in his own eyes, on the *political* problem of integrating Jews into the Soviet Union. If left to themselves, especially after 1948, this people will join in identification with Jews elsewhere, especially in the United States and Israel. In the name of a common past or current affinities Jews will resist integration into Stalin's antiuniversalist particularism, and as such become denounced as "rootless cosmopolitans." The permanent danger posed by the real foreign ties of many Jews with the capitalist enemy, with a Zionism heavily influenced by American Jews and thus the United States, with the capitalist West—"all this represents for Stalinist mistrust not only a *possibility* of infiltration but the real presence of a core of traitors . . . within" (II, 276–77).

In response, Stalin restricts whatever may strengthen their particularity as Jews and unite them with foreign Jews against other Soviet citizens—Yiddish language and culture, for example. And yet his policy has to be contradictory: kept from being Jews, they are persecuted *as* Jews. In the long run, Sartre argues, to try to "de-Judaize" without integrating Jews has only one logic: extermination. By his last years this policy led to virulent antisemitic measures.

The question is whether this policy was brought about as a deviation of sovereign praxis—its repercussion on its agents insofar as they themselves were products of their praxis of terror, mistrust, and Russian particularism—or, does it rather draw "its origin and its virulence from the old antisemitic racism" (II, 278).[15]

Certainly the Russian masses knew and shared tsarist antisemitism, and at the lower levels this remained a driving force, exploited by Stalin. Indeed, its economic basis had been destroyed by the Revolution, and thus it would have disappeared among the peasants had Stalin not revived it. In reawakening the old, racist hatred, Stalin's political antisemitism wound up dissolving in it.

> Revolutionary and particularist mistrust are insufficient to *really* believe in the Jewish peril in the Soviet Union in 1950 (even if Zionist imprudence, the facts of espionage, etc., are considered): for it is *already* necessary . . . to be racist to consider that, *among all the particular groups* . . . , the Jewish group is dangerous by essence, to attach a *real* importance to *potential* relations that Soviet Jews might entertain . . . with Western Jews. (II, 279)

Stalin not only leans on these older layers of antisemitism—common enough in bourgeois societies as well—but he "reconstitutes racist antisemitism in all its signification" while hiding it beneath historical interpretations. The earlier discussion of circularity should help explain this process. The masses are conditioned by the ostensibly Marxist sovereign praxis, which is, in turn, reconditioned by their deeper layers of antisemitism. "Stalin and his collaborators are retotalized into racists by the masses; the act, by the mediation of the entire society, returns on them to determine them" (II, 280).

Stalin's *original* intention matters little, because the process of circularity *makes it racist*. To have the masses carry out his political antisemitism, Stalin will *reinvent* their older, deeper hatreds.

> Little by little determined by the circumstances which arouse it, by the objective it pursues, by the means it creates, by the

15. Sartre's use of "racism" is certainly a bit loose. Even at its very worst, during the five years before Stalin died, Soviet antisemitism was not only light-years from Nazi antisemitism in scope and intensity, but it lacked its specific racial emphasis.

> retotalization of groups and series it carries out, by the very
> currents this retotalization produces, which, in the form of
> demands, retotalize the sovereign through this undertaking,
> this praxis is specified in the course of its temporalization into
> a spiral, and ends up by being defined as *free choice of a single
> possibility.* (II, 281)

Sartre has not at all explored the *necessity* of Stalin's antisemitism,
either as policy or in the internal structure just described. But in now
concluding he stresses, without explanation, that it was the free invention of a *single possible praxis*. Stalin overcame Marxism's theoretical resistance "to choose racism as the only possible means of rendering this
politics popular" (II, 281), and in so doing made his own praxis racist
(perhaps drawing on his own past).

Sartre's initiating question, we may recall, asked whether Stalin's antisemitism represents a deviation of praxis or a return to deeper historical
layers of antisemitism. It was of course both. His point now is that it was
free and inevitable—that "the internal transformations of the field dissolved all possibilities except *that one*" (II, 282), forcing a "free necessity
of deviation."

Why this sudden reassertion of two terms, necessity and freedom,
that have played no role in the discussion, just before announcing that
we have "looped the loop" (*bouclé la boucle*) and are ready to draw its conclusions? The discussion was, we may recall, about incarnation—retotalization of the totalization of envelopment by each event and each
praxis. We have just seen Stalin reach back into history—the crudest
depths of Russian history—in order to act in the present, and in so
doing imprison himself and the society in its past. As Soviet society
becomes further brutalized, further deviated from Marxism, and above
all further lost in its deviation, Sartre is once more stressing that it *had* to
be so.

Sartre's Contributions

Now that the entire interpretation of the Revolution's fate and Stalinism
is before us, we can appreciate its full power. On the most general level
Sartre has given us a marvelous, sustained construction-exploration, an
understanding which moves from the ever-narrowing Bolshevik rule to
the peasantry and working class and then back to Stalin. He respects the
almost infinite complexity of this undertaking and yet insists on the
praxis permeating and unifying it—and which is deviated in its carrying
out. He gives their due, as has no other social theorist, to the historical

and the structural, as well as to the resistance of matter *and* the unifying and transforming character of praxis. And, perhaps above all, he understands how human projects become *other* in their successful carrying out. This is, then, a major achievement, worth studying both as an invaluable case study of a society and for what it can teach about the Soviet Union.

For two generations the Soviet Union has confronted those who would understand it with an almost bewildering set of moral, intellectual, and political complexities. Sartre's analysis deserves to be widely read by students of the Revolution as well as by those concerned with social philosophy, because even where, and in spite of, being wrong, it contains a sharply illuminating *perspective* on the Soviet Union's simultaneous development and deformation: development *as* deformation, which never ceases to be development.

Even twenty-five years later it ranks as one of the most impressive analyses yet made of the Bolshevik Revolution's success and degeneration.[16] Avoiding both condemnatory and self-justifying one-sidedness, Sartre grasps the interdependency of success and degeneration as have few writers, doing so with rarely matched theoretical penetration as well as political balance. At the same time, without using the term, he gives a dynamic account of the phenomenon known as "totalitarianism," showing—in the Soviet case—its origins in the liberatory praxis. Having begun by demonstrating that what underlay the process was the original inspiring Bolshevik vision, and not some crude lust for power, he ends by depicting its agent, Stalin, as reawakening the depths of Russian barbarism in outliving his own historical usefulness.

Deviation is the key analytical theme and political question. It is a praxis-process in which "these men have become other men occupied in attaining other objectives by other means: and they do not even know it." Stalin finds himself caught up in, and shaped by, the praxis-process he has set in motion. Generally speaking, we have seen that the totalization of envelopment succeeds in meeting the leader's goals, but it "transforms them into other men discovering other results." The irony is that, transformed, they insist that they have achieved their original goals.

Sartre's other major achievement is to show history neither as chance and original choice nor as the unfolding of an essence over time. Rather, Bolshevism-Leninism-Stalinism were in a profound sense a single praxis unfolding *and* being created in situation, in the process changing hands

---

16. The most recent overview of such efforts is Moshe Lewin, "Grappling with Stalinism," in *The Making of the Soviet System*.

and deviating according to the new vicissitudes they had to confront. Stalinism was Bolshevik praxis in *that* situation. In correctly stressing this half of the story, Sartre avoids the retrospective wishful thinking of all those critiques of Stalinism and even Bolshevism—anarchist, Menshevik, libertarian socialist, Trotskyist, Bukharinite, Khrushchevite[17]—which insist that there was a "better way" to accomplish the same goal. Such projections reflect what I have elsewhere called the illusion of Reason and Progress—that even if the Revolution's accomplishments were rational, its disasters were irrational and avoidable.[18]

Often intellectually persuasive, such arguments are as politically abstract and groundless as championing Trotsky's *Platform of the Joint Opposition* as the "correct policy for the 1920s and 1930s" ignoring the subjective and objective political reality of the Soviet Union after the Bolshevik Revolution. Abstractly and objectively speaking, there were any number of "better" policies to follow after 1921 than the reality of NEP, followed by forced collectivization, followed by overnight industrialization, all in the context of a cautious foreign policy and domestic hierarchization. But Sartre helps us to understand the pressure causing *that* leadership, having *those* commitments, to follow *those* policies: because they saw them as the most appropriate response to *that* situation. Necessity did not impose a single praxis. The leadership *chose* it, including its monstrosities, but did so because of their formation, commitments, and situation.

Weaknesses

Certainly it must also be said that Sartre is selective, often to the point of distortion, and makes serious errors of fact and judgment. And there seem to have been enormous gaps in his reading and interest. What little analysis there is of the period before 1928 takes place in a void, making no mention of the Revolution, civil war, or the first years of the construction under Lenin. And sometimes—notably in the discussion of Stalin singularizing the Revolution—the discussion sounds more like a deductive demonstration of an abstract theme than a specific historical study.

Moreover, in his emphasis on Bolshevism as a single praxis Sartre does not mention that the Party was changing drastically by 1929. It may be that the Revolution's praxis was to become hierarchical, unprincipled, and brutalized. But it found its appropriate agents by replacing and destroying its original ones. Those in leadership were not those who had

---

17. For a discussion of these in the context of an interpretation of Stalinism, see my *The Dialectics of Disaster: A Preface to Hope* (London, 1983), 64–136.
    18. See ibid., 120.

led the Revolution. In fact, the prosecutor of most of the Old Bolshevik leadership was fated to be Vyshinsky, a former Menshevik.

A political struggle took place whose political side Sartre almost totally neglects, which was waged less in terms of the correct praxis to follow ("socialism in one country") than in terms of the prior process of Stalin's gathering the strands of power into his hands. While Trotsky and Bukharin were mesmerized by their Marxist concern for the proper "fit" between policies and the Soviet Union's social base, Stalin knew where power lay and went after it. Sartre's single-minded focus on Bolshevik˙ praxis causes him to miss its great tragic irony: the liquidation of most of the Bolsheviks by what in fact became a wholly new party, as it deviated the Revolution in constructing socialism.

A second major limitation of Sartre's analysis lies in its gentleness. At several stages of his analysis Sartre may well have brought in additional facts, readily available, to show the monstrosity becoming a caricature of Marxist hopes, to show a society's utter brutalization. Had he confessed to a praxis-process gone wild, out of circuit vis-à-vis any human standards as well as its original goals, Sartre would have fulfilled the promise of his own notion of deviation. He rather takes refuge in a combination of moral neutrality and necessitarianism. His emphasis on the ways in which the evolution of Bolshevik praxis seemed necessary to its agents and is dialectically intelligible echoes too many sophisticated justifications of Party and Stalin. Given the Revolution and the need to preserve it, it is said, everything that follows is "required," "needed," "inevitable."

Sartre never mentions the concentration camps into which perhaps one in every ten Soviet citizens entered during Stalin's lifetime, the massive scale of death under collectivization (Stalin himself spoke of ten million), the physical destruction of the Party that made the Revolution into the barbaric cult of Stalin. The point is not to interject extraneous moral judgments into a properly historical or theoretical account, but appropriately to frame the questions that an account should answer: specifically, What was the reason why one in ten people died [19] as socialism was being constructed?

The Revolution Gone Mad

I can only touch on the answer here but have developed it at length in *The Dialectics of Disaster: A Preface to Hope*. It begins with the fact that *those* leaders with *those* commitments in *that* situation felt the subjective and

19. The figure is highly debatable, and certainly requires further research to verify. Presently, however, twenty million deaths is the estimate of the most complete and care-

objective need, by 1929, to undertake a systematic and radical rupture with reality. This rupture included a genocidal attack on Old Russia itself, a mad effort to industrialize overnight, pitching the country into terror, and the creation of socialism as a grotesque amalgam of fantasy and reality.

Insofar as Sartre touches upon these themes at all, he lays them at the door of Stalin the *individual:* the disasters result from his personal idiosyncrasies at a time when praxis required to be lodged in the hands of a single individual. These *excesses* result from personal factors which are thrown into the bargain when the ruling group turns to a personal sovereign. But this analysis gives us only a more sophisticated version of the illusion of Reason and Progress: the social and historical situation calls for a rational praxis, supplied by this individual, but he inevitably injects his own irrationalities as well.

Sartre is wrong, however; the irrationalities and brutality were *social,* stemming not from will or biography or idiosyncrasy but *from the situation itself.* Rooted in Russian history and society and the international conjuncture, the irrationalities and brutality intensified to the breaking point in the world into which the Revolution was pitched after 1929. Sartre conveyed the impossible tension in his discussion of the Trotsky-Stalin conflict, but then failed to see how the situation itself made an adequate praxis impossible. Stalin understood the pressures better than anyone, and conveyed his sense of them in a prophetic speech, delivered in 1931: "We are fifty or a hundred years behind the advanced countries. We must make good this lag in ten years. Either we do it or they crush us." [20]

Of course, Stalin was correct, to the year. Without the transformation of the Soviet Union, the shape of the world would quite possibly be entirely different. Yet, in responding to the demands of an impossible situation, Stalin drove the Soviet Union to do the impossible. Strictly speaking, it was a mad project, [21] because it radically violated all historically known possibilities of development. The impossibility is given in Stalin's statement: fifty or a hundred years' advance in only ten! If it was accomplished, and in gross it was, this happened only because a mad rupture with reality—expressed in paranoia, fantasy, and extreme brutality, as well as in inconceivable achievement—became a decisive principle of the new society.

---

fully researched analysis of the scope of Stalinist terror, Robert Conquest, *The Great Terror* (New York, 1968).

20. Quoted in Isaac Deutscher, *Stalin: A Political Biography* (New York, 1967), 328.

21. I develop the basis for using *madness* to describe social policy in "Social Madness," in Isidor Wallimann and Michael N. Dobkowski, eds., *Genocide and the Modern Age* (New York, 1987).

Medvedev, following Khrushchev, has falsely envisioned Stalinist construction without Stalinist terror,[22] and Sartre's theoretically far more sophisticated emphasis on individual sovereignty has tried to tie the individual deviation to the socially required policy. But, like them, he separates individual from societal, accepting the very distinction which must be most seriously questioned. Did not the *entire process* express/focus Soviet realities every bit as much as it expressed/focused Stalin's mania?

Sartre's Second Prognosis

In 1958 Sartre, still hopeful about the Revolution's returning to itself, was not politically ready for such a conclusion, even if all of his own evidence and reflection pointed there. This certainly explains much of his enthusiasm for the Cuban Revolution, expressed only months after laying aside the *Critique* project.[23] And when he drew the conclusion in 1968, he sweepingly, and exaggeratedly, suggested abandonment of his Marxist outlook itself. But these criticisms are only possible because Sartre's analyses lead us to them—almost, we must say, in spite of himself. He gives us, in fact, the capacity for an ever-deepening look at the Revolution's deviation and transformation into *another* revolution in its being carried out.

Although he does not say so explicitly, Sartre's mounting despair over whether the Revolution can return to its original impulse seems to be implied in his final discussion of Stalin's antisemitism, perhaps including his mislabeling of it as racist. We know, and we have just seen demonstrated again, that, for Sartre, violence and lies are not a great corruption but are necessary weapons on the path forward. *Dirty Hands* eloquently testifies to this in the words of Hoederer, one of Sartre's few attractive dramatic personalities, as does *The Devil and The Good Lord,* in Goetz's climactic final words and action. As volume one shows, Sartre furthermore sees terror as a natural, understandable product of totalizing praxis, and especially of one driven to become voluntarist. It is no less than a stage of the dialectic, and thus could not conceivably draw Sartre's condemnation.

But, at the same time, the Sartre who accepts violence as necessary and liberatory[24] totally rejects any act designed to *lessen* another human

22. Roy Medvedev, *Let History Judge* (New York, 1973). For an extended discussion see *The Dialectics of Disaster,* 121–24.

23. It also explains much of his appreciation for the specificity of Cuban socialism.

24. The outstanding example is his preface to Frantz Fanon, *Les Damnés de la terre, Situations,* V (Paris, 1964); trans. Constance Farrington, "Preface," Frantz Fanon, *The Wretched of the Earth* (New York, 1965).

being: elitism, racism, colonialism, torture, or antisemitism. For Sartre, these belong to a totally detestable moral order. Indeed, this is a major theme of his work, shown as early as Sartre's biting depiction of the Corsican librarian in *Nausea*, in his account of the self-molding of a young fascist in "The Childhood of a Leader,"[25] and in the portrayal of a Southern aristocrat in the play *The Respectful Prostitute*. Sartre further dissects the psychology of the oppressor in *Antisemite and Jew* and in *The Condemned of Altona*.

The point is that Sartre does not at all reject value judgments in analyzing history: the social system that relies on diminishing human beings, especially through systematic practices, thereby condemns itself irreparably. Perhaps we can discern this logic implied in Sartre's presentation of antisemitism as being required by Stalinist mistrust. After all, is this the response of praxis to the situation, or a product of Stalin's idiosyncrasy in an already-deviated situation that calls for something different or less? Sartre seems clear enough—consideration of Stalin's own idiosyncratic brutality frames the entire discussion. It seems that Sartre is indicating Stalin's antisemitism to be that of a person and a praxis outliving themselves, deserving to be swept from the stage of history.

Deserving transformation and ready for it? In the end, does Sartre set the possibility of change in an optimistic or a pessimistic light? If we adhere closely to Sartre's own line of thought, we cannot be very sanguine. Inasmuch as Stalin socialized his particularities, they have become traits of the Soviet Union: the notion of singularization permits of no easy separations. Similarly, a Soviet Union that has given way to "racist" antisemitism will not easily be won away from this deviation, say by the fact of Stalin's death. Clearly, even after the death of the man who outlives himself, the *Critique* points to the need for a further revolutionary transformation if the Soviet Union is to become humane, democratic, egalitarian—socialist. But Sartre does not indicate the dynamic which may accomplish this, although in the next section we will see him lay its basis.

Perhaps the most telling gloss on this part of the *Critique* is *The Condemned of Altona*, written while Sartre was in the midst of the larger project. Ostensibly Franz stands for a France that would not let go of Algeria, irredeemable. But we now know the extent to which Sartre's intellectual energy during this period was being consumed by the Soviet Union. Franz had become a torturer in part out of reaction to the inhumanity toward Jews he helplessly witnessed at home, on his father's estate. And having brutalized others he had become unable to return to

25. *Le Mur* (Paris, 1939), trans. Lloyd Alexander, *The Wall and Other Stories* (New York, 1948).

the fold of humanity: he had made himself lucidly mad, self-torturing and, ultimately, suicidal. There was no way back.[26]

Is this perhaps too gloomy a conclusion about the Soviet Union? It certainly runs counter to Sartre's explicit statements. In spite of his softening the extent of the deviation, however, making it seem wholly necessary and displacing it onto Stalin's peculiarities, in wave after wave Sartre's analysis does show a corruption of Marxism in its incarnation. By and large, the logic of the praxis-process is spread before us, in spite of hopeful statements about the Party, the working class, and the peasants. We are left face to face with an account of how the building of socialism there, with the best intentions in the world, became hell. And how its rulers and perhaps even ruled could become committed to this hell as if it were heaven.

26. For a discussion, see my *Jean-Paul Sartre*, 205–13.

7 Ontological Reflections, Dialectical Conclusions

Having "looped the loop," Sartre intends to "gather in a few pages the conclusions of our study of the totality of envelopment (in the case of a society under a *personal* sovereign)" (II, 282). Now the *Critique* changes radically. Having explicitly announced his intention *not* to do so, Sartre moves from dialectical reason to "the ontology of history." Then, slowly, over its remaining two hundred pages, the manuscript loses much of its force and clarity. It ends without having directly begun its express task, to determine the ways in which history might be understood as a totalization without a totalizer. Until now I have sought to present each step of Sartre's discussion, for example of the Soviet Union, before critically appraising it. But the mushrooming difficulties of the last quarter of the work demand the reverse approach: to prepare the reader for what follows by briefly evaluating it.

The reader will have already noted an interesting difficulty that unfolds over the hundreds of pages studying the Soviet Union: each step of a largely chronological study of the Bolshevik Revolution's inner logic from the Trotsky-Stalin conflict to Stalin's postwar antisemitism is taken only as *example* of a shifting formal program. I have so far evaluated his account of the Soviet Union only on the historical and political level, although its theoretical purpose has been to illuminate the dialectic. First, Sartre seeks to explain *antilabor* in a discussion that seems immediately preparatory to studying the totalization without a totalizer. Second, he studies the Bolsheviks' deviation of the Revolution in trying to save it, in order to observe the action of a group on series. Third, he asks about Stalin and Stalinism as an example of the specific character of the totalization of envelopment. Although presumably any such totalization would be historically specific rather than general, Sartre mixes formal and historical conceptions by showing the extreme extent of Stalin's individual sovereignty. Then he discusses the workers' sexuality in order to show that *everyone* interiorizes the common project. The example of

Stalin's antisemitism shows even the sovereign individual enveloped by the totalization he created.

In a sense these analyses are hybrid, being neither wholly historical (which would mean tracing the historical dialectic explicitly and in detail) nor wholly formal (which would mean closely following Sartre's metatheoretical goal of discussing the totalization without a totalizer). Again and again Sartre insists on the formal purpose of his historical discussions, declaring for example that his only optimism is not historical but turns on being able to establish the intelligibility of the praxis-process being studied. If the *Critique* has two purposes, then, the one theoretical and the other political, they have intermingled, sometimes confusingly, throughout volume two.

From their beginning, volume two's last sections present the reader with two further problems. First, except at moments and at their climactic conclusion, they move at a markedly lower level of insight and penetration than the rest of the manuscript. Sartre often presents, yet another time, ideas he has already developed or conclusions he has already implied. If lengthy passages which restate earlier thoughts can be useful to the reader, they lack the usual excitement of Sartre's relentless pursuit of new paths and constructions. Second, the reader will also see him mention ideas he fails to develop far more frequently than elsewhere in the volume. Thoughts seem to appear out of order, examples are offered which do not fully and clearly embody the themes under consideration.

At first, Sartre's shift to ontology is itself somewhat disconcerting. Is he seeking to absorb *Being and Nothingness* within the framework and terms of the *Critique*, or vice versa, or something quite different and unanticipated? Of course, it can be argued that it is entirely appropriate, *somewhere* in the *Critique*, for the author of *Being and Nothingness* to seek to ground the being of the totalization of envelopment and the dialectic. Moreover, out of respect for Sartre's genius and his power of construction and conception—which often yield the most startlingly original results where least expected—any reader should be willing to follow his turns of direction and await his new discussions. But the customary Sartrean power and verve often desert these last pages, and the reader will miss Sartre's usual sense of single-minded mission.

Certainly, in the words of Juliette Simont, in "a decisive moment in the economy of the project," Sartre can be found to be drawing "an implacably rigorous and lucid conclusion."[1] After all, Sartre returns to *need*,

---

1. Juliette Simont, *"The Critique of Dialectical Reason: From Need to Need, Circularly," Yale French Studies*, no. 68: *Sartre after Sartre*, 110, 111.

the starting point of volume one, with an eminently dialectical circularity. And the last two hundred pages can be seen to establish the necessary ontological basis of the entire *Critique*. But in these pages Sartre can also be seen to depart decisively from his original theoretical purpose, and to do so in an extremely tortuous and often scarcely comprehensible series of discussions. To present these discussions in painstaking detail would diminish, rather than enhance, my purpose of clearly presenting volume two. The reader is likely to become lost in the process of seeking clarity on Sartre's specific points and fitting them into his larger argument. And yet they contain important lines of thought and significantly add to what we have already studied. Accordingly, I will modify the strategy used until now, of faithfully rendering each step of Sartre's analysis, clarifying his meaning, underscoring the structures and directions of his thought, and referring to volume one, to other Sartrean texts, and to the larger context in which the project developed. Instead, to best render Sartre now, and especially to make accessible the remaining riches of the *Critique*, I will present him more selectively, often omitting examples and steps of analysis that are unclear or not significant.

Needs, Labor, Worked Matter

What does Sartre mean by the totalization of envelopment? So far he has described a specific one, the Soviet Union under Stalin—a society, meaning a group working on a range of other collectivities, organized according to a specific praxis and dominated by a personal sovereign. It is unified by a labor of integration performed by the leadership and by the apparatus of coercion; by an internal link of immanence of each with everyone; and by a process of incarnation in which all individuals absorb, singularize, and reexteriorize the imperatives of the sovereign which have been imposed indifferently on all. Serially separated, the praxis of each individual is guided and organized by the sovereign, from the outside, united by the cult of his personality. Yet this vast social whole which ends up determining and deviating even its sovereign's actions, is no hyperorganism. The praxis of each of its individual agents freely produces it, and each one retotalizes his sector according to the sovereign plan. But the society does not move on its own. As totalization of envelopment, Soviet society did not simply pursue a praxis, embodied in the Plan; in its spiral movement it became lost in its own acts, deviated by them.

Sartre begins by reflecting on the *material character* of the totalization of envelopment. To study it externally, only in its physical-chemical reality, for example, as transformation of certain quantities of energy, would be to lose track of its essential character as *human labor* aimed at specific goals—to end scarcity, for example. Yet in so acting under a personal sovereign, we have seen people create a unified physical-chemical and practico-inert field, where everything and everyone is a function of, and influences, everything and everyone else. Aimed at transforming a given society in a specific direction—and thus necessarily a diachronic *temporalization,* unfolding over time—this totalization must also be grasped *synchronically.* "Stalinism" refers to the mutually interrelated structures of a specific *phase* of Soviet development, unified to achieve a certain end: the planned construction of socialism between the end of the civil war, under capitalist encirclement, and Stalin's death. The praxis, however, stems from human material need and takes place "through the total materiality of man."

Circularity

People, as we know from Sartre's abiding notion of dialectical circularity, are mediated by things to the extent that things are mediated by people. We are governed by matter to the extent that our praxis transforms it into worked matter—the practico-inert—to meet our needs. Need and praxis, themselves mediations between humans and nature, reveal another aspect of circularity: resources for meeting needs are defined by the organism and his or her needs, insofar as he or she is already socialized. But in their quantity and quality these very resources in turn recondition people: as raw materials and worked matter, valued and scarce means of meeting vital needs, they enter into the most basic social structuring, defined as it is by relations of ownership and production. In this absolutely rudimentary sense, then, the individual is determined by worked matter *as* he or she determines it.

Stalinism reveals the trajectory of a revolt against this domination, rooted in "the urgent *need* to liquidate the practico-inert" insofar as the Revolution's heritage was material scarcity, underdevelopment, and inequality. The biological unity of a personal sovereign organizes the integrated project of "transforming together and, of course, each by the other, the tools, resources, production, the producers" (II, 288). But as the inherited practico-inert was dissolved, its social structures were absorbed and reexteriorized, and their "practical reexteriorization, in a slightly different technical context, results in constituting another

practico-inert, which reconditions men, interhuman structures, institutions, and finally praxis itself" (II, 288).[2]

Thus the deviating circularity we have observed: the effort to dissolve
practico-inert concretions ends up by producing still other concretions,
which deviate its movement toward its objective. And the subsequent
interiorization of its own "drift" deprives action of the means of keeping itself on its original course. The practico-inert is thus an obstacle to
totalization and simultaneously motivates it. Can it be dissolved? It is
formally possible, elsewhere, but inconceivable, that "the only mediation between free organisms would be other organisms similarly free"
(II, 289).

Because praxis does not begin or end at a definite time but is continuous, its inert deposits react back upon and deviate it, not all at once but
by several circularities, "reconditioned from within by deposits of different ages" (II, 290). "The totalization of envelopment (in the case of the
sovereign-individual) presents itself at first as the inextricable inter-
twining of inert deposits and actions" (II, 291). Unlike sociology, which
takes these practico-inert deposits as given and determinative, the dialectic insists on the law of circularity "and its epistemological corollary,
the law of circular deciphering" (II, 291)—tracing the practico-inert deposits back to the praxis which created them.

The Human Product of Man

After these remarks on circularity Sartre begins five numbered conclusions on the totalization of envelopment, presented over the following
fifty pages. Are these conclusions intended to apply to *any* totalization
of envelopment, even including a possible one in bourgeois society, or
do they only fit Stalinism? Sartre does not say, but their level of generality seems to mark them as a transition to the ontological reflections
which will end the *Critique*.

First, "this reality is completely the *human* accomplishment of man"
(II, 291). It is this because it is produced and developed in the characteristic human way—by posing goals, by negating the past with an eye toward the future. It is also this because even under constraint, labor

2. Sartre is here rephrasing Isaac Deutscher's argument that, in seeking to modernize
brutal Russia, Stalin used the brutal weapons at hand: "Because of the nature of the means
he employed, much of the barbarism thrown out of Russian life has crept back into it" (*Stalin:
A Political Biography* [New York, 1967], 568). In Sartre's formulation, the "necessities" of a
salary differential or of repression "are partially inheritances of the abolished regime, insofar as *its* practico-inertia persists" (II, 288n).

poses its goal and carries it out. Finally, it is a human product "because the agent is a man, and a man, be he a slave, is sovereign in his work, *even if* the practico-inert alienates its results as the worker objectifies himself in it, even if the work is sold as commodity, even if it stands as an enemy force and is realized as a 'loss of substance.' He must indeed *do it*, this labor. Which is to say that he wills it" (II, 292). No matter that it becomes the *being* of the thousands and millions who carry it out—their serial impotence, their *exis*, their destiny. Its every last characteristic remains *exclusively human*.[3]

Controlling Circularity

Second, it appears as antihuman. We have seen the ways in which "things have produced men and given them a false consciousness of themselves, of the past and of their future goals" (II, 292–93). To this considerable degree the totalization of envelopment appears antihuman. Not inhuman, which suggests domination by the natural world, but rather marked by the peculiar antihuman character that emerges only in human society.

Might it be possible to avoid the inert negation of man by his product which has so dominated volume two? In returning to this question, Sartre deepens a line of thought which will become decisive for the final pages of the *Critique*. Is there, we might ask, an alternative—in any societal praxis—to the deviation represented by Stalinism? Had the urgency not been so great, had leadership and masses been culturally more homogeneous, had capable people been less scarce, had all the other urgencies overwhelming the Bolsheviks not been present, then it might have been possible to become aware of the deviation, to control and reduce it. Even so, however, even with far better results, the formal law of circularity would still apply.

The dialectical law of circularity is not imposed by scarcity, we may conclude, but is inherent in praxis itself. And we have seen why: by entering and altering the original practical field, worked matter makes its demands on the praxis that created it. The original praxis must in time become another praxis, one that may seek to sustain or dissolve, but must in any case take account of, these material results of past praxis. And so, as they effectively alter things, human beings are effectively altered by them—under any and every condition. This remains true even in a totally self-conscious, cybernated economy, where planning would

3. This section should be compared with "Materialism and Revolution," 222–28.

condition circularity by a sort of corrective feedback designed to over-come the negative feedback in which their products deviate the agents.

But having stated this as a formal law of all praxis, Sartre in a remark-able vision now leads us back to the historical-materialist hope of tran-scending it. Conquering scarcity does not mean *dominating* nature but, quite the contrary, being able to submit to it without mystification. A sci-entifically and technically advanced society, "far from pretending—like Stalinist society—to escape from circularity, would submit to it in order to govern it and, by means of a system of compensating devices, would automatically correct the deviation by its effects" (II, 294). This is precisely the point Sartre will develop toward the end, as the *Critique* reaches be-yond the domination of the practico-inert.

Comprehending Circularity

Third, a more immediate question is whether the involuted process of circularity even permits being comprehended. As we have seen, the individual agent him- or herself becomes changed as the totalization of envelopment proceeds. Although positivist reason cannot grasp this, the dialectic must acknowledge that deviation is an "antidialectical con-ditioning of the dialectic, it is sovereign praxis insofar as it is (partially) itself antidialectical" (II, 295).

Still, it is intelligible, not as the absurd society-model of sociologists, which loses all contact with history and praxis, but as we have seen with Bolshevism and Stalinism, through moving back and forth from "sover-eign praxis to the masses and to new modifications of the practico-inert to return afterward, through new abstract and statistical determinations to the sovereign reconditioned by the new results of his action" (II, 297).

Unity of the Human and the Antihuman

Fourth, deviation is not limited to collective actions, however, but can be seen, and for the same causes, in constituent (individual) praxis. Sartre takes fatigue as a universal example, applicable to any society or social class. Repeating an urgent action again—digging a trench to build an earthworks—leads to a growth of fatigue which makes it more and more difficult to repeat the same act. The worker becomes less and less able to reproduce his act because *it* has produced inert modifications in his body: lack of the consumed resources, accumulation of wastes and toxins. And these in turn modify his action because of their effect on the prac-tical organism. His gestures become less precise and effective, his attention relaxes, he makes mistakes. This is a reformulation of the process Sartre described in *Being and Nothingness*, which explored the different ways hikers live the physiological facts associated with tiredness and, more radically, separated the physical state from how consciousness chooses to live it (*EN* 530–42; *BN* 453–64). Here, in spite of our best efforts to avoid it, the physical dominates consciousness.

Situated Meaning versus Desituated Signification

In a second example Sartre introduces a new direction, insisting on understanding a garishly dressed woman as a "suspended synthesis of the human and the antihuman," in terms of "the person's *meaning* [*sens*] and not the signification of her behavior" (II, 304). Once more, Sartre is contrasting dialectical with analytical reason. Meaning is connected with praxis-process as an intentional if deviated human product; signification is read from the outside, these links severed. This leads to restating the distinction between taking Stalinism as model and as adventure. The model, formulated by analytical reason, claims the various structures as prototypes, universalizing them by detaching structure from its *temporal* character.

On the other hand, Stalinism's meaning, grasped only by dialectical reason, is inseparable from its "unique and unmatched" unfolding as a specific history. Locating its meaning requires a regressive-progressive study which returns (with a sense of their ultimate destiny) to the original practices, choices, and tensions and moves forward in time to reconstruct the main lines of the entire history as it unfolded in time. "This, to employ a word we used just now, is Stalinism-as-adventure, containing in itself its own temporalization, and not Stalinism-as-prototype . . ." (II, 306). The historian studying Stalinism will himself retemporalize the praxis-process, reconstituting its meaning, as he studies its documents.[4]

The Being of Meaning

Meaning, which can be read in an event by the situated historian, is not the same as the totalization of envelopment as produced by historical agents. "Can it be said that there are *meanings* of the synchronic totalization and not *a single one*" (II, 308)? We have seen that Merleau-Ponty was

---

4. Similarly, to anticipate the later study of a totalization without a totalizer, the *meaning* of the ancien régime, in all its contradictions and complexity, is temporarily reproduced in the playing of a Bach fugue on the clavichord—and can be grasped intuitively in our enjoyment of that fugue today.

left with this conclusion after abandoning Marxism as a philosophy of history. While each level and sector may have its own meaning, increasingly a whole is taking shape which mediates between each of the partial meanings. But this does not make meaning relative to the historian's knowledge. As in the Bach fugue, which conveys to us the ancien régime's meaning, "each real phase of a historical adventure has its *flavor* [*goût*] which is, in each, the objective presence of the whole" (II, 308). The historian does not create this meaning but only makes it explicit and, because it is past and transcended, renders it an *object*. Even if the structures he reveals are in some sense a function of his knowledge, this does not relativize the meaning of the praxis-process: his limiting presuppositions and method situate *him* in relation to the totality he studies as much or more than they situate the totality.

Certainly scanty documents, weak methods or class prejudices, may limit his understanding, and a change in any or all of these would deepen and enlarge his grasp. Indeed, "as we shall see later," a given totalization takes on its full meaning only on the basis of human history as a whole. The future will bring fuller historical syntheses and will be accompanied by new methods. The progress of universal history, and the need to situate each historical object within it, will impose "an infinite task" on the future historian. In a sense, then, it is his *being* that defines the current historian's knowledge as relative.

At the same time, by participating in the historical changes of his lifetime, the historian will transform the meaning of the past. For example, peoples of the past formed relatively closed and distinct totalities, which made past history into a *pluralist* history, as in the relative noncommunication of Asia and the West until the end of the last century. Such factors as industrialization and its drive toward a worldwide economy, colonialism and decolonization, industrialization under Communist control, "lead the historical process for the first time to totalize concrete and current humanity, that is, the two billion men today working on earth, whose needs, labors, products of these labors, and diverse social orders that they create react on each other, on the condition of each individual, and, for the first time, in the unity of a mutual conditioning. Starting from that point, *the previous pluralism is unity*" (II, 310).

This anticipated "one world" of the future redefines the past and gives *its* unity as the destiny of past struggles. It becomes the lens through which the entire past and present will be appreciated, the truth and direction of all history. In this sense the historian does not *impose* a certain meaning—the convergence of two totalities—but, rather, through changes in his own situation, *discovers* it. In other words, "he *constitutes* it through a temporalization which envelops him and totalizes his partial action with those of all the others" (II, 311).

A Turning Point

Fifth, Sartre has been arguing forcefully against any pretense that we can know independently of being situated. We have just seen that the researcher cannot place himself *"at the point of view of the inhuman* to know and understand historical reality" (II, 312). He cannot begin with nature and act as if history was one of its dialectical hypotheses—an external dialectical dogmatism used by orthodox Marxists (I, 143–51; 122–28; 24–32). Nor can he pretend to situate the object studied in relation to the researchers without in turn situating them in relation to the object—the dogmatic and positivistic idealism of conservatives. Each effort at *de-situation* tries to make objectivity, "the object itself being revealed," into an *absolute reality* and to strip it of its *human* meaning and source. This destroys its character as temporalization and ignores the temporalizing agent and his praxis as genuine center of the dialectic.

These preliminary *ontological* remarks, having clarified the situated character of the *being of meaning* (*l'être du sens*), now provoke another question: what is the *real-being* of the totalization of envelopment? By this, Sartre claims not to have in mind ontologically examining the complex structures of the dialectical unity of human and antihuman. "This difficult problem is the province of an ontology of history, not a critique of dialectical reason" (II, 311–12). What matters for us is "simply" how to view the totalization of envelopment—through a "positivistic nominalism" or a "radicalizing realism"?

If all historical totalizations can be grasped only in relation to their agent's or observer's situation, in what sense can they be called *real?* Or, on the contrary, as Sartre will say later, are these relative beings dependent on consciousness in the manner of Berkeleyan ideas? In constantly pushing beneath given assumptions, a radicalizing realism might ask: If we are always *inside* the human project—and those who claim to see it from the outside, such as proponents of analytical reason, radically distort it by severing it from the human praxis that creates it—then what guarantees do we have that it has an outside, a material reality independent of us?

On one level this is the appropriate next question of the *Critique*. But as Sartre develops it, it becomes a rather startling change of direction. (The editor of the *Critique*, noting that Sartre's "purposes expanded along the way" [II, 311n], acknowledges this by beginning a new chapter here.)

In *Being and Nothingness*, which after all was subtitled "An Essay on Phenomenological Ontology," its equivalent question led to the "ontological proof" for the existence of the world beyond consciousness—which took only two pages. Sartre could conceivably do the same here, taking care to guarantee the reality of the totalization of envelopment and then returning to his main purpose. Instead, after over eighty pages mostly devoted to drawing conclusions about the specific totalization of envelopment that appeared in the analyses of the Soviet Union (pages 230–311), the remaining quarter of the volume will now focus directly on various connected ontological themes (pages 311–401). As it turns out, Sartre will launch the discussion by asking about the totalization of envelopment, but then will reconsider certain basic structures of being. If we recall volume two's initiating questions, as well as their specific substance (to let the synchronic structures elaborated in volume one "live freely" in a diachronic study, to pursue the Meaning and Truth of History by exploring the question of a "totalization without a totalizer"), it is clear that Sartre's return to ontology will carry him decisively away from his original purpose.

Does Sartre's change of terrain suggest abandonment of the implicit postulate that has guided the entire *Critique*, namely that everything is situated in history? On every page, praxis has been seen as the ultimate source of the human world—and praxis, unfolding in time, deviated by its material products, is precisely history. Volume one laid out a variety of structures *in order to* then see them active in and produced in human history.[5] In volume two the enveloping totalization, unfolding over time, is the concrete meaning of the dialectic and can be expected to recondition and give concrete definition to each of its individuals and abstract structures. The very notion of circularity, although posed independently of history, falls *within* history as Sartre speculates about a circularity guided by human praxis which avoids deviation. And certainly the force of deviation is weighed historically as well: the specific scar-

5. It might be possible, had one not read volume two, to agree with André Gorz's description of the two distinct and equally necessary stages of Sartre's project: moving from the abstract and ahistorical analyses of *Being and Nothingness* (which set out to show that the individual is not "governed from outside or behind by external and unconscious determinisms") to (in the *Critique*) "analyze the reality of alienation as necessary—*practicalnecessity in *this* world, which cannot be transcended by a simple subjective conversion, and which becomes intelligible only if one goes beyond the framework of the reflexive cogito, not in order to abandon it forever, it is true, but rather to return to it constantly" ("Sartre and Marx," *New Left Review*, no. 37 [May-June 1966], 41–42; republished in *Western Marxism* [London, 1977]). But by the time we have studied volume two it is clear that *everything* is framed historically, and the deepening and correction of Sartre's first attempt at ontology goes behind it to situate *Being and Nothingness* in history.

cities encountered and engendered by the Bolshevik Revolution were decisive to the extent and character of its deviation. Furthermore, the thoughts Sartre has just presented about meaning tie it, internally, to history: the unfinished character of the past waits on the present just as those acting and understanding in the present take shape in a specific past and no other.

But now Sartre's intention of looking at fundamental structures of the totalization of envelopment *outside* history seems to shift drastically from these central themes of the dialectic. Does inquiring about its being place the totalization of envelopment *outside of* history? Does Sartre now situate history within a larger nonhuman, nondialectical framework, which limits its every act and understanding?

The ontological question is an essential moment of the *Critique*, Sartre argues, "since it decides about the relations of Being and Knowledge and since it again calls in question the very basis of the situated dialectic" (II, 312). It is needed to guarantee our knowledge and the reality of the dialectic: "indeed, once we recognize the existence of a totality of envelopment, considered as the temporalization of praxis-process, we will discover that our *situated analysis* was incomplete, and that it can only free itself from indetermination by calling into question the ontological reality of the enveloping totalization" (II, 313–14).[6]

Being and Nothingness, we may recall, revealed no such worries. For Sartre, his Husserlian starting point, that "all consciousness is consciousness of something," began by placing all being *outside* of consciousness. This meant, on the one hand, that "subjectivity is powerless to constitute the objective" (*EN* 29; *BN* lxii); on the other, that "consciousness is born *supported by* a being which is not itself" (*EN* 28; *BN* lxi). This last point is indeed the "ontological proof" of the being of the in-itself. Why now, we might ask, fifteen years after publishing the ontology that made his reputation as a philosopher, does Sartre seek anew to *guarantee* the reality of human activity and its products?

The answer shows how far Sartre has come from Merleau-Ponty's characterizations of him in *Adventures of the Dialectic*. His theoretical shift toward historical materialism appears on every page of a study tracing the praxis-process of the subject constituting the objective world. But if the

6. As Simont has written, in reply to an early evaluation by this author of Sartre's turn to ontology, the following is at stake: "to prove that the dialectic cannot be accused of idealism, that is never simply a method or a theory of knowledge, but that it *is* and that Being is dialectical, that the dialectic has being and that this being is that of being itself" (*"Critique of Dialectical Reason,"* 111). Simont convincingly demonstrates the importance of *grounding* the *Critique* to avoid the accusation of idealism. The problem remains that Sartre abandons his main *and unanswered* concern: is history dialectical?

world's very givenness to intentional consciousness once guaranteed its reality, Sartre's new emphasis on praxis-process jeopardizes the autonomy upon which he leaned for his "ontological proof." The new emphasis on praxis-process thus requires him to rethink key terms of his earlier ontology.

In modulating toward his ontological discussion, Sartre returns to a famous theme of Marxism. But as a new twist he emphasizes the importance of providing the material anchoring to free historical materialism from the accusation of Berkeleyan idealism: "it is men who make History; and as it is History which produces them (insofar as they make it), we understand as self-evident [*dans l'évidence*] that the 'substance' of the human act, if it existed . . . would be *on the contrary* the nonhuman (or, strictly speaking, the prehuman) insofar as it is exactly the discrete materiality of each one . . ." (II, 316). To clarify this is to indicate the theme to be developed below: if praxis is the human, then a totalization of envelopment, and any individual life within it, must be understood as the interiority of praxis relating to the antihuman, which is exterior to it and conditions it. In other words, reality is more and other than the human praxis-process Sartre has been describing. If that were all there was, we would be dwelling in a world which is totally absurd and unintelligible because totally human. It would have no outside, no materiality, no guarantee that what we see and act upon *is* what it *seems*.

Comment: The Appropriate Question?

Yet Sartre has in no way prepared for posing such questions. Consider the state of the argument: we have witnessed single totalization of envelopment, that carried out by a personal sovereign under conditions of a revolution's degeneration-fulfillment. From a formal point of view this praxis-process is the least illuminating for understanding history, which seems to happen without anyone intending it, or the dialectic, which emerges from conflict rather than project.

Speaking politically, volume two has been a study in the deviation of the Bolshevik Revolution and the dialectical freezing of the historical dialectic. The illuminating power of this study does not extend to being able to tell us anything about whether other societies have their own forms of unity—about whether bourgeois society, for example, is a totalization of envelopment in *its own way*.

Sartre has, we might say, provided certain tools for solving the riddle of historical totalization, while avoiding hyperorganisms, and for illuminating the structures between individual and collectivity. But he has enabled us to grasp totalization only as a single praxis, therefore only in its extreme case—the totalitarian one leading to a Stalin.[7] The question that remains, announced repeatedly in volume two but never to be carried out, points to most other historical societies and, indeed, to the historical process itself. How can there be a totalization without a totalizer? Today this means first dwelling on bourgeois societies, whose operating principle is that of the autonomy and magical coherence of millions of separate praxes. And then it means seeing how separate societies cohere into "one world."

Indeed, it is of the very nature of the dialectic that it can be methodologically validated only if it is substantively true, and it is substantively true only if history itself turns out to cohere as a totalization of envelopment. We do not yet know whether human life unfolds in such an overarching and internally unifying praxis-process: questions about its ontological status seem to appear premature at best until the other studies are sketched.

Moreover, Sartre has turned to the question as a parallel to his brief sketch of the real-being of meaning.[8] This quite appropriate methodological aside has emphasized the objective and real character of meaning, its inevitable relationship to the historian who grasps it, and its potentiality for being redefined by his praxis and changes in his world. It has distinguished *meaning* from the totalization of envelopment by distinguishing the historian's subsequent reflection from the agents and their actual praxis itself.

Now, instead of recovering his main thread, Sartre will reflect on the totalization of envelopment by returning, at the end of his last major philosophical work, to rethink a major theme of his first, being-in-itself. His goal, we might say, is to integrate his two major philosophical works, on the one hand providing a historical-materialist basis for his ontology, and on the other providing an ontological basis for *Critique of Dialectical Reason*. He now generalizes as if he had answered the necessary prior questions, and draws his conclusions as if they fit all social forms. He implicitly builds on the scattered suggestions we have seen him plant about bourgeois and other societies and about the totalization of envelopment in general.

7. And he has only performed a progressive analysis, which leads us from the individual to the social; in his own terms a regressive analysis is needed, which moves from the social to the individual.

8. Simont mistakenly seeks to place the ontological study in the light of *meaning*, grasped later, from the outside by the historian, rather than seeing Sartre asking about its being from *within* the totalization of envelopment, from the point of view of its agents. See "*Critique of Dialectical Reason*," 111–12.

Being-in-itself: The Outside of Human Praxis

Sartre now begins to explore being-in-itself as the pole of history that remains forever autonomous to human praxis. The possibility that a cooling of the sun would end history from the outside (not from within, as in the case of a nuclear holocaust) throws into sharp relief the fact that our human projects take place in a universe which is indifferent to them and are conditioned by forces which are *on principle* unknowable and uncontrollable. Even expanding human scientific technique would not remove this exteriority, any more than our ability to artificially create humans would remove their dependence on an exterior infinity "whose characteristic—seen by our lenses [*lorgnette*]—is to support or destroy practical individuals with equal indifference . . ." (II, 318n).

Our every act is marked by a kind of impotence. This is the limitation of practical beings living in a material universe they did not create and which is on principle indifferent to them. If this limit defines praxis-process from the *outside,* it also does so from within. The fact that every one of our successes must be tolerated by the universe marks it "as a reality which is not the basis of its own possibility" (II, 318). This "being-in-transcendence penetrates and qualifies praxis-process right into its interiority" (II, 319). This being-in-itself of praxis-process, this exterior limit of all totalization, is its "unassimilable and irrecoverable reality."

Reflection on death can perhaps help us grasp this "being-in-itself of the enveloping totalization."[9] When, after a violent death, the next of kin experience their loss, they sense that "comprehension in interiority reaches its limit" where death is concerned. Lying outside of history as its limit, and being the limit of life, death qualifies life and history in transcendence.

Every action within history is marked by an implicit comprehension of its fragility, its radical conditioning from outside and the danger that its agents will be deprived of the human possibility of making history. When a death occurs, "history is revealed to fighting individuals and groups as *riddled:* its deaths are billions of holes which pierce it; and each time, through this fundamental porousness, the fragility of praxis-process is given in experience, as the universal presence of its being in exteriority" (II, 324).

---

9. Note Sartre's terminological shift from the whole, the totalization of envelopment [*la totalisation d'enveloppement*] to the enveloping totalization [*la totalisation enveloppante*], which actively envelops individual praxis in its *praxis-process.* As I pointed out above, sometimes Sartre uses the two interchangeably, but sometimes the change signals a shift of emphasis from how the totalization affects individuals to the societal and historical praxes-processes.

Thus, then, the *être-en-soi* of history, its irremediable, omnipresent, unchanging ontological status. If nearly the whole of the *Critique* took place from within the human adventure, focusing on its praxis and its products, Sartre now looks beyond and insists that "its ontological status *also* comes to it from the external world" (II, 325).

Toward a Synthesis of Being and Nothingness and the Critique

The terrifying fact that there is an *outside,* which we cannot reach, permits no intuitive knowledge and is in fact beyond all knowledge. The optimism—Marxist as well as bourgeois—that tries to define being solely in terms of praxis refuses to take account of this transcendent and nonhuman determination of humanity. This is not to quarrel with Marxism's analysis of a whole in-itself economic realm which has not yet been transformed into an economy for itself. It is worked matter, an inert exteriority arising only through human mediation. But this is only half the truth.

To suggest the whole truth Sartre now takes the striking step of opposing one side of his thought, "historical realism," to the other, "the situated method." Without explicitly indicating they are his, he seeks to reconcile the ontological strand, developed in *Being and Nothingness* and here misleadingly called "historical realism," with the dialectical and historical strand developed in the *Critique.* The first, as I noted, radically distinguishes being-in-itself from being-known or being-acted-upon, refusing to dissolve all being into praxis. As he formulates it here, the second "reveals significations, laws, and objects, as it reveals them in modifying and being modified by them" (II, 327).

Each position is correct, but each, taken separately, wanders off into an idealism. By itself the "situated method" makes everything historical and leaves nothing outside to guarantee the material reality of the praxis-process and its products. The idealism for which he criticizes "historical realism" no doubt refers to the radical separation between being-in-itself and being-for-itself, which has given rise to frequent criticisms about Sartre's dualism and the for-itself's unmotivated total freedom. Presumably, then, *Being and Nothingness* requires the *Critique,* and vice versa. The next pages seek to transcend the limitations of both partial works. "It is precisely to show the synthesis of the two truths into one totalizing ontological truth that our abstract experience of *Being-in-itself* is of use" (II, 327).

To do this, Sartre launches into a meditation on being-in-itself as the exteriority of the totalization of envelopment. This is far and away the least accessible part of the *Critique*. In it Sartre is trying to outline what he knows to be unknowable, the premise of experience, which must forever lie beyond experience. Death has indicated this being-in-itself, but it is not at all identical with it. It is, rather, the "exteriority of our history and our life, as well as of our world itself."

Exteriority and Interiority: The Martian

His strategy for contemplating the exteriority lying beyond our own interiority is to observe us from the point of view of the Martian of science-fiction. This Martian lives at such a superior level of knowledge and technique as to make our history seem to be a "cosmic provincialism," our retarded world appear no better than a rat colony. He sees us as we can never see ourselves—from the outside, as we are objectively. He sees both our projects and the vast in-itself universe which remains external to and uncomprehended by us, upon which we act and which conditions us.[10]

The point is, in addition to establishing that we are not adrift in a Berkeleyan universe consisting only of ourselves and our ideas, that an objective and exterior account of the human adventure—one which sees us as we *are*—can only come from outside the human species.[11] This external objectivity of being is an implied pole of our every interior account. Trapped within it, we never leave *our* practical field, *our* projects: Sputnik expands the field but never for a moment leaves it. Outside lies being-in-itself, which by definition is that which overflows consciousness and is the center of "infinitely infinite relationships with the entire universe" (II, 333). Sartre's purpose in these remarks is to provide a new "ontological proof," one that begins with the interiority of praxis and, "far from transforming interiority into a dream, guarantees to it its absolute reality" (II, 339).

Even knowing about an impending interplanetary disaster coming from "outside" a hundred or a thousand years ahead would change nothing of our current concerns: "we would have to live, eat, work, struggle against exploitation, against oppression and colonization" (II, 337) within our universe because these urgencies are rooted in our needs.

10. Sartre adds an interesting note, arguing that the West sees the socialist world this way: they have intellectual tools we lack, we are their object. He suggests that America's "Great Fear" was in part due to this feeling (II, 330–31n).
11. This, of course, would be the gravamen of Sartre's extended critique of analytical reason—that it presents human reality from a perspective beyond the species itself. See chapter eight below.

Two Absolutes

Sartre here rethinks *Being and Nothingness* in ways that reflect his absorption of historical materialism: praxis, not consciousness, points to a being outside of itself; the interaction, not the opposition of in-itself and for-itself, seems to matter most; and Sartre is less concerned with the for-itself's activity as negating the in-itself and more concerned to see the in-itself as boundary of the for-itself's activity. To say that all praxis, as activity for-itself, takes place within the in-itself does not dismiss praxis as an epiphenomenon but, rather, restores its absolute reality. Even a Martian, hypothetically able to see our history as *exis* located within a context inaccessible to humans stuck inside, could not grasp it as praxis, in its inner logic and meaning, without entering into it. *Being and Nothingness* gave these two regions of being a kind of theoretical equality, treating them as absolutely essential components of our world. Until now the *Critique* has wholly emphasized praxis, which, even in its deviation as process, was a historical, not ontological product of the for-itself. In returning to the in-itself as the border of the human project, for historical-materialist reasons, Sartre reemphasizes that the in-itself and the for-itself are two absolutes which reciprocally envelop each other.

This means that the *being* of a given historical event—say the insurrection of August 10, 1792—has two sides. First, it is for-itself, a specific moment of the French Revolution grasped as a totalization of envelopment. As such its logic has been presented by the *Critique* to this point, within the world of the for-itself. Second, this event, seen in the larger universe, is "the interior limit of all exteriority" (II, 341). On the one hand, the dialectic, logic of practical interiority, stops at "this line without thickness" where our praxis leaves off, and by this very token the exteriority reaches its limit at the exact same point.

The dialectic of practical interiority, a radically different intelligibility than would apply to being-in-itself, is therefore incapable of being modified or completed by the transcendent absolute, which always remains heterogeneous to it. But if this is so, the deviations, delays, and ignorance belonging to temporalization are its own exteriority: it engenders them *itself*, in its own circularity. The in-itself is the boundary of all praxis, all history, but human activity configures it *as* in-itself. Moreover, the in-itself as exteriority is limited by interiority, which is "produced in the in-itself as limit of dispersion, as passive synthesis, as produced and maintained unity of systems, as relative isolation of a material totality . . ." (II, 338).

As I indicated earlier, by this point Sartre has already devoted far more

time in the *Critique* to establishing the independent reality of being-in-
itself than he did in *Being and Nothingness*. Were his goal to return to the
purposes of the *Critique*, he could now do so without further delay. Instead, the specific ontological question about the being of the totalization of envelopment, required to guarantee its material reality, now
opens out into a major recasting of other central ideas of his earlier ontology. He will consider a number of familiar themes: the primary relations that develop between being-for-itself and being-in-itself; the goals
of the for-itself's activity; the question of whether the for-itself invents or
finds the structures discovered in being-in-itself; the different ways of
knowing the in-itself; the products and their uses, of the for-itself's activity on the in-itself; and the logic governing the entire process.

Need

Sartre's rethinking of his ontology begins, appropriately enough for
someone influenced by historical materialism, with *need*. Volume one
had already set out the first principle: "Everything is to be explained
through *need*; need is the first totalizing relation between the material
being, man, and the material ensemble of which he is part" (I, 194; 166;
80). In fact, the subsequent dozen pages of the first volume covered
much of the same ground as the reflections to which Sartre returns at the
end of volume two, but not from an explicitly ontological perspective.

The organism's first need is simply to persevere in being. But the organism must perpetually and actively restore itself in order to survive. It
pursues a kind of "organic unity," which refers to its ontological status as
an organism and to its "perpetual repair of damage." The organism's
exis, then, refers to its refusal of dispersion in exteriority and its active
pursuit and achievement of stability. "Organic life is, in fact, permanence *as exis*: it condenses itself in the renewed instant of passivity, and
the repetition of the *same* functional operations is transformed into the
repetition of the creation *of the same object*" (II, 357). Its goal, then, is the
organism's biological integrity, its negation of change and inertial projection of stability.

The organism's need leads to a projection of a future unity. The ontological status of this unity is drawn from the living being and "from
this perpetually maintained unity which constitutes the being-in-itself of
the agent and the transcendent framework of all temporalization . . ."
(II, 344). Other organisms might subsist in a kind of organic circularity,
an *exis* which implies the organism spontaneously operating on itself, in
its own interiority. This *exis* is characterized by a fundamental repeti-

tiveness—as in the case of digestion, circulation, or the functioning of organs such as the liver.

Under conditions of scarcity, however, the organic cycle is broken by a shattering characterized by "the investing presence of inorganic exteriority and the impossibility for *these* organisms to directly transform mineral substances into integrated elements of the living substance . . ." (II, 360). If the human goal is biological integration, the organism must become its own instrument in order to achieve it. Indeed, history is a brutal rupture with this cyclical repetition. Praxis, in unifying the practical field and creating a multiplicity of practical organisms, breaks organic circularity, substituting instead its own spirals of reconditioned conditioning.

The organism begins by seeking its own biological integrity. It will become agent by posing this end, beyond the organism's current state. This goal, *"living* integrity," is "an absolute category, whose origin is neither the inert nor life but the shifting relations of these two statuses . . ." (II, 365). With this category we have reached the practical and material basis of all ontology.

The Organic and the Inorganic

Praxis thus originates in the fact that the organism is incapable of spontaneously reproducing its own life, and that life itself can integrate and transcend nonlife. Its action is "the negation of the organic by the organism insofar as it is attacked by the outside and insofar as it wants, in exteriorizing itself, to rediscover the functional interiority which determines it" (II, 364). In other words, the organism, seeking to "restore" interiority, transcends its original, untenable situation, seeing the surrounding materiality as "the diverse to be unified." The organism defines it as its own practical field, and makes it the basis of all practical creation. Until life itself can be synthesized and integration can take place more or less spontaneously and without reference to the external world, what must be integrated is a "totality of inert processes" whose unity completely depends on action.

Sartre emphasizes the "until" as a way of focusing on the relationship between the organic and the inorganic at the base of praxis itself. Praxis cannot produce life, but (so far) only "passive syntheses of physicochemical substances" (II, 347). Life produces itself, and we can act on it by using inorganic substances and techniques, as in the case of medicine, surgery, and biological experiments. "But it remains that, in all these activities, life is a prerequisite which, under one form or another, always has to be given. To sow, grain is needed, to fertilize a sea urchin with seawater, the sea urchin is necessary" (II, 347). Praxis that seeks to modify life must begin like any other praxis, then allow the organic movement of life to take over and realize its goals according to its own internal laws.

"Thus historical praxis is characterized as relationship of the organism to the inorganic or as its relationship to other organisms by the common mediation of inorganic inertia (in *the agent* as in those *acted upon*)" (II, 349). Praxis tears inorganic substances from the world of dispersed exteriority and marks them "with the seal of life without communicating this very life to them" (II, 349). Man consumes organic substances (plants, animals) as well as inorganic ones (water, air) for his own survival, without however being able to synthesize the former. Instead, he uses passive syntheses—tools, implements—to mediate between (his) life and (their) life. Creating life would be radically different praxis than our own. It would transform inorganic matter into life by integrating it; its living action would itself directly result in living action rather than passive synthesis; and it would realize its creator's aims by its own autonomy. Neither scarcity nor the in-itself/for-itself dialectic would thereby be suppressed, but the practico-inert would be diminished and history would thereby be profoundly transformed.

This is, to be sure, a hypothesis of science fiction whose purpose is to show the unique character of our dialectic and our history. Different from other possible and actual beings, we work only with and on the inert but we do not consume it; we consume only organic matter. Were we not thus doubly limited, but were, like plants, directly linked to mineral substances, then our action would disappear or be minimal, and scarcity might give way to abundance. If we could directly and immediately create life, our action would "thicken" in the created organism. Instead, it is a transcendence of the organism which must escape us "to mark the inorganic with its seal" (II, 351).

Acting on the Dispersion: Unity

The human organism, driven by need, goes outside of itself into the milieu of inertia and scarcity. This in-itself first exists, before any praxis, in a state of dispersion proper to it—the nonrelationship of its elements. Unity is a product/requirement for an organism who, in order to survive, must create passive syntheses of the inorganic. As a result, our first step must be to unify the practical field, and preserve it as unified—unified by the objective of maintaining the agent's organic integrity.

In so doing, however, our first synthesis perpetuates the very dispersion we originally encountered by gathering its elements as a *multiplicity*
within the newly created practical field. At the same time, this is a partial
operation aiming at unifying an isolated part of the field. This "unified
solitude" becomes isolated from the infinite dispersion and, as *this*, becomes separated from *that*, uniting the in-itself whole as *dispersed*. The
dispersion thus paradoxically enters into each singular operation: as the
unity imposed on a local passivity, as the temporary multiplicity that ar-
rests the dispersion.

The unity is objective and real, even if imposed from a distance. It becomes an interior and practical link between each element of the dispersion, sustaining itself on the physical and physiological planes. As we
wrest our practical field from the dispersion, then, we discover the "immanence of everything in everything," which is none other than the "law
of interiority" (II, 353).

Unity and Passive Syntheses: The Passive Humanity of the Tool

Unity, then, is our own goal and our way of organizing the practical
field. Our praxis is unifying activity, forging in the very idea of unity the
"regulatory schema of all human action" (II, 354). And this act in turn
involves attacking and disintegrating the organic, as it is encountered in
nature by the human organism. Farming is such an attack, and uses inorganic substances as well as ideas of unity to restructure the organic in
order to meet human needs. Inorganic products, such as farm implements, are united by the passive inertia we build into them—the metal
coheres after casting and lacks the power to disperse itself.

In this sense, a tool's inertia is an affirmation of organic being. Praxis is
its very source and the organic being's survival its raison d'être. Its very
transcendence is given in the tool: it "refers to the action which produces
it and which uses it, indissolubly linked . . ." (II, 358). Praxis (practical
unification) and its product (functional unity) point us to "*the passive humanity of the tool*" (II, 358).[12] Tools are produced in and for the organism's
praxis, whose goal is to maintain its *exis:* the organism's perseverance is
the "profound truth" of the tool's inertia. "Through it, in a reciprocity of
perspectives, the organic becomes practical (*exis* is made affirmation as

12. The reader may be startled by this formulation, especially after comparing it with
the strikingly different interpretation of tools in volume one: "In the most adequate and
satisfactory tool, there is a hidden violence which is the reverse of its docility" (I, 293; 250;
183). The shift is characteristic of the new and unaccustomed tonality of the entire final
section.

act) and organic practice (the *function* of the tool, as coagulated transcendence and signification, becomes function of an organ, as mysterious and condensed life of a whole)" (II, 358). In a tool's unity action has become organic *exis* insofar as the tool itself contains the goal of perpetuating life as its ontological function and as its meaning.

Acts, Tools, Machines

The equilibrium of natural function is ruptured by the act which goes outside of itself and seeks to directly alter the universe according to an objective. The tool absorbing and being made what it is by the act, is in its passive unity the "very unity of the act *'in person'*" (II, 361). We can best grasp this by considering that the tool is a "materialized (inorganic) mediation between the agent and the inert thing" (II, 361) he or she would have it work on. It designates, in its very passivity, how the worker should use it. It further suggests the action which uses it, because it operates on and unifies diverse materials, and can itself be subdivided into a series of partial actions. The act, operating on an inert and diverse multiplicity, "can be reduced, according to techniques, into a multiplicity of tasks accomplished by a multiplicity of individuals" (II, 362).

With the discussion of tools, Sartre has completed his major ontological reflections and is ready to bring them to bear on the themes of the *Critique*. However, before returning to an explicit discussion of the dialectic, he explores several other matters. In one discussion, stressing the ontological novelty of passive syntheses, Sartre crosses another boundary he had earlier indicated as impassable. These syntheses, such as tools, "reflect both the organic, the inorganic and the act as mediation" (II, 370). In *Being and Nothingness* Sartre had distinguished that which, upon interaction, becomes consciousness, being-for-itself, from that which becomes the material world, being-in-itself. The integration of the two, the in-itself-for-itself, was relegated to the status of a necessary but impossible fantasy, goal of an endless quest. Here Sartre, after looking both at the realm of organic inertia and the human *exis* which is this realm's goal, advances a full step beyond the perpetual oscillation forecast by *Being and Nothingness*: we live in a world of humanized inertia so constituted as to serve the goal of a stabilized humanity. This is not at all an ontological fantasy, but a constant reality of our daily life. The passive synthesis has an autonomous ontological status because "it *is not reducible to anything*—neither to the organic nor to pure dispersion . . ." (II, 370). Sartre is speaking, of course, of the entire practical field and every unity within it created by human action.

Sartre also poses the relationship to praxis of knowing, perception, and invention. To know is to unify the inert and diverse practical field, with an end in view. Even the decipherings of perception "always represent the sketch of a praxis." As in the discussion of the historian earlier, invention is behavior which both reveals—finds—what is there *and* unifies it. "The point is that the unification of the means in view of an objective is a real activity which discovers actualized relationships in integrating terms in an inert synthesis" (II, 374). Knowing is the most elementary form of this praxis, which discovers what is there as it creates it.

Sartre also returns one last time to the discussion of geometric and conceptual thought. Earlier in his ontological reflections he spoke of essences and conceptual thought in general as passive syntheses which are, indeed, antihuman. In them human products, "abstract and inert entities," seem to act passively on men. However "this captive thought" can be dissolved by analysis or explored by dialectics, "it is reborn endlessly as 'natural' thought of man or rather as thoughts which things produce, in totalizing circularity, by their reconditioning of men" (II, 359).

Essences, however, are worked matter which become models in exteriority of such-and-such an organism, and become linked to the free praxis of another organism insofar as it uses the other one. Therefore their external and inertial character reflect a certain alienation. In reality, however, even the most abstract knowledge of geometric figures—which pretends to be a "discovery"—"is nothing but a passive synthesis *carried out by a generating act,* that is, by a construction which unifies a totality of points or of places by a rule . . ." (II, 374). Such figures, it may be claimed, are constituted of relations in exteriority, hypostatized and separated from their human source and its synthetic acts. But it is praxis, after all, based on need, that supports the original unity.

In addition to these insights, and the new light they throw on similar discussions in *Being and Nothingness,* it is worth noting the thread running through them. In each case Sartre is trying to champion the dialectical view of the entire process over the analytical view of each separate act being indifferent to each other one. Dialectical comprehension "restores to us the indissoluble unity in which an organism is designated in its inertia by an exterior material insofar as this organism itself or its restoration (or its preservation) define the operation starting from the projected future . . ." (II, 380). This indissoluble group of acts, in unity and in a certain order, involves performing a set succession of inert syntheses to achieve a future organic consequence, the living being's survival. When we watch a worker's gesture, we may or may not be able to foresee all the acts which precede and follow it. "But what counts is the 'presence' of the future in this gesture . . ." (II, 380). No matter how external each operation of a division of labor is to each other one, together they are a totalization whose each element can only be grasped in terms of their goal. It matters little that a whole praxis, using analytical reason, deploys its elements in an inert succession of exteriority. These elements equally belong to, are integrated in, an interior temporalization—understandable only by dialectical reason.

Analytical Reason, Dialectical Reason, and Machines

After repeatedly distinguishing analytical reason from dialectical reason, Sartre is now ready to do so definitively. He will rest on the opposing/interconnected themes of exteriority and interiority that have wound their way through these reflections. To put it most simply, the dialectic is the interior logic of the entire project he has just described, whereby the organism, in a "passion of thought," exteriorizes itself and undertakes its project of survival in relation to inert materiality. Temporarily ignoring itself as organism, and using analytical reason as its tool, the organism-agent focuses on successive states of inert matter. Analytical reason is the reason of this exteriority established by and within the dialectical project: "thus it can be named our first machine" (II, 384).

Guided by "creative invention," this reason is led, naturally and necessarily, to produce machines. "For machines are only itself [analytical reason] as unified exteriority and itself is only a machine to produce machines" (II, 384).

To understand tools requires more than this "reason of dispersed exteriority"; it requires, rather, a comprehension which can see them in relation to the teleological structures of praxis. Normally, a machine expert visiting a factory sees what is taking place within a pregiven definition of rationality. Thus, for example, *these* machines here are measured insofar as they lower costs by reducing accidents and raising productivity. In creating them, their inventor is responding to practico-inert demands of the process: how to reduce the costs of accidents without crossing a certain threshold of additional cost.

The inventor makes *himself* the tool of the situation, mediating between inert demand and new deployment of matter to satisfy it. The operations of his positivist intellect do not grasp the entire process in its teleological perspective of bettering human life, but only respond to prior demands. "And the inventor as singular individual is in addition conditioned by his own needs and by his desire (for money, glory, honors, etc.)—that is, by the incarnation in his practical person of the objective exigencies of the ruling class" (II, 386). His is "the thought of inertia," "the thought of things," a "thought-thing." The expert *"under-stands* a machine . . . when he uncovers and unifies its structures and its movements starting from the objectives pursued by the inventor . . ." (II, 387). From his point of view, there is *no* difference between a machine in action and a man in action. Only a dialectical praxis and its counterpart, dialectical reason, can synthetically grasp, and thus fully comprehend, these inert demands, structures, and mediations. Thus we have seen that a "broad and dialectical thought sustained and surpassed a technical thought which drew its unity from it . . ." (II, 386).

Dialectical intelligibility sees the inert determinations, the processes and transmutations, as "rigorously and irreversibly oriented toward an end by the synthetic and creative movement of labor, under the control of a positivist Reason always watched over by totalizing praxis" (II, 388). From its perspective, "human action is irreducible to any other process insofar as it defines itself as practical organization of inert multiplicities . . ." (II, 388).

Ontology and Dialectical Reason

Sartre's interest in ontology thus returns us to dialectical reason and, with it, to an explicit materialist emphasis which points to the ultimate foundation of both. If the organism (for-itself) and exterior dispersion (in-itself) are irreducible ontological starting points, human survival wholly depends on the sort of interaction Sartre has been describing. Thus the materialism of Sartre's return to ontology in the *Critique* revises *Being and Nothingness:* to survive, the human organism must unify and rework the dispersion, must interiorize its exteriority and exteriorize its interiority. The process in which the human being must become a worker, an agent, is central to Sartre's rethinking of ontology. Exterior dispersion becomes practical field, tool, and machine, as the human organism itself becomes inertia, tool, and machine in order to survive.

Sartre's unique and often-repeated argument about dialectical circularity remains central to this discussion: matter transforms us to the degree that we transform it. As we have seen, analytical reason, agent and product of this transformation, is incapable of even envisioning it. A tool, it only plots and grasps the passage from one inertial state to another. A striking feature of Sartre's discussion of this "thought of machines" is that men are shown to "become machines" by drastic self-diminution. Our inventor of machines, for example, governed by instrumental reason, sacrifices his capacity for the dialectical comprehension of the whole and fits himself into single and limited tasks within it.

Now, at the end of the *Critique,* Sartre returns to dialectical reason to insist on its capacity to grasp the *telos* and logic of the whole. Dialectical reason is affirmed against its practico-inert products as never before in the *Critique*. In the major analysis of volume one, the group, formed to combat the threat of death that emerges under conditions of seriality, slowly collapses into seriality in order to perpetuate itself. In the major analysis of volume two, we have seen the Bolshevik Revolution, undertaken to assert human control over the historical process, give way to the grotesqueries of Stalinism in order to save the Revolution. In concluding the ontological exploration which reconstructs the basis of both *Being and Nothingness* and *Critique of Dialectical Reason*—and which must be placed at the center of Sartre's mature thought—he suggests an escape from this overwhelming circularity. And to this discussion he now adds two striking but appropriate lines of thought.

Sartre first emphasizes the ultimate purpose of the entire process, the organism's survival. And, second, he for the first time explores the extent to which human beings can avoid being imprisoned in the law of circularity by gaining control over the entire process. The two pursuits are deeply interconnected: satisfying human needs, the material spring of the entire dialectical process, holds out the only hope for liberating humans from its practico-inert consequences.

Guided Circularity

In the very first circularity, the organism is affected from the outside by the results of its praxis on the in-itself. The primary relationship of interiority to exteriority has turned out to be "the ontological and practical basis of the dialectic as totalization perpetually reconditioned by the dispersion that it totalizes, and ceaselessly retotalizing the multiplicities that each of its practical syntheses produce in interiority" (II, 344). We also know that the progress of positivist reason, as reflected in the development and accumulation of machines, leads to a constant deepening of our own domination by the inertia of our products. But for the first time Sartre explores the opposite possibility, equally inherent in the notion of dialectical circularity—namely, that the development and extension of praxis, and its fuller and deeper organization of the practical field, may reach a point of being able to *"liberate praxis* in affirming the commutativity [mutual interchangeability] of all elements of the practical field . . ." (II, 389). Once we project the total decomposition of the organism into inorganic processes, we can equally project the total subordination of the practical field *to the organism.*

Sartre roots his speculation in the *permanence* of the organism—both as agent and as a point of orientation—and, in turn, in the permanence of the organism's needs. Because our goal remains "assuring human organisms the possibility of living" in this indifferent universe, circularity and its alienations will reach an unbridgeable limit. "Hence, despite the dissolution of the biological organism into the inert, the practical organism remains, because the living organism with its functions and its needs has not disappeared either" (II, 390). Even the hypothetically total absorption of the organism into "an immense circuit of machines" must still refer to their goal. Ruled over by practical agents they are incapable of reproducing, the machines fill the needs of the very biological organism they deny.

Until now, Sartre suggests, the process of circularity has only been seen as a *negative* one, entailing growing passivization of the human. But now Sartre speaks of a *guided* circularity, one which the organism-agent controls rather than undergoes, "to direct the *reactions* of the inert, to foresee repercussions and to use them to directly or indirectly recondition the organism through its inertia" (II, 391).

How? Sartre does not have in mind either synthesizing life or making the inert assimilable by the organism (for example nourishing the organism on the inert). Rather, he foresees acting on the organism's functions, conditioning them, regularizing them, slowing down some and accelerating others, raising "for a definite time the individual's practical capacities and resistance . . ." (II, 391). An example would be to help the organism survive by replacing some of its organs by inorganic systems, as when an artifical organ—an inert object, product of human labor—is introduced into the organism. The basis for this speculation is that the kind of machine, manufactured in the perspective of interchangeability which governs machine production, performs a labor for us, under our control, for our ends. "In other words, this machine is *action* of man at the heart of the organism; in certain conditions and for certain functions, the organ can be replaced by a product of action and the function by the action of this product" (II, 392).

In spite of everything, then, the original purpose of praxis remains its abiding purpose. Praxis, we have seen, results in our constructing means. "It is the restoration and safeguarding of the organism, as end projected in the future, which will determine the place of the means and its function in the environment" (II, 392). The organism's *needs* cannot be assimilated by the practico-inert world, however infected by circularity, which is constructed to serve them.

On the one hand, then, Sartre's vision of deviating circularity reaches its limit as he projects the total absorption of human praxis, and thus the human organism, by the practico-inert world it creates. He speculates on whether everything and everyone can become a means, in a world where man is totally mediated by things. Yet outside the series, unable to be absorbed in it, lies its original end. "The direct movement of praxis remains that of an organism (or of an organized group) which tries to make *its material environment* into a combination of inert elements which are favorable to its life" (II, 392). The practical field, which for so much of both volumes of the *Critique* had developed an overwhelming life of its own, is now more appropriately seen as *means,* a however complex and distorted network of mediations between two moments of life.

The Evanescent Act

After a bit of reflexive preparation for the conclusion "of this brief study," Sartre continues to explore the implications of his new emphasis on the "untranscendable end" of human praxis in our history: "to save life" (II, 394). He now argues that "praxis is originally a relationship of the organism to itself through the inorganic environment, and, when the goal is attained, this relationship suppresses itself" (II, 394–95). This means that the organism, when its needs are met, preserves in itself no trace of the inert synthesis which made this possible. If action is only the negation, by praxis, of the negation, need, "it is relative, transitory, commanded by life; it abolishes itself in life, which dissolves it in itself as it redissolves and reassimilates its inert-being" (II, 395).

The original and fundamental trait of action, then, is its evanescence. Of course its passive syntheses remain after the satisfaction of needs, to be used again, "inertia being put in the service of life" (II, 396). These "absolute realities" are the objectification of action. "At the moment of success, the agent is both dissolved by the organism and preserved under form of passive synthesis by the inorganic; better, action, insofar as its inert result prolongs it, becomes the simple relationship of the 'mechanical slave' to the organism . . ." (II, 395–96).

Sartre does not forget his earlier analysis of the practico-inert and its deviating effect. Certainly, insofar as these "realizations" are posed for themselves and lead to modification of other men and objects, "the action of each and all is reconditioned by its own products . . ." (II, 396). Looking at this prospect with his new emphasis, he now speaks of how we must cope with it by readjusting, overseeing, or correcting.

Action Is Not Autonomous

But action, "absorbed by its end, is, on the contrary, supported, prolonged, posed for itself and developed by the very demands of its products" (II, 396). And the agent himself is one of these products. He diverges more and more from the organism he is and serves. He takes on his own structures, his own needs, his own *exis*, as if he were entirely separate from the organism. As the division of labor progresses, his actions may have less and less to do with the reproduction of life—thus posing "his own end as untranscendable, his own objectification as his very reality" (II, 396). For example, in exploitative societies, some members of the ruling class give themselves to totally gratuitous activities, such as the arts or sports. Action seems totally autonomous, radically separate from the organism undertaking it.

Sartre concludes with five extremely dense, numbered observations which refute the apparent autonomy of action and its products and instead tighten their ontological relationship to human needs. This may seem a rather odd way of framing the *Critique*'s last pages until we recall that the ontological reflections were also *preceded* by five numbered observations—and that their thrust was precisely in the opposite direction! In short, in spite of the fact that volume two does not follow Sartre's plan, was never finished, and was withheld from publication during his lifetime, even its most difficult part has a remarkable coherence and, indeed, ends with a surprising sense of resolution.

Earlier, Sartre emphasized the deviating circularity of praxis-process, while now he attacks any autonomy claimed for the product of praxis. In concluding by firmly rooting praxis in need, he will place decisive boundaries on the deviation of praxis-process. This will have far-reaching consequences for his analysis of the Soviet Union. In a powerful climactic argument, then, the *Critique* suggests that any freezing of the dialectic can only be temporary, insisting that dialectical reason will always rise beyond its products.

First, "the action which is posed for itself is reduced to producing a passive synthesis: the absolute end it gave to itself, in fact, defines it rigorously . . ." (II, 397).

Second, the agent of this action becomes defined by this passive synthesis, which both engenders positive reason and reflects back the inorganic image of the agent's organism. In cutting itself adrift from its end, action would destroy any point of view making it possible to prefer *this* to that.

Third, the world of ends-in-themselves has no sufficiency of being and can only exist on a twofold basis: "the perpetuation of the organism as the *transcendent end of action*, the dialectic itself as law of creative transcendence of all these means toward the goal and as dissolving in itself all inert syntheses" (II, 397).

The Practico-Inert Revisited

In the fourth point, four pages long, Sartre looks at the practico-inert for the first time through what I have been suggesting are the new lenses of the final pages of volume two. The products of action, as we know, themselves impose antihuman demands on future action, deviating it from its original goal. We have seen in Stalinism, for example, the Revolution's deviation in order to save itself in specific historical conditions, and its consequent subjection to the very conditions it creates. The structured inertia it produces becomes a *new* and autonomous set of ends to which future praxis is alienated. This analysis, we recall, was the structural basis for deep pessimism about the Soviet future.

Now, however, in returning to the practico-inert, Sartre presents a more solid basis for hope as he explores what precisely it means to speak, in industrial societies, of man living for the machine. He does so by repeating the argument he has been developing for the past dozen pages, but now in relation to the practico-inert. Both it and its weight on us are possible for one reason and one reason only: "*at bottom [foncièrement]* the totality of the economic process and the organization of work *are related to the conservation of the organism*" (II, 397–98). The point is not that economic crises may occur, or that capitalists care about the lives of their workers, but simply that "neither the practico-inert, nor oppression, nor exploitation, nor *this* alienation would be possible if the immense and heavy social and economic machine were not supported, conditioned, and set in motion *by needs*" (II, 398). The worker is willing to sell his labor power only for one reason: to live, in an environment of scarcity. *This* is why he obeys the machines.

To be sure, even after the worker's vital needs are met, practico-inert conditioning substitutes itself for organic demands, just as the well-fed, well-housed, and well-clothed manufacturer continues to pursue *his interest*, obeying the logic of his property. Sartre's key point is that the very basis of "interest," in *everyone*, is the need to survive. In the world of scarcity the generalized survival-urgency is communicated to the machines themselves. The equivalence of human agent and machine is based on the ever-more complex pursuit of their "always identical and untranscendable end: the perpetuation of life" (II, 399).

Consider a social revolution, which stems from the contradictions between existing forms of the practico-inert:[13] revolutionary struggles break out *"in the name of need."* In 1789 structural contradictions took on their explosive force and led to the replacement of one ruling class by another "because the people lacked bread" (II, 399). The fantasy that human acts might be purer and more rigorous if wholly divorced from need is the opposite of the truth: without need we do not even have "the dream of acting" (II, 399). With this underlying urgency Sartre reaches the basis of historical materialism: a theoretically autonomous sector of activity may indeed by governed by its own laws, but these in turn reflect a praxis born out of need.

Sartre now clearly reveals the links between each step of his argument.

> Scarcity lived in interiority by the organ is the inorganic being produced as negative determination of the organism: and this lacuna, insofar as the entire organism is modified by it, *is need*; but need, in turn, insofar as posing its suppression as absolute end through the inorganic milieu, is *the materiality of action*, its reality and its basis, its substance, its urgency. By need, the individual, whoever he may be and however gratuitous may be his act, acts under pain of death, directly or indirectly, for him or for others. (II, 400)

This threat, grasped above all by historical materialism, is the real secret of the practico-inert.

Action and Dialectic

Finally, Sartre turns to the ontological status of action. It lies between the organic and the inorganic as their mediation, laying claim to an entirely new status, which only the dialectic can grasp. We have already seen that the inert is characterized by permanence, the organism by repetition, and action by its transitoriness. If action casts aside the ordinarily cyclical character of organic life, it keeps its goal, the organism's restoration. Yet it does this in a *noncyclical* way because it rearranges the elements of the practical field and in so doing transforms the organism. This irreversibility—meaning that a *different* environment and a *different* organism are created—is the ontological status of action. Because its purpose lies beyond itself, in the organism's restoration, action itself can never be a unity but only a *unification* whose meaning points ahead.

Certainly this "alienating arrest, the stasis of action, can come from

---

13. Under "forms of the practico-inert," Sartre includes both productive forces and production relations. The second seem more clearly practico-inert: a historically produced structural dimension within which the forces function.

the social regime . . ." (II, 401). Labor may be divided in such a way that no worker totalizes it and everyone does minute and elementary tasks. "The man whom the regime defines *in his reality as agent* by the number of needles he places per hour on the dashboard dials and, *in his organism*, by the means it gives him to satisfy his need is alienated and reified; he is an inert synthesis" (II, 401). But these states are contradicted by the motor of the entire process, workers' praxis. In its essence, praxis cannot be limited to *that*.

In the end, the logic of the process and the principle of understanding—the dialectic—reasserts itself as what it always was, the essence of human action. As such it cannot be suppressed. "*Action* struggles against its own alienation by matter (and by men, it goes without saying) insofar as it is dialectically posed as the unifying temporalization which transcends and conserves in itself every form of *unity*" (II, 401).

Sartre's discussion reaches its climax in his last words, as he concludes with a ringing reaffirmation of dialectical reason that insists on the inherent impossibility of human products' triumphing over human praxis:

> Thus the dialectic appears as that which is truly irreducible in action: between inert synthesis and functional integration, it affirms its ontological status of temporalizing synthesis, which is unified in unifying and in order to unify itself and which never lets itself be defined by the result—whatever it is—that it has just obtained. (II, 401)

Comment: The Positive Purpose of Our Product

In this ontological discussion, we may note, the *Critique* has moved in a fundamentally new direction. Until now, Sartre had been above all concerned with the logic of circularity—of various praxes-processes of alienation and deviation. He had explored how human products rise up against the praxis that produces them, to the very point of transforming the human intentions themselves. In this sense the deep structure of Sartre's analysis generated or traced an undertow against which his positive hopes for the unfreezing of the dialectic in the Soviet Union could scarcely be sustained. Now, after shifting from history to ontology—thus in moving to what is both a far more abstract and far more fundamental level of reflection—Sartre has limited circularity by indicating the positive human purpose of the material world created by praxis.

Having begun this discussion of ontology with need, he affirms that this starting point remains inscribed in our tools, our action, and our organism itself. Although this affirmation comes too late to affect the *Cri-*

tique's main lines of development, it is of major importance in Sartre's thought.

His first discussion of tools was in *The Emotions*, where he talked about the world humans had created without reference to its purpose of meeting our needs: "This world might be compared to the moving of the coin-making machines on which the ball-bearings are made to roll; there are paths formed by rows of pins, and often, at the crossing of the paths, holes are pierced through. The ball-bearings must travel across a determined route, taking determined paths and without falling into the holes. This world is *difficult*."[14] When Sartre returns to the problem in his postwar writings, most notably in "Materialism and Revolution," it is with a somewhat altered perspective. The world of labor now contains a "liberating relationship" between man and things.[15]

Until this point the *Critique* had actually returned to Sartre's original pessimism, and indeed, with its discussion of the practico-inert, had sought the structural root of this *difficulty*. Its major shortcoming in this respect was to not sufficiently appreciate the original purpose of this overwhelming world of tools.[16] Now, however, Sartre has accomplished just this. Were he able to return with it to his account of Stalinism, a new perspective might be possible on the Soviet Union. Its deviation from Bolshevism could be fully and explicitly acknowledged, on the one hand, along with whatever possibilities for a humane socialism lie within, and might be regenerated by, the material basis of Soviet life.

More generally, could these ontological reflections be incorporated into the whole of the *Critique* project, a different sense of history might emerge—one which removes the negative tonality from the practico-inert and casts it, appropriately, as positive *as well as* negative deposit of human praxis. Partial victories in the struggle for human dignity achieve a practico-inert status in laws and institutions, as do praxes-processes of societal survival. The practico-inert thus becomes material guarantor as well as obstacle: that a specific level of equality and dignity has been won by everyone; that workers and women have certain rights; that blacks will not be reenslaved; that the poorest members of society will be fed.

Of course, in suggesting this I am taking a full step away from Sartre. His emphasis even in these last pages has not been on a *positive* practico-

14. *Esquisse d'un théorie des émotions* (Paris, 1939); trans. Bernard Frechtman, *The Emotions: Outline of a Theory* (New York, 1948), 58.

15. "Materialism and Revolution," 240. In *What Is Literature?* Sartre talks negatively about the world of tools because it requires that we substitute "a set succession of traditional procedures for the free invention of means" ("Qu'est-ce que la littérature?", *Situations* 1 [Paris, 1948]; trans. Bernard Frechtman, *What Is Literature?* [New York, 1949], 41).

16. See my *Jean-Paul Sartre*, 252–71.

inert, but on the persistence of human needs beneath the practico-inert. Even here, at the conclusion, Sartre is still *opposing* praxis to the practico-inert. Only it is a praxis which, being anchored in need, refuses to submit finally and fully to its products. Nevertheless, his concluding interest in its human purpose gives us reason to cast a whole new light on the world of the practico-inert.

8 Conclusion:

The Sartrean Dialectic and the Crisis of Marxism

Has the *Critique* met its goals by the end of volume two? Sartre himself thought not, and concluded in 1969 that the volume would "probably never appear."[1] In the words of his bibliographers Michel Contat and Michel Rybalka, "Sartre was interrupted when he realized that the elaboration of the second volume—which, it may be recalled, was supposed to reach the level of concrete history—required a sum of readings and historical research representing the work of a lifetime for a philosopher, or, for a group of researchers, the work of many years."[2] Any appraisal must also bear in mind that Sartre himself saw fit to publish only a small extract, in English, during his lifetime and that, in the words of André Gorz, "the manuscript is not only unfinished but unpolished, had never been reread and is full of wandering (though interesting) digressions and excursions sometimes leading nowhere."[3]

Yet volume two follows directly on the heels of the published portion of the *Critique*, continues its very same analyses from the very same problematic, and comes to a halt with the original goals still in mind, not long after volume one's appearance, never to be resumed. In this sense it is rather unlike Sartre's unfinished ethics, attempted anew at various stages of his career.[4] Although Gorz's appraisal is certainly correct, we have also seen that much of volume two is classic Sartre, and deserves wide reading and discussion. It concludes with a certain sense of closure, even if by the end its original goals have not been met. In spite of its uncompleted form, the entire *Critique* comprises a single coherent

1. Interview quoted in Michel Contat and Michel Rybalka, *Les Ecrits de Sartre* (Paris, 1970), 481.
2. Ibid., 340.
3. Letter to the author, September 14, 1980.
4. What we have of his first efforts, *Cahiers pour une morale*, differs markedly from his later efforts. See Sonia Kruks, "Sartre's *Cahiers pour une morale*," *Social Text*, Winter/Spring 1986; and Robert Stone and Elizabeth Bowman, "Unpublished Dialectical Ethics of Sartre: A Summary," ibid.

work of over 500,000 words. Moreover, its finished studies, the vastness of the project, its complexity, and the great stakes assure us that the *Critique*'s achievement and failures will be debated for years to come.

There are, of course, many possible frames for evaluating Sartre's achievement (for example, the usefulness of the *Critique* for the social sciences), but it seems fitting, at the end of this exposition and commentary, to return to the questions with which we began. Sartre himself set the *Critique*'s task as being to validate historical materialism, and this issued in volume two's goal of understanding history and societies as "totalizations without a totalizer." The larger project, we have also seen, takes on its specific meaning within Merleau-Ponty's break with Marxism, *Les Temps Modernes*, and Sartre. This conflict between philosophers—deliberately muted from the one side if not the other, issuing in two books on dialectic and an unfinished manuscript—contains one of the major debates of the twentieth century. Accordingly, from the first page of volume one to the last page of volume two, the *Critique* is self-consciously bound up with the fate of Marxism. Sartre's strict concern, to establish the validity and parameters of dialectical reason, cannot be separated from the project of saving historical materialism from the acid bath of post-Marxism. To do so, Sartre must rescue historical materialism from the agnosticism that sees history as detotalizing as indifferently as it totalizes, that sees praxes but not trends, that taboos revolutionary visions.

For the *Critique* to meet its goals, then, means presenting a convincing argument for historical materialism in the face of post-Marxism. We have seen Merleau-Ponty reject Marxism on the most basic philosophical level, for pretending to base praxis on a historical truth, inscribing socialism in facts, claiming to root it in forces that are "already there." And we have seen Sartre set out the challenge this rejection lays before him: to show human praxis as the source of the Meaning and Truth of History.[5] In other words, accepting some sense of historical truth, of tendencies and structures "already there," while in turn showing their source in praxis. Sartre sought to meet Merleau-Ponty's challenge by transcending *both* terms of the debate. He sought to develop a Marxism that answered Merleau-Ponty by linking orthodox Marxism's sense of the world's weight, unreified, with Western Marxism's sense of subjective praxis, solidified. This massive undertaking has entailed at least four major interconnected and overlapping projects in volume two.

5. "We must show how it is possible," we have seen him say, speaking of the dialectic, "for it to be both a *resultant*, though not a passive average, and a *totalizing force*, thought not a transcendent fate, and how it can continually bring about the unity of dispersive profusion and integration" (I, 154; 131; 36).

First, Sartre has tried to clarify dialectical reason as a mode of thought, and to show why it is more adequate for grasping human reality than its alternatives. Second, he has tried to show that the dialectic is indeed the logic of history, even in its deviations. Third, he has sought to demonstrate, through analysis after analysis, that all deposits, structures, trends, and other substantive social and historical "realities" are in fact practico-inert deposits or processes whose source is human praxis. And finally, building on this last direction, he has taken on the burden of demonstrating society and history as being "totalizations without a totalizer."

The Critical Dialectic Clarified

How far has Sartre gone toward fulfilling these purposes by the end of this unfinished manuscript? Obviously, the *Critique* gives out before completing the final goal; but it goes remarkably far toward meeting the other three. Sartre leaves us with some of the decisive starting points of an adequate philosophically based social theory even while failing to answer its main question.

First, he leaves us with a series of descriptions of dialectical reason as overarching comprehension which integrates its antagonists into a larger framework. Sartre's intention of establishing the dialectic "as the universal method and universal law of anthropology" (I, 138; 118; 18) while "being the movement of History and of knowledge" meant first clearly distinguishing the dialectic from its contending modes of thought (I, 141; 120; 20). The dialectic is not, Sartre tells us again and again in both volumes, analytical reason, positivist reason, instrumental reason, or sociology. The urgency of Sartre's criticism of these kindred forms of thought is best conveyed by his remark, near the end of volume one, that analytical reason is a "permanent threat to the human" (I, 790; 668; 710). As bourgeois thought, Sartre insists, it is the intellectual principle and ideological reflection of a society that separates human beings in order to oppress and dominate them (I, 877; 741; 800).[6] The dialectic, on the other hand, places the human being and human projects at the center of human thought, indeed, roots the thinking in the projects.

Analytical reason first appears in volume two under the guise of the abstract calculations of military schools analyzing a battle, sifting through the possible strategies to find the single best one. Its perspective on the

6. It is worth noting that Sartre had first sounded this theme well before becoming a Marxist, in the introduction to the very first issue of *Les Temps Modernes*, where he cites the "spirit of analysis" as characteristic of bourgeois society ("Présentation des *Temps Modernes*," *Situations* II [Paris, 1948], 17–18).

human condition is external: first, in seeing any struggle from the outside, as if every combatant were not situated and committed, and second, in viewing every possible action as if conditioned in exteriority rather than as praxis interiorizing and reexteriorizing its situation. Likewise, our boxers would be seen from the outside by analytical reason, as it watched them undertake a given strategy chosen from dozens of possibilities, with equal indifference to their individual projects.

Analytical reason is further external as it seeks to break down its object into factors, parts, or components. It *separates*. Then, from the outside, with no self-consciousness about what it is doing or why, it reconnects what it has separated. This multiple exteriority of analytical reason is also visible in one of its characteristic products, the *concept*, which is abstracted from singular objects and presented as if it were external and prior to them. The "model" is the sociological version of this—for example as applied in ahistorical presentations of "the Soviet model of industrialization." Such a "model" is often studied as the response to the equally unsituated "need" to industrialize, not by looking at the specific logic of a specific society at a specific moment in history. All such approaches posit a transcendent reality *served* by individual praxis or *exemplified* by singular individuals, separating both project and comprehension from *these* historical individuals who undertake either.

In reflecting on the Soviet experience, abstract and desituated thought would look for alternatives to Stalin without considering the historical specificity of *that* experience. Thus, for example, it may search for another dictator to accomplish the same tasks, perhaps with greater flexibility and less brutality. At its most intolerable it proposes a perfectly abstract being—the "angel"—capable of doing all that "needed" to be done without any of Stalin's specific personal idiosyncrasies. This approach, of course, reads the project from the outside, much as analytical reason tries to read all significations from the outside, cut off from the *sens*, or meaning, intentionally put into a given object by praxis.

Dialectical reason, on the contrary, grasps its object from the inside, first tracing it as a specific praxis responding to the specific exigencies of a specific situation. Sartre stresses the impossibility of a desituated, wholly "objective" account of social reality as strongly as he rejects any adherence to fixed universal laws.[7] Even our knowledge of the dialectic is a specific praxis, situated in a given history. The dialectic's main traits, then, are its praxis-rooted interiority and specificity. But these traits are not those of any dialectic, but distinguish the "critical" Sartrean dialectic

7. See the illuminating summary of the elements of dialectical Marxism—which, however, makes no mention of Sartre—in Warren, *The Emergence of Dialectical Theory*, 65–89.

from the "dogmatic" or "transcendental" dialectic which Merleau-Ponty resignedly saw as the natural terminus of Marxism.

The transcendental dialectic is as blind to praxis as is analytical reason. Thus we have seen Sartre fully agree with Merleau-Ponty's perception of orthodox Marxism. In the hands of Engels and Plekhanov, or even Trotsky, it imposes an a priori logic *on* human beings, whether of history, class, world revolution, or some other abstract universal. It, too, would see our boxers externally, making them little more than the expression of some larger social reality which gives them their identity. And it too would see itself as looking at the world with the eye of God, detached, objective without subjectivity, universal. Engels, for example, takes dialectic as a transcendent law which imposes itself on individuals, much as Plekhanov, like Hegel, sees the large process of history designating the individuals who carry it out.

Sartre again and again attacks as his special bête noir, implied or even explicit in much orthodox Marxism, the appeal to a "hyperorganism"— a general social entity moving on its own which somehow determines individuals and their action. He rejects this as strongly as Merleau-Ponty had rejected the notion of a truth inscribed in being which praxis or the Party need only "realize." Sartre's rejection, however, seeks to validate an historical materialism which does not lean on a hyperorganism.

In carrying out this goal, Sartre resolves the original antagonism between analytical, instrumental, or positivist reason and dialectical reason—not, as Lévi-Strauss mistakenly argued, by equalizing the two,[8] but by strictly subordinating the former to the latter. Sartre sees the dialectic as the master logic, situated within praxis and capable of visualizing the entire social praxis-process in all its displacements and deviations. Analytical reason is not false, then, but only limited. This "first machine" is properly only a tool of the dialectic, one that ignores its own premises and historical specificity, is blind to its being situated. Its mistake is to try to view the human condition from the outside, as if it had a privileged position which allowed absolute knowledge. It presumes too much, then, in trying to pretend that its technical and external vision of an instrumentalized process conveys the whole of human reality.

The Critical Dialectic Criticized

Drawn together, Sartre's scattered discussions present an important clarification of the dialectic as a mode of comprehension. He would

8. Claude Lévi-Strauss, *The Savage Mind* (Chicago, 1966), 245–69.

agree that there is a use for the military schools' analyses of battles, just as there is a use for "models" and "essences." But, he would argue, like machine building on the one hand and its guiding human purpose on the other, these modes of thought are used *by* a larger dialectical reason whose premises and purview stretches far beyond their limits. Certainly the test of this reason lies in its announced ability, to illuminate the battles, models, and machines—indeed all the details of histories and societies—in relation to the praxes-processes which envelop and make use of them and which they constantly escape and redefine.

But before assessing how far Sartre has met his other goals, I want to underscore a major problem of his definition of the dialectic. We have encountered a certain amount of confusion in his single-minded emphasis on specificity as the dialectic's distinctive trait. Again and again we have seen Sartre oppose the particular plane of existence to a hypothetical, and presumably unreal, general plane. He attacks the general plane as pretending to autonomy, as imposing itself upon individuals, and ultimately as the alienated product of individual praxis. Sartre's quite appropriate attack on hyperorganicism and dogmatic Marxism leads to a systematic rejection of the entire plane of generality and a crude defense of individual singularity as the only plane of existence. In so doing, Sartre is throwing out the baby with the bath water.

But we have seen Sartre, no less than any philosopher, think with and in terms of such generalities—for example, the most general realm of being-in-itself—even while fiercely trying to explicitly deny them. Sartre has again and again shown that he thinks in terms of general characteristics—whether of boxing as a whole or the notions of incarnation and contradiction or antilabor—both because this is the only possible way to think and study and because he seeks to know the general structures of another general praxis-process, the dialectic.

For Sartre, as well as for Aristotle criticizing Plato's independent world of ideas, general knowledge of the general plane of things is decisive for any conceivable comprehension, let alone praxis. Certainly as Aristotle already knew, this does not mean that this general plane has a substantive existence separate from its concrete incarnations. But, equally, as Aristotle also knew and Sartre repeatedly demonstrates, no concrete singularity is conceivable which does not in some way partake of a whole network of generalities. If some forms of reason can discuss and analyze them as autonomous, to the point of Platonism's affirming their separate existence or "lazy Marxists" explaining all specifics from them, such misuse only confirms their status as a legitimate and abstractable plane of concrete reality.

There is no particular *as such* any more than there is a general *as such*. A totally specific being lacking general, socially communicable (and thus common) traits and structures would have no identity, would resemble a person without language, an object without meaning. A pure particularity, like a "world of boxing" made up only of other particularities, would be indecipherable, incomprehensible. For what we recognize and know and communicate in this specific object is a dimension which is nowhere and everywhere at once—its general features. They are indeed embodied here, and always only here or there or elsewhere (even if they can be thought abstractly as if they had only a mental existence). This means that the individual object or event is always general and particular at the same time. Both layers are absolutely necessary for there to be an individual, yet may be thought distinctly. Both are abstractions from the concrete reality which can be grasped, depending on our focus, as the individual-member-of-a-general-class or the species-embodied-in-each-of-its-members.

If Sartre is right in insisting that history and the dialectic are always specific, he makes them less comprehensible by rejecting the general structures operative in them and through which they are thought and comprehended. We have seen, for example, his rich concept of incarnation, deprived of any resort to the general, equivocate and confuse even as it illuminates.[9] But we have also seen that this animus in no way undermines Sartre's brilliant attempts to present the dialectic in action.

The Sartrean Dialectic in Action

If the dialectic is anything, it is above all the practical activity—the praxis—of specific individuals. In studying this activity, Sartre lays special stress on its encounter with and absorption of materiality, under conditions of scarcity, to the point where it becomes deviated from its original intentions and then deviates the intentions themselves. Indeed, the only explicit Sartrean "law" of dialectics is the "law of dialectical circularity." In Sartre's analysis our sense only grows of the dialectic as a tool of comprehension. Other modes of thought stand mute before the

9. Sartre is, after all, seeking a way of clarifying the *mediations* called for first by Merleau-Ponty and then in *Search for a Method*. But the project itself loses its meaning if analysis simply moves from a specific gathering of individuals—the society—to a specific individual. The decisive question, which he will triumphantly return to later, in the last volume of *The Family Idiot*, is how the specific individual absorbs and furthers the social environment within which he is situated. Of course, even there Sartre will answer this in a specific study, without explicitly clarifying the theoretical issues posed here. See my *Jean-Paul Sartre*, 343–52.

monstrosities of history such as "socialism in one country," forever missing the logic whereby opposites in conflict, mediated by the larger group, produce a grotesque result originally intended by neither. But Sartre uses the dialectic to illuminate the meaning and social purpose of an absurd, unintelligible, and inherently self-contradictory idea—as well as seeing how this idea is a praxis that went astray.

Beginning with the commitments and praxis of the Bolsheviks, say, in the mid-1920s, dialectical reason enables us to see not some abstract "best solution," but why *a specific* path evolved out of the contradictory situation Bolshevik praxis had created. The dialectic, then, is the logic of praxis—the specific praxis of specific individuals incarnating specific totalities in their action and being redefined by the specific results of their prior praxis. Because it connects rather than separates, it allows the most contradictory, indeed, absurd results to be linked with the intentions producing—and disavowing—them. The primary link illuminated by the Sartrean dialectic is between praxis and the inanimate matter in which it is inscribed, which absorbs, reflects, and alienates it.

One of Sartre's great achievements in volume two, in study after study, is to use the materialist dialectic to show, against both Hegel and dialectical materialism, how human praxis becomes deviated by its products. The "law of dialectical circularity," after all, is that matter determines human beings to the extent that humans determine matter. The point is not that praxis somehow becomes directed from outside by something material which remains exterior to it. Rather, and more profoundly, one praxis inscribes itself on the material world under specific, inhospitable conditions, and its successor encounters the very situation created by the first. Each praxis must then absorb into itself as its new situation, to be transcended by yet another step of praxis, the antihuman result it has generated. Thus the terms "interiorize" and "reexteriorize" are central to Sartre's dialectical lexicon. They emphasize the inability of any more purely external mode of thought to grasp the praxis-process of human action in the world. Even as praxis is inscribed in matter and deviated, it remains human: their intention, their practice, their project place human beings at the heart of the dialectic, and make its continuing law the transcending of the results of prior intention, practice, and project.

We have seen Sartre develop one of the great interpretations of the Bolshevik Revolution's fate. In it he presents the deviation of Bolshevism into Stalinism *in order to survive*. Aside from its importance for Soviet studies, this discussion traces what became of the dialectic in the hands of its first historical practitioners to take power. If the "totalizing activity of the world" had led to a "divorce of blind unprincipled praxis and sclerosed thought (I, 166; 141; 50)," Sartre's study shows how Bolshevism moved further and further from its original premises. While not discussing the dialectic as Stalin's frame of reference—and thus without exploring how the "dogmatic" dialectic was a necessary handmaiden in the praxis-process—Sartre traces the Revolution's deviation.

Can the post-Stalinist reordering be expected to lead to a revival of a historical dialectic leading back toward a less oppressive socialism? We have seen Sartre equivocate on this issue, while presenting ammunition for both sides. Strictly speaking, however, Sartre cannot answer this question by the end of volume two. Approaching it depends on having first answered at least two others: does history have a meaning, and can there be a totalization without a totalizer?

Praxis and Process: A Basis for Historical Materialism

Volume two's greatest accomplishment requires perhaps the least commentary, for it has already been anticipated by nearly the whole of volume one, although its full implications become clear only by the end of the manuscript. Beginning with his discussion of the group's taking on inertia to perpetuate itself—the pledge—Sartre describes the processes whereby praxis sediments inertial structures. Volume one traced each step from the group to the institution, then analyzed social classes and their interests along the same lines. Volume two first explores the praxes of incarnation and contradiction and conflicting praxes yielding a product, antilabor. Then Sartre traces the praxis-process leading to Stalinism.

In a sense, all other studies are preparatory to this one, for it is by placing the dialectic in history and tracing the development of a specific praxis-process that Sartre answers Merleau-Ponty. He develops the basis for a genuinely historical materialism—an outlook neither abstractly subjective, as Merleau-Ponty described Western Marxism, nor abstractly objective, as he discussed orthodox Marxism. He explains indeed the ways in which tendencies can be lodged in the facts themselves without thereby ceasing to be praxis.

Sartre goes so far as to show that the manipulated masses must actively maintain their very passivity. Indeed, under Stalin the Russian workers' praxis remains human even where it is confined to retotalizing what has already been laid out by the sovereign. Positivist historians misread this, seeing only active ruling forces acting on passive masses, but in fact the dialectic's first principle of praxis illuminates the way in which active masses are treated as inert physical forces whose free action must be regenerated for the leadership's goals.

By the end of volume two, Sartre, after having rethought the ontology of *Being and Nothingness* to place praxis, based on need, at its center, has convincingly demonstrated that if the dialectic is anything, it is human practical activity. He has achieved the monumental breakthrough of finding praxis at the basis of structure, everywhere the eye can see. In studying this activity he has laid special stress on its encounter with and absorption of materiality, under conditions of scarcity, to the point where it becomes deviated from its original intentions, and then deviates the intentions themselves. But even then, all inertial social structures, all processes, are created and maintained *at every moment* by praxis.

"How," we have seen Sartre ask at the beginning of volume one, "can praxis in itself be an experience of necessity and of freedom, since neither of these, according to classical logic, can be grasped in an empirical process" (I, 193; 165; 79)? By the end of volume two, Sartre has answered this most difficult question by demonstrating praxis as an a priori basis of a variety of its inertial deposits. Again and again, throughout the *Critique*, we experience praxis cohering into structure, inertia dissolving back into the praxis from whence it came. Here is where Sartre makes good on his promise of seeing human activity, however deviated, as the human world's source. He gives us the ability both to see praxis *and* its freezing into structure—in one and the same act, in one and the same process, in one and the same product.

The Totalization without a Totalizer Revisited

"If dialectical rationality really is a logic of totalization," Sartre asked early in volume one, "how can History—that swarm of individual destinies—appear as a totalizing movement . . ." (I, 193; 165; 79)? While Sartre does not directly tackle the theme of the totalization without a totalizer by the end of the *Critique*, volume two takes a number of steps to prepare the discussion. In fact, its first third carefully prepares the way until, preoccupied with the Bolshevik Revolution, Sartre begins to ask other questions. Each small step of his early discussion deals with conflicts which totalize—the boxers, the subgroups, Trotsky versus Stalin. In fact, the formal fruits of this study of conflicts sustained and mediated by larger social entities—the "world of boxing," the group, the Bolshevik Party—were the themes of incarnation and contradiction. They specifically clarify the relationship between particularities and larger entities.

Sartre did not move beyond these preparations into a full-scale study of the totalization without a totalizer. In fact, by the time we reach the end of the book, we cannot fail to notice that much of Sartre's exposition of the dialectic takes the opposite path to the one he announced. The Soviet Union under Stalin follows a very particular dialectic: that of a society needing to be totalized by an individual totalizer and thus increasingly terrorized and totalitarian. The single specific totalization of envelopment developed in the *Critique* has deliberately placed itself in the hands of an individual sovereign, so that the conflicting mass of praxes would not fatally fracture their unity. And so, after preparing explicitly to treat a fragmented and conflictual society and history, Sartre has wound up studying a case of a single comprehensible praxis-process. Whatever the dialectic *might be* then, as a "totalizing movement" unifying a "swarm of individual destinies," the particular one Sartre leads us through is the one terminating in Stalin.

He does, however, leave hints of the paths such an analysis might follow, and a few pages of notes. We may recall, first, that his reference to a boxing match at the time of the Munich crisis clearly suggests that historical events are totalized freely, spontaneously, individually, and collectively—without a totalizer. Secondly, his reference to the Bach fugue conveying the flavor of the ancien régime, as well as to boxing in general, suggests that societies' histories, structures, tensions, and contradictions are totalized and singularized—incarnated—without resort to a single sovereign praxis. Third, his discussion of "one world" suggests the diachronic destination of history without a single person guiding it: toward larger and larger totalizations, which, eventually, become a single vast totalization of totalizations. Plurality is slowly dissolved, universality slowly achieved.[10] Finally, among the notes he made in 1961–62 we can find twelve pages of theoretical reflections on "totalization in nondictatorial societies," followed by four pages of thoughts on one such society, Venice (II, 436–51).

The Sartrean Dialectic among Others

Provocative as these suggestions might be, however, they are only that— suggestions. Sartre broke off work on the *Critique* without sighting his goal, and remained unable to secure historical materialism on a decisive front. As Sartre well knew, the key question of any social thought remains: Does a "cunning of reason" or some other force, logic, or unifying

10. This is a strictly formal analysis, suggesting no value judgment—just as Sartre's earlier discussion of *progress* in the liquidation of subgroups suggests only a fuller unification of the group, not its improvement. One world is not a better world. Does Sartre fall back on unification as progress because he refuses to philosophically incorporate other terms of value judgment?

power give direction and meaning to human history and to fragmented and conflictual societies?

At the beginning of volume two we have seen Sartre clearly lay out what is at stake: "Marxism is rigorously true if history is totalization; it is no longer so if human history is decomposed into a plurality of different histories." We are still on an a priori level, but the abstract principle is decisive: Do the conflicts totalize or are they produced by the totalizing movement of the whole? If this can be demonstrated, then "the materialist dialectic as movement of history and of historical understanding need only be proven by the facts it illuminates . . ." (II, 25).

It is possible to "solve" the problem in advance by stipulating a single force—God, Reason, hyperorganism, Progress or collective unconscious that somehow rules social life. Sartre appropriately attacks the idea of a being, whether Society or History or Progress, which acts *on* us and *through* us independently of our own projects. Yet Hegel was also right to raise the troubling question of "history as the slaughter-bench at which the happiness of peoples, the wisdom of States, and the virtue of individuals have been sacrificed . . ."[11] His "cunning of reason" suggested a distinction between the conscious intentions of individuals and a larger process working itself out through their uncomprehending and colliding actions.

If this is the main thrust of Hegel's dialectic of history, what is Sartre's? By comparing Sartre to Hegel, Marx, Stalin, and a contemporary of Sartre of equal stature, Herbert Marcuse, we can better understand his project and its thrust. First, we may ask, what meaning of history does the dialectic produce? And second, who is it that produces it? For Hegel the meaning of history was the progressive overcoming of alienation and the realization of freedom. Hegel's dialectic was operated by an agent, Reason unfolding in history, which was synonymous with God. For Marx the dialectic led to the classless society, and the agency for accomplishing this was the proletariat. According to Stalin the goal of the dialectic was *this* particular society, the Soviet Union, "where the social ownership of the means of production fully corresponds to the social character of the process of production . . ."[12] For him the agency was "the party of the proletariat." Marcuse, writing with Walter Benjamin's hope "for the sake of those without hope,"[13] identified as agency those on the margin within advanced industrial society and at its periphery.[14] He saw *nega-*

11. Georg Wilhelm Friedrich Hegel, *Reason in History* (Indianapolis, 1953), 27.
12. Joseph Stalin, *Dialectical and Historical Materialism* (New York, 1940), 32.
13. Herbert Marcuse, *One-Dimensional Man* (Boston, 1964), 257.
14. Marcuse himself found it necessary to explore the deformation of Marxism in the Soviet Union. See *Soviet Marxism* (New York, 1961).

tion as the dialectic's key theme. His emphasis denied the transcendent unfolding of Progress, and he refused to identify the dialectic with any traditional social force. But he also envisaged a free society no longer dominated by the struggle for survival or domination, in which, for the first time in history, the full and harmonious development of each individual would be the goal.

Sartre's emphasis and agency contrast with every one of these thinkers. It should be clear that the *Critique* is far more agnostic and less certain about the shape of history than any of the others. Unlike the others, Sartre is *asking* about the meaning of history, not advocating a meaning. Progress and History are as problematic at the end of the *Critique* as at the beginning.[15] As far as the agency is concerned, Sartre leaves us with two. Formally speaking, the center of Sartre's dialectic is the particular individual whoever he or she may be, with whom all praxis begins and ends. The agency Sartre focuses on in his historical study is the revolutionary party-cum-bureaucracy whose praxis is successively displaced and deviated to the sovereign individual.

Perhaps Sartre's agents differ so from the others because he is not presenting a vision of history or a projection of social transformation but a *critique of dialectical reason*. He seeks to establish the terrain and limits of the dialectic, in order to develop the a priori analysis that will then permit historical materialism to be validated. Thus even if his Marxist-inspired inquiry into the meaning of history cannot help but be a substantive one, and can scarcely be separated from real forces and events, the core of Sartre's pursuit is *meta*theoretical in character, and must be judged accordingly.

Theory Separated from Praxis?

Even so, we must pause to note how remote Sartre's general project of carrying out a *critique* of dialectical reason would sound to the Lukács of *History and Class Consciousness*. If "materialist dialectic is a revolutionary dialectic"[16] there must be a "necessary connection" between theoretical consciousness and political action. Lukács insists—as Sartre does not—that the essence of the dialectic "is inseparable from the 'practical and critical' activity of the proletariat . . ." (20).

For Lukács to inquire about the dialectic is to ask about the practical activity of the proletariat: "If the meaning of history is to be found in the

15. In fact, his 1961–62 notes contain twenty-four pages of largely inconclusive notes on progress. (II, 410–33).
16. Georg Lukács, "What Is Orthodox Marxism?" *History and Class Consciousness* (Cambridge, Mass., 1970), 2. Further references to this work will be by page number only.

process of history itself and not, as formerly, in a transcendental, mytho-
logical or ethical meaning foisted on to recalcitrant material, this presupposes a proletariat with a relatively advanced awareness of its own
position, i.e. a relatively advanced proletariat, and, therefore, a long preceding period of evolution" (22).

Even his eventual antagonist, Merleau-Ponty, had agreed with Lukács
that the Marxist dialectic is inseparable from the class struggle. For
Lukács its revolutionary character becomes distorted out of shape by
any effort to make it into an a priori and universal method of comprehension independent of the "self-knowledge, both subjective and objective, of the proletariat at a given point in its evolution . . ." (23). Lukács
seems to rule out, a generation in advance, any kind of *critique* of the
dialectic:

> All attempts to deepen the dialectical method with the aid of
> "criticism" inevitably lead to a more superficial view. For "crit-
> icism" always starts with just this separation between method
> and reality, between thought and being. And it is just this
> separation that it holds to be an improvement deserving of
> every praise for its introduction of true scientific rigor into
> the crude, uncritical materialism of the Marxian method. Of
> course, no one denies the right of "criticism" to do this. But if
> it does so we must insist that it will be moving counter to the
> essential spirit of dialectics. (4)

The Lukács of 1919 would certainly regard the *Critique* in this light.
After all, the totalizing character of reality is precisely what is in question for Sartre. In this sense Sartre even tends to separate the dialectic as
method from the dialectic as content—the tools of dialectical reason are
developed in volume one *in order to then* be deployed in volume two for
determining whether history is dialectical. He seeks to construct a universal and a priori understanding of the formal conditions of history,
one which places praxis, but not yet the proletariat or the class struggle,
at its center. In Lukács' optic, which views the dialectic by emphasizing
the unity of theory and practice and the transcendence of philosophy in
proletarian revolution, Sartre separates the dialectic from politics and
philosophy from the proletarian struggle. The Lukács of 1919 would see
him as regressively ascending to an intolerable level of abstraction from
the real conditions of human life and conflict.

Such putative accusations might indeed be compelling had the Lukács
of 1919 remained as Deputy People's Commissar for Education in a victorious Hungarian Soviet Republic. Or had his Western Marxism become the official one rather than a youthful folly dutifully renounced

by a thinker who withdrew into literary and aesthetic questions. Lukács's thought itself became increasingly remote from the class and the struggle it had sought to serve. *In fact,* and not just in theory, theory became separated from practice. We have already seen Sartre explain this in *Search for a Method:* real history forced the break.

And yet neither Sartre nor Merleau-Ponty realized that dialectical Marxism kept developing, even in defeat. As Perry Anderson succinctly captures it,

> from 1924 to 1968, Marxism did not "stop," as Sartre was later to claim; but it advanced via an unending detour from any revolutionary political practice. The divorce between the two was determined by the whole historical epoch. At its deepest level, the fate of Marxism in Europe was rooted in the absence of any big revolutionary upsurge after 1920, except in the cultural periphery of Spain, Yugoslavia and Greece. It was also, and inseparably, a result of the Stalinization of the Communist Parties, the formal heirs of the October Revolution, which rendered impossible genuine theoretical work within politics even in the absence of any revolutionary upheavals—which it in turn contributed to prevent. The hidden hallmark of Western Marxism as a whole is thus that it is a product of *defeat.* The failure of the socialist revolution to spread outside Russia, cause and consequence of its corruption inside Russia, is the common background to the entire theoretical tradition of this period.[17]

The richest current of Marxist thought to develop in these years between Lukács and Sartre, that originating in the Institute for Social Research, first of Frankfurt, later of New York, bore the stamp of defeat. More academic than political from its founding in 1923, it reflected the enormous psychological distance from active politics of all those who, in Anderson's words, "were statutorily debarred from the revolutionary unity of theory and practice demanded by the eleventh thesis on Feuerbach."[18]

The *Critique* follows along this path, sometimes unconsciously, in fundamental ways a work of theory apart from praxis. But for a Sartre barred by its bureaucratized and Stalinized character from genuine interaction with a Communist Party or a workers' movement there were simply no alternative paths open. His thought was not, could not be, tied to a political force. His own political trajectory shows this definitively. In writing, as founder/editor of *Les Temps Modernes,* and as activ-

17. Perry Anderson, *Considerations on Western Marxism* (London, 1976), 42.
18. Ibid., 60.

ist, Sartre himself had tried again and again, without ever feeling successful, to connect thought and action.[19]

The fact of living amidst a blockage may well have limited Sartre's ability to search for the meaning of history demanded by his project. Indeed, Sartre followed his most intensive period of work on the *Critique* by writing *The Condemned of Altona*, a play whose hero, Franz, commits suicide because he is "unredeemable." Sartre himself pointed out the parallel between Franz and France during these years of the Algerian War of Independence. His eulogy of Merleau-Ponty and interviews at this time strike an even more despairing posture, climaxed by the self-lacerating anticolonialism of Sartre's remarkable preface to Frantz Fanon's *The Wretched of the Earth*, Sartre's Europe-castigating translation of Euripedes' *The Trojan Women*, and his general abandonment of Europe and turn toward the Third World.[20] Sartre's hope for a new political direction, which originally animated the *Critique*, seemed to fade even as he was struggling with it.

No doubt, Sartre was not as aware as were the members of the Institute for Social Research, for example, of the ways in which this alienation entered into his concepts themselves.[21] Aware or not, the pressures and absences removing the *Critique* from real struggles had been defined by history itself. Yet, years later, like the work of the more self-conscious Herbert Marcuse,[22] its analyses were to become political tools in his lifetime.[23]

Sartre's Individualism

The long- and short-term political situation may well have played a role in Sartre's dropping the *Critique* before finishing it.[24] So may have the project's daunting length. I would suggest that we have again and again

19. See my *Jean-Paul Sartre*, 157–79.

20. See ibid., 209–13; 303–8.

21. Marcuse's *One-Dimensional Man* is probably the best example of a social critique painfully aware of itself as lacking the agency which could make it historically true. Interestingly enough, it was published at almost the same time as *Critique I*.

22. For an excellent discussion of Marcuse's lifelong project of rethinking Marxism—and its political effect—see Douglas Kellner, *Herbert Marcuse and the Crisis of Marxism* (Berkeley, 1984).

23. This point is developed by Poster, *Sartre's Marxism*, as well as by Gorz, "Sartre and Marx."

24. In a similar vein, André Gorz suggests that "Sartre dropped *Critique, II* because at the time he didn't see what relevance his conclusions could have. They could not improve his relations with any existing social or political force or current" (Letter to the author, September 14, 1980).

come up against a third reason within the pages of the *Critique* itself. It is indicated in the last word of the complex debate between Sartre and Merleau-Ponty that has framed much of our discussion: Merleau-Ponty's fleeting comments, in notes for his unfinished *The Visible and the Invisible*, made upon reading the *Critique* in May and June of 1960. Sartre's philosophy of history, he noted there, "is finally a philosophy of 'individual praxis,' and so history is the meeting of this praxis with the inertia of 'worked matter,' of authentic temporality with what *congeals* it . . ."[25]

Merleau-Ponty sees the same problem in the *Critique* as he saw in Sartre's earlier work. Sartre himself foreshadowed the difficulty in the remainder of the question cited above, about how "that swarm of individual destinies" can "appear as a totalizing movement": "and how can one avoid the paradox that in order to totalize there must already be a unified principle, that is that only active totalities can totalize themselves" (I, 193; 165; 79)? In other words, can we really expect to add individuals to individuals and somehow *arrive at* a larger totality? Does the totality not have to be given in advance, at least in the form of a totalizing force, in order for it to appear at the end?

The *Critique* undertakes a remarkable gamble, namely that larger totalizations can be explained from Sartre's starting point of individual praxis. On the one hand, we repeatedly witness his unremitting attack on hyperorganisms and all forms of generality; on the other, a missionary desire to explain all of social reality through individual praxis. The result is both awe-inspiring and chaotic, penetrating and sloppy to the point of incoherence. And above all, it remains unfinished.

Why? I have shown elsewhere that Sartre's starting point of individual praxis, meant as a heuristic device, becomes the substantive core of the entire analysis. The problem is that as Sartre construes individual praxis, its intrinsic links with larger totalities can never appear. Without presuming these social links at the outset, as the very basis for the individual's identity, we will never understand how this individual, alone or as a member of a class in conflict, will naturally build larger totalities.[26] Sartre dismisses sociality just as he dismisses generality, brilliantly making use of it when necessary, but theoretically refuting it (as the hyperorganism) at every chance.

A totalization without a totalizer is inaccessible to Sartre's thought *on principle*. From the very beginning Sartre makes all social relations an external process, mediated by a Third who remains outside any two individuals in question. He mistakenly links the gardener and road mender

25. *Le Visible et l'invisible* (Paris, 1964), 312. See also 307.
26. See my *Jean-Paul Sartre*, 263–70.

only from the outside, as if they were not already linked—and inter-dependent—as members of the same society.[27]

The same objections hold whether we take the cogito or individual praxis as Sartre's starting point: the individual has had to use language to describe his or her experience; he or she has had to *become* an individual, in a certain society, shaped by a certain history; he or she has done this according to certain customs, traditions, legal codes, and other political and social practices; he or she has had to eat this morning before coming out to work or to contemplate, and this satisfaction of his or her survival needs took place according to a certain division of labor, at a certain level of the development of productive forces. All of this, every bit of it, is pre-supposed in the first Cartesian "Je pense" or the first act of striking the sod with a hoe.

The thinking individual may indeed discover his or her own thinking to be self-evident and therefore the correct starting point. But a second kind of self-evidence is also needed: the self-evidence of all that is *presup-posed* by the first thought or act. Without both self-evidences, of the cogito as well as the individual's concrete existence, our comprehension will fix itself to one or another of two equally inadequate polar opposites: the isolated individual or the hyperorganism. Without both "poles," the self-evident self-consciousness and the self-evident society, being given at the outset, there is no thought, no knowledge. Most "solutions" of the problem take hold of a single pole when the truth needs rather the ten-sion between the two, the constant going-and-coming of concrete reality.

In reacting against one side, Sartre tends to hypostatize the other, just as Plekhanov, for example, has reified its opposite. Sartre was blocked from seeing sociality by a number of factors, including his intense op-position to the "lazy Marxists" who imposed an artificial general knowl-edge without even studying events. His own "ideological interest"[28] in his earlier formulations and a network of commitments would have made it extraordinarily difficult to shift his thought to accommodate two *equal* starting points rather than a single principle of Cartesian self-evidence.[29] At the same time, Sartre was far too penetrating to rest easy, and, refusing to avoid the issue, actually took his starting point as the

27. See my critical analysis of *Critique I* in ibid., 265–70.

28. In the film by Alexandre Astruc and Michel Contat, Sartre himself discusses how he developed an "ideological interest" in the concepts and formulations of *Being and Noth-ingness* which he found it impossible to renounce upon his encounter with Marxism. See *Sartre by Himself*, 65–67.

29. Of course, we have seen him oppose his two major works to each other at the end of volume two, and reconcile them by finding *need* behind the principles of *Being and Nothing-ness*. The difficulty with *sociality* is that no acceptable sense of it was available to Sartre.

guiding thread to the other pole! As in the quote above, he is well aware of the issues: without positing it in advance, can one ever hope to arrive at the totalization? The answer turned out to be no, and it defeated the *Critique*.

A Corrective: Sociality without Hyperorganism

In all fairness, however, we might ask whether anyone else has solved these problems. Indeed, since Hegel, specifically within and against the orthodox Marxist tradition, no thinker mentioned above has even posed them. Even at its peak, as Perry Anderson points out, classical Marxism did not develop an answer to how contending subjects totalize social structures and history. It was precisely Sartre himself, in this monumental exploration containing Marxism itself in the balance, who articulated, moved toward, and then abandoned the problem of the totalization without a totalizer. His, as Anderson argues, was "the largest promise that perhaps any writer has ever given in the twentieth century" but, alas, "was not to be kept." [30] After noting that Sartre abandoned this urgent problem and never again reopened it, Anderson comments: "In that pregnant act of desistance, and the silence that ensued from it, much of the subsequent intellectual fate of the French Left was—we can now see—being decided." [31] Sartre's failure opened the door for the current wave of post-Marxism.

However, as I have suggested, the problem is not at all irresolvable. I would propose one major corrective to Sartre's formulations which would enable us to free his rich insights from their limitations: lodging the concept of sociality alongside his focus on individual praxis. With the wisdom of hindsight it is possible to extend, correct, and supplement Sartre, and to read a change back into his thinking which would render it more true to experience and adequate to our situation. Of course Sartre would fiercely argue against this, taking the "correction" as diametrically opposed to his most basic principles of explanation. Whether it is radical revision or correction is for the reader to judge: I will argue that accepting society as an equal pole to individuality preserves Sartre's basic perspectives and adds to their capacity for insight.

To begin with, we can build on approaches left to us by Sartre himself. Three key discussions give us the basis for an understanding, which Sartre's other commitments kept him from pursuing. First, we may recall from the discussion of subgroups and contradiction, that the conflict be-

30. *In the Tracks of historical Materialism*, 36.
31. Ibid., 37.

tween subgroups in a city under siege is resolved by the community *as a whole*. The conflict itself is carried out *within* a larger praxis, set of needs, traditions and goals, and is resolved by a kind of "diffuse mediation of the entire group." A totalization is effected here in which each subgroup is simultaneously a double agent: both of its own particular interest and of the larger group. The nonparticipants who mediate the conflict do so as members of the group, in effect totalizing spontaneously and collectively without being directed to do so by a single individual. Second, although Sartre does not develop this in as much detail, the antilabor produced by classes or subgroups in conflict is a collective product of the both of them. It, too, is a totalization without a totalizer.

A third theme, also undeveloped, appears in Sartre's 1961–62 notes: those of us working on, and struggling against each other within the same *practical field*, by this token enter into reciprocal relations with each other. This relationship is one of *immanence* "insofar as the impossibility of living together in the field is itself defined through the impossibility of not living together" (II, 443). We coexist, yet the field does not provide enough for all of us to coexist. Although Sartre does not say it explicitly, we fight each other *and* cooperate. "The whole question is that totalization is always indirect; it takes place through worked matter and with the mediation of men. It is because the practical field is a sealed unity that man recoils this sealed unity upon other men. In short, matter unites through the intermediary of man" (II, 448).

In each above case, although Sartre does not sufficiently develop this, conflict must move within an agreed-upon framework. Like our two boxers, antagonists appeal to common rules, values, institutions, traditions. They are part of a *larger collectivity*, which their own conflict in part or whole seeks to further *from their own point of view*. The same is true of the conflict that led to the Ateliers Nationaux in 1848: the French working-class leaders made this demand as a statement of *social* policy. Class conflict is not usually about separate groups seeking their own total victory and the other's death[32] but, rather, involves contention over larger social goals between mutually interdependent social groups. Sartre usually loses sight of this interdependency, this common institutional, legal, and historical mooring, although his examples cited above enable us to decipher it. This is what I describe as *sociality*.

I would suggest that societies resemble armies under siege, or revolutionary parties contesting a given praxis, *every bit as much as* they resemble two deadly enemies locked in violent conflict. The second is

32. This is, however, precisely how Sartre described class conflict in France after 1871. See *The Communists and Peace*, part three.

Sartre's usual way of seeing class conflict, the first my way of seeing the praxis-process of *antagonistic cooperation* in which we live most of our lives. Long before the French workers demanded Ateliers Nationaux from the French bourgeoisie of 1848, these two classes were joined by a—however antagonistic—praxis-process of cooperation to ensure their *common* survival.

More complex and basic than Sartre's description of the group's formation would suggest, this original societal activity of individuals and classes shapes, defines, and makes there be individuals with a common territory, economic processes, institutions, traditions, value structure, and language. These do not behave independently of the individuals involved—*the state* can only execute someone if specific individuals carry out the sentence. But neither do the individuals act independently of their social being. Indeed, even their rebellions and revolutions take place in terms of shared—equally social, even if not yet dominant— needs and convictions. Even a revolutionary wants to gain power over the collective social processes in order to reshape them.

Societies may be shifting collectivities of groups, series, and other social formations, but I would also suggest that their members share a residual sense of themselves, capable of being reactivated in times of danger, *as a group*, struggling together to assure their *common* survival. The true picture is an often contradictory and mystified one, because in a given country social survival has become indissolubly linked with social privilege and disadvantage, because external danger is often manipulated, along with a sense of a group under siege, as a means of sustaining privilege and disadvantage. Sartre's portrayal of class conflict is thus inadequate insofar as it projects the crude assertion of one group *over* another, rather than individual classes' contending claims upon both each other and the larger society, *mediated by* the larger society. Victories rarely involve sheer brute force; what they invoke, rather, are the very praxes-processes of mediation Sartre has described in his analysis of subgroups in conflict.

While Sartre is right to see it as nothing but all the individuals sustaining it, society does in fact take on a force of its own. Society is an "it" not only because it may oppose itself to us, but above all as *our collective being*. As ground and basis for each individual life—as internal and not merely external force—it gains a certain autonomy over each and every one of us. It functions independently of any particular individual. But *not as a hyperorganism*. Like a species, it will no longer exist if all of its individuals are destroyed. But it certainly can, and does, impose itself with overwhelming force and autonomy on any given individual. Even if

it is resisted *here,* elsewhere it remains the collective force of its dominant individual members' and classes' pasts. shared commitments,
structures, praxes, and values. The vital social plane of everyone's existence, as well as their forms of interaction, it is at the same time so dependent on these individuals that it disappears if they are destroyed. But
when new individuals appear, in the same territory, they will sooner or
later constitute themselves as a society.

Thus this entity, society, is simultaneously everywhere and nowhere.
It is our complex sets of ways of being together, on every level. It is in fact
a collective, contradictory praxis-process interiorized differentially by its
members according to (in today's world) their sex, race, class, national,
ethnic, and religious origin. It is both practico-inertia (as a *culture* and
set of *values* transmitted from generation to generation) and praxis (as
interiorized and reexteriorized by everyone). As such it includes language, customs, ethics, the heritage and fruits of prior social struggles,
and paths for every conceivable individual action. And, equally as such,
it is the basis, everywhere, for individual identity (which is inconceivable
without it).

We are, then, simultaneously singular and social, generating our general layer under forms and according to practices we have interiorized
and now continue to reexteriorize, even as it generates us. Thus we
shape our general forms of interaction at every moment even as they
shape us. No, it does not move on its own, this society kept alive at every
moment *only* by the praxes of millions. But were we to withdraw our own
praxis and resist the whole, it would continue to act as if "on its own,"
still sustained and kept vital by millions of *other* praxes—unless, in a
revolutionary crisis, a critical mass withdraws its support from certain
decisive structures.

Incarnation is useful for describing one direction of this interaction, although nowhere in his work does Sartre provide keys to understand the
other directon of the praxis-process—the social pole. The individual interiorizes and reexteriorizes some social *thing* but does not in any way
create it. Indeed, in Sartre's analysis its logic eludes us from beginning to
end, except for the one case where it supposedly is totally under the
command of a single individual. In fighting against the general dimension, Sartre sought to uphold the individual; but in so doing he made the
individual's social layer—and thus the individual—unintelligible. Our
view "corrected" in part with keys Sartre himself has suggested, we may
be able to see these shared, presupposed, and constantly sustained lay-

ers of bourgeois society, of the Soviet Union, and of the larger praxis-process of history.

General Uses

One implication of this "correction" of Sartre is that the fruits of prior struggles for human dignity are interiorized by each of us as part of our deepest social as well as personal identity. I suggested at the end of chapter seven that Sartre's emphasis on needs allows us to look at the positive deposits of practico-inertia, even if Sartre himself had not gone this far. They wait to be reassumed and projected forward as the meaning of history. It will not be a meaning given by some hyperorganisms or imposed *on* us, but a meaning interiorized and reexteriorized from among a series of practico-inert possibilities.

History does not have a single Meaning, given and waiting, or a Truth, awaiting to be deciphered. It rather bequeaths us several possibilities and tendencies, and our task is always to decide which of them, if any, we choose to interiorize and carry further. History is already, in this one world of ours, a totalization without a totalizer, one operated by a few who are more or less conscious of doing so and by many who cannot see the praxis-process in which they live and its directions. Within this one world, nontotalitarian societies are equally totalizations without individual totalizers—and are equally driven forward by the sheer inertia of existing social institutions and their need.

Sartre's dialectic holds out the promise of illuminating this shadowy world in which we grope. Freed from its antipathy to value judgments, for example by the discussion at the end of volume two, it would find tendencies in a given social praxis-process, as well as in the strands becoming knit together increasingly under the rubric of world history, to both meet human needs and achieve genuine progress. It would also locate tendencies destructive of those needs and thus worthy of being described as regressive. Raised to its full height, the dialectic may enable us to see, the better to take control of, where we are going.

A Specific Use

To glimpse a specific use of the Sartrean dialectic we need only return, at the end of our journey through *Critique II*, to Sartre's chosen example, the Soviet Union. After all, Merleau-Ponty's post-Marxism turned on the fate of the Bolshevik Revolution, and Sartre's chosen task was to free the

dialectic from its Stalinist sclerosis. How might these "corrections" enhance his ambivalent analysis of future Soviet prospects? The haunting
question is, in the third decade after Sartre tried to free up the dialectic
by assessing how the machine had become jammed, has the Soviet
Union become decisively deviated from the original goals and praxis of
the Revolution? Or is some kind of revival conceivable which can recreate, at a higher level appropriate to an industrialized socialist society, the
original vision in whose name the Revolution captivated and polarized
the world? How will the Soviet leadership relate to such a revival?

In the *Critique's* last pages, Sartre reminded us of two unshakable
touchstones which, taken together, will help answer these questions:
need and the human dialectic's triumph over its products. Sartre's analysis emphasized that the Bolsheviks' enormous urgency about building a
modern industrial society lay at the heart of Stalinism and the deviation
of the Bolshevik Revolution. Only later, however, does he suggest that
the purpose of this immense apparatus might limit the extent and nature
of the deviation. Similarly, his final words reaffirming the dialectic suggest the resiliency of humanity in the face of its creations. Added to a
bedrock layer of need *in the name of which* all praxis is undertaken, this
resiliency suggests a permanent basis sustaining revolutionary long-
ings—until they are met.

In these and other ways, then, there are limits to deviation. The human being can redefine reality, forget the past, live monstrosities and
barbaric lies, but it cannot totally repress its humanness. To this we must
add the reality of classes in the Soviet Union, and thus of profound differences of power and privilege, which at least partly and above all in
spirit contradict Soviet ideology. And also, as Sartre has said, the existence of a bureaucracy, whose charter is to lead the social transformation—and then disappear. Nor must we neglect the fact that no amount
of deviation could completely efface a codified and institutionalized
revolutionary history, which has, like the Civil Rights Act in the United
States, become, with the struggles that created it, a practico-inert layer of
social life. That the Soviet Union is a society, and not a mere agglomera-
tion of individuals, acts as another limit to possible deviations. Each citizen is a member of that society, shares in its practico-inert world of
rights, traditions, institutions, expectations, social promises.

Today's deviations are rooted, in spite of all rewriting of the past, in
heroic parents, a heroic past, liberating ideas. Indeed, even Stalin's *Dialectical and Historical Materialism,* positing universal laws governing all of
reality, taught dogmatically, its view of history terminating in *that* society, retains a subversive, revolutionary thread: the notion of bringing

history under the conscious, collective control of its subjects. Marxism retains a liberating core which must remain a constant thorn in the side of Soviet rulers who teach it, live by it—and deny it in their daily practice.[33] This is, after all, one of the main reasons why Marxism has been so compelling to so many in the worldwide wave of New Left activists, in spite of repeated revolutionary defeats and betrayals, as well as histories of deviation.[34] One whole side of it, with all its gaps, weaknesses, and omissions, remains revolutionary and liberating—in Moscow even when taught as catechism, at Harvard even when studied as falsehood. It is both a practico-inert accumulation of the liberatory heritage of Western society and a remarkable set of tools. Among other things, it provides keys for looking at potential contemporary conflicts in the Soviet Union.

Sartre's dialectic, however, will not enable us to do so unless we shift its habitual focus away from the vicissitudes of power. Unlike Marcuse, Sartre does not look for contradiction, negation, fault lines, the possibility of explosions. Indeed, even at its best, Sartre's analysis failed to convey the catastrophe of Stalinism. This weakness is especially relevant to our current task because much of what appeared—and still appears today—as consensus in the Soviet Union (and thus as successful deviation) resulted from a terror so great that virtually every Soviet citizen was a potential "enemy of the people." Today's docility, generally regarded in the West as based on a still effective if softened totalitarianism, is in part rooted in the generational coma into which Stalin pitched Soviet society. A revival of opposition, fed by a revolutionary past and slumbering revolutionary ideology, based on real social contradictions, perhaps even instigated by the leadership, is only a matter of time.

Sartre had hoped, we know, for a reformist evolution of the Soviet Union, led by the Party. If, however, one dialectic unfolded within the ruling group and between them and the masses, a very different one, filled with contradiction, was contained within the first. Accessible through the negative and conflictual sense bequeathed us by Marx and Marcuse, but also through Sartre's concept of the practico-inert and his emphasis on need and the dialectic, it may one day become dominant and point toward a revolutionary transformation of Soviet society. The dialectic cannot, of course, predict the outcome of that transformation— or, indeed, whether a new Russian Revolution will not itself become deviated. But if we cannot predict its shape or moment of appearance, we can at least be prepared for the coming of the future Soviet Solidarity.

33. For comments on this, see Marcuse, *Soviet Marxism*, 121–78.
34. For a discussion of this, see Anderson, *In the Tracks of Historical Materialism*.

Guide to Pagination

Sartre's manuscript of Critique II consists of 781 pages, without titles or other divisions into chapters or sections. In editing the text for publication, Arlette Elkaïm-Sartre has divided it into three parts and twenty chapters, with chapters further divided into sections. Her titles stress Sartre's formal concerns. My own organization of this study into six chapters presenting Sartre's argument does not completely correspond to Elkaïm's. Accordingly, the reader may find the following guide useful.

Index

Communist Party of France (PCF), 5–9
Communist project, affirmed by Sartre, 23–24
Communists and Peace, 8, 12, 17, 30, 31, 131–32n
Concept, 79; and analytical reason, 60–61; as the general, 67; and praxis, 207–8. *See also* Analytical reason
Concrete universal, 66, 72
Condemned of Altona, 182–83; 234
Conflict: between subgroups, 84; between working class and bureaucracy, 130–31
Conquest, Robert, 180n
Contat, Michel, 219, 236n
Contradiction, 3, 41, 227–28; and class struggle, 73; and group, 76, 87; introduced, 45; realized only in conflict, 90; and reunification, 89; source of, 78–81, 83, 88; between subgroups, 77–78; in USSR in 1920s, 108–9, 112
Cromwell, Oliver, 99–101
Cuba, 29, 63, 106, 154, 181
Cunning of reason, 229–32. *See also* Hegel, G. W. F.
"Czechoslovakia: The Socialism That Came in from the Cold," 149n

Death: and history, 198–200; real not symbolic in boxing, 61–62; and revolutionary continuity, 99
Degradation, 99–100
Desituated understanding impossible, 191–93
De-Stalinization, and critique of the dialectic, 29
Deutscher, Isaac, 139n, 180n, 188n
Deviation, 100, 123, 127, 147–48, 176–77, 184, 190–91; of Bolshevik Revolution, 3, 119–20, 161–64, 168, 226; within history, 194; reaches its limits, 213–18; and scarcity, 163; social source in USSR, 180; and Stalin, 150; to.stay the same, 98–99
Devil and the Good Lord, 8, 30, 181
Dialectic and dialectical reason, 221, 243; affirmed, 242; and analytical reason: 3, 13, 42–44, 46, 52, 138, 190–91, 208–9, 223–24; and antidialectic, 115, 188; critical dialectic not dogmatic, 28–29, 35, 37, 72, 97, 125–26, 193, 221–23; and future unity, 207; according to Hegel, 3; and history, 35, 37, 115, 241; as human creation, 35; proceeds from individuals in action, 4, 33, 36–37, 43–44, 223–24; jammed in Soviet Union, 21; key terms

of, 1; Merleau-Ponty's critique of, 13, 21; and negation, 21, 230–31; and ontology, 3, 185, 193–97, 209–10; and praxis, 59–60, 215–16, 218, 225; Sartrean, among others, 229–31; and scarcity, 44; as self-development, 33; subjective versus objective, 26–27, 127; and totalization, 33, 36, 197; as universal method, 4, 35; uses of, 225. *See also* Marxian dialectic
Dirty Hands, 30, 171n, 181
Disadaptation, 94
Dreyfus affair, 98

Elkaïm-Sartre, Arlette, xvi, 2n, 150n, 193
Emotions: Outline of a Theory, 217
Engels, Frederick, 27, 35, 223
Entretiens sur la politique, 5n
Exis, 189; described, 53n, 155–56; and organic integrity, 205–6
Exteriority, 127, 166, 199–200; and analytical reason, 42; inorganic and need, 203; and interiority, 138n; from within, 145

Family Idiot, x, 74, 225
Fanon, Frantz, 234
Flaubert, Gustave, x, 63
Frankfurt School, 4, 16, 26, 233
Freedom: alienated in Soviet history, 117; and Marxism, 5
French Revolution, 21, 30, 81–83, 161–63, 201
Freud Scenario, xi

Garaudy, Roger, 11
Gorz, André, 194n, 234n
Gramsci, Antonio, 16, 26
Group, 239; creates subgroups as specialized apparatuses, 77; group-in-fusion, 2, 39, 76; Party as would-be permanent, 130–32; and subgroups, 45, 83–85; reunifies itself in conflict, 45; and series, 114–16, 130–31; as totalization of envelopment, 86
Guérin, Daniel, 21

Hegel, G. W. F., 3, 29, 34, 74, 223, 226, 230, 237
Hirsch, Arthur, 9n
Historical materialism, xv, 9, 122, 215, 220, 227–29
History, 115; according to Plekhanov, 161–62; all of, in each boxing match, 75; ambiguous? 114–15; explained by per-